THE SYRIAN JEWELRY BOX

Praise for

THE SYRIAN JEWELRY BOX
A Daughter's Journey for Truth

"Carina Burns has looked within herself, faced her demons, and developed the courage to share her journey of love, perceived betrayal, angst, and regenerative love. I first knew Carina before she learned of her adoption. She was a typical carefree teenager enjoying the 'good life' of a third-culture expatriate kid. Only recently have I reconnected with her. She has quite a story, a gift she shares with passion. Carina Burns is truly 'becoming' in every way imaginable."

—**Richard Maack**, junior high school principal, Saudi Arabia

"One cannot expect to walk in on a life that is so private and has been like that for years and not find similarities that will taunt you and challenge you to resolve those issues that have long been contaminating your life. When you realize that the issues you have unpacked have left your life naked and painfully raw from the death of your natural beliefs, *The Syrian Jewelry Box* will become your anecdote. Carina's story holds the key to a delightful celebration of self and trust. By following the well-worn steps to a full and sustainable recovery, you will be able to elevate yourself to your rightful place in the sun."

—**Barbie Lightbody**

"We are shaped by the experiences we go through in our lives. These experiences aren't always good unfortunately. We can't however allow these bumps to hold us back from riding the wave of life. This is exactly what Carina Burns did; she managed to catch the wave. Luckily, she washed up on my shore last year."

—**Mansour Al Zamil**, deputy general manager of
Al Zamil Heavy Industries Ltd., author of *Historic Jeddah
1969 Through the Eyes of Joseph Rourke Jeddah, Saudi Arabia*

Praise for

WHAT DO YOU MEAN I WAS ADOPTED?
7 Steps to Acceptance, Gratitude & Peace

"'What do you mean I was adopted?' At fifteen, Carina Burns had to ask that painful question when she found out she was adopted. Her compelling book reveals how she reached deep inside herself to find the strength and courage to deal with the emotions arising from the revelation of her adoption. Her stirring book then offers strategies to help those in similar circumstances. I highly recommend you read it."

> —**Joe Soll**, LCSW, Psychotherapist and author of
> *Adoption Healing…a Path to Recovery*

"*What Do You Mean I Was Adopted?* is easy to read and offers great insight to how children can feel and react about adoption. Even though it is a story of adoption, it can be transposed to any area of life: secrets always come to light, and once they do they can have a devastating effect. And forgiveness is the only way toward peace and acceptance of what is."

> —**Aminata Toure**, accounting supervisor, Kettler Management

"*What Do You Mean I Was Adopted?* is a wonderful resource for those just beginning their journey of healing from the identity crisis often associated with adoption. Carina's experience and willingness to share is priceless!"

> —**Pattie Meyers**, The PM Companies

"Carina's book shows you how to become empowered by the sometimes shocking and traumatic experience of adoption. It is a must-read for anyone who is adopted."

> —**Richard Krawczyk**, Author of
> *Ultimate Success Blueprint* (TheMrBlueprint.com)

THE
SYRIAN
JEWELRY
BOX

A Daughter's Journey for Truth

CARINA SUE BURNS

New York

THE SYRIAN JEWELRY BOX
A Daughter's Journey for Truth

Published in New York, New York, by Morgan James Publishing. Morgan James and The Entrepreneurial Publisher are trademarks of Morgan James, LLC.
www.MorganJamesPublishing.com

The Morgan James Speakers Group can bring authors to your live event. For more information or to book an event visit The Morgan James Speakers Group at
www.TheMorganJamesSpeakersGroup.com.

A free eBook edition is available
with the purchase of this print book.

CLEARLY PRINT YOUR NAME ABOVE IN UPPER CASE

Instructions to claim your free eBook edition:
1. Download the BitLit app for Android or iOS
2. Write your name in **UPPER CASE** on the line
3. Use the BitLit app to submit a photo
4. Download your eBook to any device

ISBN 978-1-63047-582-6 paperback
ISBN 978-1-63047-583-3 eBook
Library of Congress Control Number:
2015902359

Cover Design by:
Rachel Lopez
www.r2cdesign.com

Interior Design by:
Bonnie Bushman
bonnie@caboodlegraphics.com

In an effort to support local communities and raise awareness and funds, Morgan James Publishing donates a percentage of all book sales for the life of each book to Habitat for Humanity Peninsula and Greater Williamsburg.

Get involved today, visit
www.MorganJamesBuilds.com

For Dad, who gave me my story,
For Mom, who gave me the miracle of life,
And for my brother
With everlasting love and gratitude

CONTENTS

FOREWORD

Carina Sue Burns, in *The Syrian Jewelry Box*, has written a compelling page turner of substance and impact. In this personal memoir she conveys the confusion, disorientation, and ache of learning as a teenager that the father she has adored is not her biological father. And when she learns this by way of her own doing, her mother provides her no additional information about this man.

From then on everything is shifted. Every action, every encounter is examined in light of this revelation. Nothing for her is as it seemed.

In my experience as a psychotherapist I met with people grappling with turbulent, and disquieting adoption issues of various kinds. This book is pitch perfect in portraying many of those.

Ms. Burns chronicles her progression toward her current internal equilibrium, and reveals how fraught it was with swerves, including superheated affairs. And she takes pains to be clear that she is speaking about her journey rather than as a spokesperson for adoptees, or as evangelist for adoption practices.

—**Kenneth W. Christian**, PhD, Psychologist and author of
Your Own Worst Enemy: Breaking the Habit of Adult Underachievement

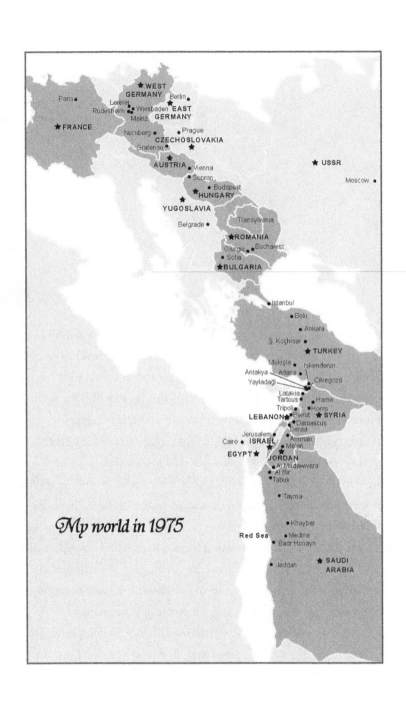

My world in 1975

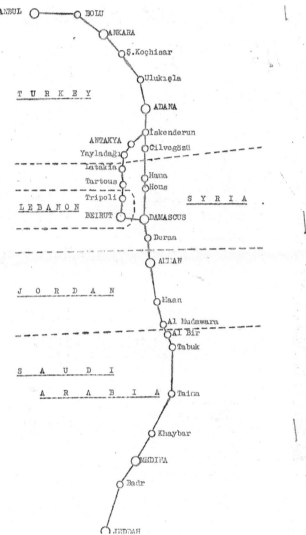

İSTANBUL O——O BOLU
                    O ANKARA
                      O Ş.Koçhisar
                      O Ulukışla

T U R K E Y
                       O ADANA
                       O İskenderun
ANTAKYA   O Cilvegözü
Yayladağı   O
    Latakia   O
    Tartous   O   O Hama
    Tripoli O   O Homs
L E B A N O N   S Y R I A
   BEIRUT O   O DAMASCUS
                       O Deraa

                       O AMMAN
J O R D A N
                       O Maan
                       O Al Mudawara
                       O Al Bir
                       O Tabuk
S   A   U   D   I
   A   R   A   B   I   A   O Taima

                       O Khaybar
                       O MEDINA
                       O Badr
                       O JEDDAH

Original map used on the trip.

PREPARING
FOR JEDDAH
Saudi Arabia (1968)

I ingested mouthful after mouthful of plump sweet grapes. Intoxicated, I plopped down on the freshly mowed grass with my back against our weathered picket fence, inhaling their tantalizing aroma. I found it difficult to stop after eating just one grape, so I stuffed my mouth full. These were no ordinary grapes—they were Concord grapes, whose vines occupied the entire rear fence. The crisp day of inviting light-blue sky was just ending. Spring of 1968 had sprung. I was eight and a half years old.

"It's time to come in now, Carina," Mom called from the kitchen window.

Mom sat back against a colonial captain's wood chair, resting her right elbow on the chair's arm, hands clasped on her lap. She appeared deliriously happy. "You're just in time—come sit with us in the kitchen. Dad and I have some news we'd like to discuss with you and Dennis."

Leaning back in the other captain's chair, Dad raised his interlocked hands, placing them comfortably behind his head, and threw Dennis and me a wink. Knitting my brows, I plunked myself into the last chair next to Dennis, who sat Indian style and twirled his red toy bomber plane.

"Schatzi, how would you like to live in Saudi Arabia?" Dad tilted his head sideways at Mom and chuckled, as if asking her for the first time.

Dad often used this German pet name for Mom. It is similar to "sweetheart" as he affectionately addressed Mom, as he did on this evening.

"Where's Saudi Arabia?" she responded, betraying excitement.

"I'm not exactly sure." He grinned like a Cheshire cat. "Let's pull out the map and find out."

I glanced from Mom to Dad and decided there was no way she could resist the charm of his twinkling blue eyes and pirate's grin. "Du, Raytheon wants me—wants *us*—to move to Jeddah, Saudi Arabia, for a two-year assignment," he said, using the familiar German *du*, meaning "you," as an endearment term with Mom. "I need to go soon. You and the kiddies could take a plane to join me later, in three months."

"Du, this is wonderful news." Mom mirrored his grin. "I'm ready for a change. After all, we've been here four years now."

Dad shot up from his chair and pointed to the map spread out on the round pine table covered in a vintage tablecloth. He showed us where Saudi Arabia was located. He and Mom exchanged secret smiles over this huge change, practically ignoring how Dennis and I felt. I tucked my chin into my chest and jutted out my bottom lip. I didn't want to leave all my friends, like Cindy Pratt, my best friend. I didn't want to leave Cleveland Elementary School or Shnuky, our spunky black-and-white tabby with a tub fetish. What would happen to him?

Both Mom and Dad were eager to go, but what about me? Didn't I matter? I glanced at Dennis and figured that he didn't want to leave either—he was only six years old.

I blurted out, "Who's going to be able to play 'who can eat the most rhubarb until you pucker up' or spray each other with the garden hose in the kiddie pool with the Dione boys and their sister, Susan?" I was on a roll. "And what's Shnuky going to do without his favorite spot to sleep?" I often found him curled up asleep in our porcelain bathtub—without the water, of course.

"Yeah, Dad!" Dennis whined.

Mom stood up and hugged Dennis. Dad gave me a warm hug. "I know it's going to be hard to leave your friends, it always is. Listen, there's one thing for sure—you guys will make lots of new friends. I promise."

I left the kitchen and threw myself on the couch in the living room.

"Can't Shnuky come with us, Dad?" Dennis whined on. "Why can't our friends visit us in our new home?"

"Maybe you could try writing to your friends," Mom said.

"It's not fair that we have to leave all our friends behind. I don't want to write to them. I want them to visit us," I said with a pout.

Dad reassured me with a heartfelt gaze. "You know we love you guys, right? On the compound, there are so many families with kids. I bet you'll make new ones in a flash."

"What's a compound?" I blurted out, still frowning.

Dennis wrinkled his nose. "Yeah, Dad. What's a cawpound?"

"It's where a community of families lives in houses next to each other, surrounded by four giant ten-foot walls. There's a guard desk where we have to sign in before entering the compound. I saw pictures of the place. You'll love it—the compound reminded me of one giant playground."

"What about the playground?" I asked, betraying some curiosity despite my mood. Besides I could never stay mad at Dad for long.

"There's a huge swimming pool, tennis courts, a basketball court, and even a baseball field," he said. "In the same area, there's a movie theater with free movies and a recreation center where you guys can play ping-pong. There's even a snack bar next door."

Sucked into the exotic adventure of a foreign land with a giant playground, I threw a peek at Dennis—he showed off his angelic white teeth. Obviously he liked the idea of a giant playground. I thought of something else that greatly appealed: I'd never have to wear a dress.

I glanced at Mom and wondered what she saw in this whole idea of moving. She was my loving, nurturing mom, who had a passion for cultivating her day lily garden—sometimes preferring quiet moments to chitchatting.

"Schatzi, I want to ask you something." Dad said.

"Yes, Du?"

Dad wrapped his arm around her shoulders. His sky-blue eyes crinkled with merriment. He had beautiful eyes, I thought—eyes with a perpetual sparkle.

"How about we invite *Tante* Peg and *Tante* Loretta over on Easter Sunday one last time before we leave for Jeddah?"

She nodded in agreement and smiled softly.

·····

When I later told my best friend, Cindy, about the move, we promised to write each other and always remain best friends, but I took it one step further.

"Wanna be blood sisters?"

"Blood sisters?" she exclaimed, wrinkling her brow.

"You're not afraid of pricking your finger, are you?"

"Nah, just a little nervous, though," she said, and then looked at me biting her lower lip.

"Well good, cuz we'd each have to get a needle to prick our fingers, and then you press your bloody finger against my bloody finger . . . and that's what makes blood sisters!"

"OK, follow me," she said. "We could get the needles from my mom's sewing drawer."

I was relieved that she approved, and now we were equally excited. I followed her while she fetched two needles from the sewing drawer. Then we headed for her bedroom where mahogany twin beds stood out against the pink flowery wallpaper.

"Are you sure we're ready for this, Carina?"

"Are you kidding? This is gonna be great!"

Cindy sat on her India Rose bedspread, and I settled in opposite her, on the other bed with an ivory blanket bed covering. In preparation, we each grabbed a tissue from the box of Kleenex on the nightstand.

"Are you nervous?" Cindy asked.

"Well, maybe a tiny bit," I said with tight lips.

We grabbed the needles, still facing each other, and hung our legs over the edge of the beds.

"OK," I said. "Let's do it on the count of three. . ."

We counted together: "One, two, three…" We pricked our index fingers at the same time, then pressed them together so the blood mixed.

"Blood sisters forever!" we squealed in unison.

"For life!" Cindy shouted, just as we dabbed the blood from our fingers with tissues.

"Now, would you teach me to braid my hair like yours?" I asked.

"Sure, but we should do it in the bathroom. It would be easier," Cindy said.

I'd always loved Cindy's thick blonde hair and how she braided it. I wondered, did she get up early to braid her own hair, or did her mother do it for her? Did she wash it every day or every week? But most of all, I wanted my shoulder-length blonde hair to be braided just like hers.

She showed me every move and I keenly observed her in the mirror.

"Now it's your turn," she said.

I pulled a wad of hair with both hands, separated it into three pieces, found my own way of holding all three strands between by hands, and used all ten fingers. I placed one strand over another, alternating between the three. I managed but remained unsatisfied.

"It always turns out better when you braid my hair," I said.

"But if you practice braiding every day, you'll get it, I promise," she said with a convincing giggle.

I noticed the time. "Hey, I gotta go home, but this was the best afternoon we've ever had, right?" I waited for her approval.

"Yeah, it really was the best time ever."

We walked to her front porch.

"See ya at school tomorrow," I said. As I ran home, I wondered how many afternoons were left for us. Now we were blood sisters forever. I never wanted to forget this cozy life of my perfect childhood. Soon it would be just a memory.

THE ARRIVAL
Jeddah, Saudi Arabia (1968)

My only memory of our flight aboard a Saudi Arabian Airlines jet was the touchdown at King Abdulaziz International Airport in Jeddah. It was August of 1968. I sat up in my window seat and rubbed the sleep out of my eyes with my fingers to stare at the runway's bright lights. My head swam. I shifted in my seat with thoughts of Cindy, Shnuky, and our next-door neighbors. Would this foreign land be everything that Dad promised us it would be? My heart throbbed with excitement at seeing Dad again. We hadn't seen him for three long months.

The stewardess opened the door. A wave of oppressively hot sticky air, jet fuel, and hot tarmac filled our cabin. Still, a welcome relief to the strong cigar smoke, smelly socks, and body odor of a long flight. I could always detect the ladies' designer perfume amidst the smell. Then there was the lavatory cologne which all the Saudi men doused themselves with immediately before landing. My nose was assaulted.

I stepped out of the plane's cabin down the steep steps to the tarmac. Mom followed, holding Dennis's hand.

Habitual airport sounds under an ebony sky hovered over us, but my eyes focused on the lonely and brightly lit building.

"What time is it, Mom?"

"It's midnight," she said. "Dad's waiting for us on the other side of the customs stand."

"What's customs?" I asked.

"It's a place where we have to show a policeman some papers so that we can get into the country, but let's not worry about that now, Carina," Mom answered absent-mindedly.

"It's too hot and sticky!" Dennis whined. "When are we gonna see Dad?"

Mom slowly shook her head in frustration. "Come on, kiddies, hang in there—I know this heat isn't making it easy for us, but we need to walk across the runway to that flat building where your father should be waiting for us. I promise you'll eventually get used to this heat." She touched my shoulder. "Always stay close to me."

Beads of sweat formed on my face, and my armpits felt damp. This had to be the hottest place I'd ever experienced. *Have I walked into a pitch-dark oven?* I thought to myself.

"*Yallah, Yallah, Imshi!*" people shouted around me. I heard the expression everywhere and thought it meant *let's go*. I soon learned from my Arab friend Mansour "The word is *Ya Allah*, which is a calling to Allah, requesting his mercy or support. People now use it out of context: Yallah, meaning with Allah. Let's go in the protection of Allah."

Yawning, I said to Mom, "How long were we on that plane? I want to see Dad; I can't wait."

To this day the combination of hot humid air, jet fuel smell, and hot tarmac reminds me of that unforgettable adventure. An adventure of a lifetime.

"We left Boston over fifteen hours ago," she said, looking weary from the flight. "We'll soon see Dad, I promise." Then she added, "Imagine, we're finally in Saudi Arabia. The people here are called Arabs."

As we walked along the runway, I saw men in long white robes. The women were dressed in all black. Young children wore clothes similar to what Dennis and I wore, although many boys also wore the traditional white robe.

We were herded toward the flat building beaming under bright lights. Dad was nowhere in sight. *It'll be swell when we're finally a family again*, I thought. I grinned, anticipating him being close. I missed his engaging smile; he always made me feel loved and special. It seemed like ages ago that I felt his closeness. Maybe he could still arrive home with Danish pastries on the weekend. Jeddah's exotic smells, heat, and chaos thrilled me yet filled me with trepidation.

We entered a huge crowded room with a ceiling fan that turned slowly and circulated hot dry air.

Many of the Arab men wore red-and-white-checkered headdresses with a black cord to hold it in place. Arabs mostly had light brown skin and dark hair and eyes. Although men traditionally wore the white robe, occasionally one might have a gray or brown robe with a colorful trim. Some wore just a white cap over their head; others wore the white cap with a white scarf that dangled above the shoulder. *What a bizarre way of dressing*, I thought, staring secretly at them.

I stared at men holding hands and kissing each other on the cheeks. I stared at women in black gowns. They all wore a black long-sleeved, floor-length dress and gazed at me with dark eyes through an opening in something that covered their faces.

Body odor from sweaty clothes, cigarette smoke, cologne, and various designer perfumes assaulted my nose again. Saudi's constant guttural chatter echoed in the massive room. *"Ma'Assalama … Shukran… Al Salamu Alaikum… Wa Alaikum Al Salam…."*

"Yallah, Yallah, Imshi," the women said, motioning their hands toward their children.

After being herded around, we placed our luggage onto a long table against a wall. This must have been the customs place Mom talked about. An Arab officer ordered loudly for us to open our suitcases. Three uniformed Arabs rummaged through every article of clothing and summoned us to repack and close them up. We ended up at a kiosk where Mom handed the stern black mustached Arab a stack of blue little books. He opened each one separately and slowly looked inside each. I stared at him while he lifted his head to scrutinize us. Then with a loud stamp he gave everything back to Mom. The man raised his hand and waved us on.

"Mom, why is every woman covered up over her head?" I asked.

"All women must wear a veil, which covers their entire face except the eyes, and the long black robe covers their entire body," she said, not answering my question. "Before you know it, we'll be used to it." Mom raised her brow, trying to persuade me.

"Hmmm, weird. I don't want to wear that, Mom. Do we have to?"

"No, but we will have to wear some sort of long robe. Don't worry about it now, though," she reassured me.

Then I saw him.

"There he is!" I squealed. "I see Dad! I see him, Mom!"

I jumped up and down, shaking my hands in the air and hoping he could see me. He looked darker than I remembered.

"I see him too!" Dennis yelled, almost at the same time. He jumped up and down, waving his arms like a cheerleader.

We rushed into Dad's open arms; Dad gave Mom a hug and a kiss on the cheek.

"Hey, guys, so how was the journey?" he said. It was way too long, very long, we told him.

"Dad, how come your face looks dark like an Arab's?" I asked.

"After three months in the sun, I now have a tan—and you guys will have one too, real soon." He turned to Mom and grinned. "Well, at least we're a family again, Du. You and the kids are here now." Dad gave his *joie-de-vivre* laugh. I felt loved, safe, and protected. I had a good feeling that we'd finally arrived home again. Even though it happened to be in a different land, I looked forward to the adventure unfolding before me.

"Ready, guys? I'll show you our villa downtown where we'll be living for a few months until our house on the American compound is ready."

"Aw…but, Dad!" I said, while I scuffled my feet in the dirt. "You told us we would make loads of friends on a giant playground."

"Yeah, Dad," Dennis echoed.

"Guys, I'm sorry, but if people are still living in the house, we can't live in it, right? Just hang in there for a little while."

Dennis and I pouted.

"Come on, we'll still have a good time. It'll be fun. Trust me." Dad winked at each of us. We grabbed our belongings and followed him, carrying a suitcase in each hand.

"Dad, how come the men here are all dressed in white?" I asked.

"Well, Carina, have you noticed the women are all in black? By law this is their custom or way of dress. Someone once told me that men wear white because it reflects the sun and women wear black because they don't wish to wear clothes that draw attention to them." He tilted his head in my direction, ready for more questions.

I didn't ask any; I just shrugged, wondering at it all. I'd stepped inside an exotic world and decided to let it all just unfold in front of me.

Dad turned to Mom suddenly. "Guys, follow me, and our driver will take us to our temporary home."

"Mom, I smell something stinky and sour like rubbish," I said, scrunching up my nose.

"Yeah, Mom, I smell it too," Dennis copycatted me.

"I know. You will probably smell it a lot around here. Try holding your nose to ignore it," Mom said, staring at us with a long face.

We followed Dad to a used blue Plymouth with a driver in the traditional white robe and red-checkered headdress seated at the wheel. The driver got out and helped load our belongings into the trunk as Mom, Dennis, and I climbed in back. Dad sat up front. Our Arab driver raced crazily through a maze of honking traffic, men clothed in white robes riding bicycles or mopeds. Jeddah's nighttime polychromatic show tangoed with a variety of spouting water jets emerging to my side. Smells of hot sand combined with camel or donkey odors wafted through the open windows. Neon lights lit the downtown with hallucinogenic greenish, reddish, and bluish hues.

We passed an iron gate that opened from a white square pillar topped off by a white cement ball. The long driveway, flanked by a huge eight-foot wall, led us to our three-story villa. It was a huge white square box with no ornamentation that reminded me of the Bauhaus Museum in Tel Aviv. The front porch light was on. Mom and Dad escorted us to our rooms.

"Dennis and Carina, you can explore in the morning after a good night's sleep…okay?" Mom said. I noticed her bloodshot, puffy eyes from all the traveling.

"But it's too hot," Dennis whined.

"It's really way too hot, Mom," I added.

"Think of all the friends you'll soon be making on the compound and fun stuff to do—I bet that would take your mind off the heat," Dad humored us, poking his head into our room.

"It'll be tough," I griped.

"Aw, all right." Dennis yawned.

I thought about my favorite bedtime story, "Rapunzel," and how I also wished to have long golden hair like hers when I grew up and be carried away by my prince.

<hr />

The next morning, I woke up sweating from the lingering muggy air and unfamiliar surroundings—it felt like mid-afternoon. I peeked outside my bedroom window and noticed that a round white car was parked in the elongated driveway. The driveway was made of rectangular tiles that formed expanded narrow rows of both sky blue and cloud white. Was that our car? *It's funny looking.* A desert-colored cement wall separated us from the main dirt road. Rummaging through my suitcase, I hastily slipped on a white-cotton T-shirt and a pair of red/white-striped shorts, eager to see my family downstairs and greet the day's new adventures. As I bounded down the hall, I glanced up at the cathedral ceilings of our striking Bauhaus-style villa. I wandered throughout a gigantic interior maze, searching for the kitchen with a clueless face. The cacophony of occasional cawing, barking, meowing, and chirping startled me. My armpits grew wet from the moist air. I inhaled a loamy odor that reminded me of a dirty camel or dried moss. A few white cement steps landed me on the third floor.

I wandered along the hallway and stopped at a small door ajar. A clammy breeze wafted past me. I tucked my blonde hair behind my ears and peeked through the opening onto a flat open-air roof, used for laundry. Nothing hung from a desolate clothes rack in the left-hand corner. But I had a view of the town.

Desert sand- or white-colored villas three, four, or five stories high sprawled above the skyline. Farther out, occasional cream-colored tall buildings jutted out of the sea of villas.

I looked across the street, and at the edge of the balcony of another three-story villa stood a white square covering with three beautiful white wood-like intricately carved arches. White posts supported the overhang connected to two below which held up another canopy. Again, three white arches appeared to be made of wood, their intricately carved edges resembling embroidered lace. A small square awning decorated the ground-floor entrance. Trees four or more times my height bloomed with white or red flowers. They provided shade for an occasional three-story house adorned with colorful magnolias.

I headed down the deep and narrow hallway past my bedroom. Finally, I happened upon the dining room adjacent to the living room. Dad sat at the dining room table, sipping a cup of coffee. Dennis scarfed down toast.

"Morning," I mumbled. "Dad, it was too hot and sticky to sleep last night."

"You and Dennis can sleep on the rooftop tonight, on the canvas cots we talked about."

"That'll be cool!" Dennis said.

"Dad, why was there a funny-looking car in our driveway?" I asked. "What happened to the other car?"

"You don't remember taking a taxi home yesterday afternoon?" Dad chuckled.

Geez, everything is a complete fog to me.

"Think about it, we couldn't all fit inside the small white car with our suitcases. That small round car is called a Volkswagen Beetle," Dad said. "It's also the name of an ugly fat black bug. You'll see them a lot around here—the insect, not the car—but also cockroaches and scorpions, some of which are poisonous. The clear white geckos are everywhere. You'll see them scurrying up and down walls."

"Yech! Those sound gross," I said. Except for the tiny lizards that raced up and down the walls, the rest of the critters made me want to scream.

"Not me. I like bugs, but I wouldn't want 'em in my bed," Dennis said.

"What are scorpions, and what do they look like?" I asked, hoping they weren't another bug.

"Come here, let's find a picture." Dad dug out some magazine and showed us the ugly black slippery-looking arachnid.

"Well, guys, when we visit some sand dunes in the desert, I will be sure to point them out; but *always* check your shoes for scorpions or any other creature crawling inside." He gave us one of his meaningful chuckles. "OK, guys?"

I rumpled my forehead. "Where's Mom?"

Just then, as if bidden, I caught the pleasant whiff of Mom's flowery fragrance as she stepped into the dining room.

"I'm coming. Du, I need some coffee," she yawned in her sleeveless cream-colored dress.

Dad gazed at her endearingly. "I made a fresh pot just for Du. And here's some toast, Carina." Dad set a fresh piece on my plate. He turned back to Mom. "Du, why don't I call our neighbors? They have a girl and a boy Carina and Dennis's ages. Yasmeen would be around your age, Carina, and Mustafa is exactly your age, Dennis. I told them how you'd soon be arriving from America."

Dad got up out of his chair and headed toward the push-button phone on the wall. He spoke in Arabic.

"*Al Salamu Alaikum, Ismee* Joe Rourke…Carina, Dennis, Renate arrived from *Amreeca.*" Dad raised his voice a notch while fingering the tangled white chord.

Dennis and I sat glued to the conversation that we didn't understand. Hopefully we could figure out whether or not they could come by keeping a close eye on Dad's facial expressions.

"*Ma'Assalama.*"

Dad reattached the long white earpiece against its wall mount.

"Wow, Du, I'm impressed with your knowledge of Arabic." Mom looked at him with widened eyes.

"Thanks, Schatzi. I learned the basics before you and the kiddies arrived."

"So what did you tell them, Dad? Do they want to meet us?" I asked.

"Can we play with them, Dad?" Dennis butted in.

"Whoa, slow down, not so fast. Come on, you guys, and Schatzi, you too— Yasmeen and Mustafa will be waiting next to the front gate to meet you and maybe play with you guys."

Dennis and I dashed out the front door with Mom and Dad trailing behind. We then waited in anticipation near the wrought-iron gate.

Within a short while an eager and cheerful lean eight-year-old dark-skinned girl appeared. I was sure she was an Arab. She looked at us through big dark brown eyes. She had shoulder-length curly black hair that framed her olive face. She wore a bright green dress with an orange daisy pattern, frilled at the bottom. I couldn't help noticing her pink fluorescent flip-flop sandals. She threw us a broad smile. A stick-thin young boy—probably her brother—emerged from behind. He tucked his chin in toward his chest and guarded a grimace. He wore a white short-sleeved T-shirt over khaki shorts with black flip-flops. Dennis and I cautiously ventured toward them.

Resting my right hand on my chest, I said slowly, "My name is Carina."

Dennis mimicked me. "My name is Dennis."

They inched toward us and the girl quietly pronounced what sounded like "Amreeca" just as she rolled the letter "r." Her brother laughed.

I repeated, "Hello, my name is Careena." I pointed to Dennis and mumbled quickly under my breath.

"Say 'my name is Dennis.'"

"I know, I know! Stop bossing me around, Carina."

Patting his chest swiftly with his right hand, he repeated, "My name is Dennis."

The girl placed her hand on her chest and repeated over and over, "Hallow, Yasmeen." Then she pointed to her shy brother and said "Mustafa" a couple of times.

"Yaasmeeeen and Mustaafa," I repeated.

Dennis tried his best with an attempted "Yaazameeeen Mustfa."

"Let's teach them hopscotch, Dennis," I announced.

"No way, I'm not playing any girl's game." He backed away.

Although I didn't have any chalk, I grabbed the nearest pebble and threw it in front of me then hopscotched over make-believe squares from our driveway's tiles as fast as I could. I tried not to fall, gasping but determined to make our new friends happy. I leaned over, scooped up the pebble, and threw it farther. I quickly gestured toward Yasmeen. "It's your turn, go ahead." I flicked my hand toward her.

Yasmeen's forehead wrinkled over her big brown eyes as she danced to the distant pebble, scooping it up like a feather and beaming from ear to ear. She threw Mustafa a glance and raised her right hand, cupping her fingers, then motioned them toward him. Mustafa puckered his lips and shook his head.

While Yasmeen and I frolicked in a game of hopscotch, Dennis and Mustafa eagerly chased each other across the tiled driveway, then climbed on top of our parked Beetle.

Yasmeen and I became best friends. Behind us, Dennis and Mustafa laughed during the time that they mimicked us hobbling side-by-side toward a yonder pebble. After a single-legged attempt they both fell flat on their behinds. We turned toward each other giggling.

I looked at Yasmeen and said, "I'm eight years old."

She peered playfully at me with a scrunched-up nose.

I noticed Mom approaching us.

"Carina, she probably doesn't understand. Try using your fingers to help you count to eight so she can understand what you're saying." Mom looked pleased. Then she meandered toward the villa.

"Good idea, Mom. OK," I said loudly, hoping that she heard me. I raised my right hand forming a fist and then slowly opened it beginning with my thumb and went through every finger ending with my middle finger on my left hand; then I said, "Yasmeen, I am eight."

Her dark eyes opened wide and she began gesticulating with her fingers and said, "Wa-Hid." She raised a finger.

"*Wahid.*"

"WAA-Hid," she emphasized.

"Waa-hid," I tried again.

Dennis appeared half smiling. "What did you say?"

"Don't but in. Yasmeen is telling me how old she is." I frowned, throwing him a glance.

"Aw, come on, Creena, let us in."

"Aw, OK." So I gestured over to Mustafa, bending my index finger toward me.

Mustafa left his sister's side with a faint grimace and placed himself in front of Dennis.

Copying his sister he stared at Dennis and began with "*Wahid.*"

"Wahd," Dennis said wide-eyed, with pursed lips.

"No, Dennis, Waa-hid," I repeated.

"That's not what he said…nah, I don't want to," he whined.

Grinning from ear to ear, Yasmeen slowly echoed, "*Wahid.*"

Hoping that Dennis still kept quiet, I quickly tilted my head, rubbed my hands, and bellowed "Waa-Hid!"

Yasmeen gasped. "*Ith-nane.*"

I reverberated with "*Ith-nane.*"

I extended my long arms over my head at the same time that I flicked my hands to the right then to the left, smiling. Yasmeen began to jump up and down mimicking my gesticulations as she gasped joyfully with "*Thalatha!*"

I stopped jumping and followed suit a tad easier. "*Thalatha.*"

Next she came out with "*Arba'a.*"

I repeated, "*Ar-ba'a.*"

"OK," I said and waved my palms out, indicating that I had it.

Yasmeen giggled, showing only her upper teeth. I meandered over to the Beetle with Yasmeen at my side, hoping the boys would follow us.

We all climbed on top of the Beetle, squishing each other on the rooftop next to the open sunroof.

"Hey guys, look up, I want to get a picture of you," Dad yelled from the rooftop.

We looked up at Dad, who stood way up on the roof and snapped away. A minute later, he inquired from the doorway, "How would you guys like to see the *souq*[1]—the downtown market?"

Mom reappeared in the driveway as we all waved goodbye.

"Goodbye," I shouted.

"Gooodbi," Yasmeen repeated and waved. Mustafa let out a faint "Gwooodbiy" and let his right hand flicker up.

Dad said something to them in Arabic.

"What did you say?" I asked.

"I told them we're going to the *souq* but that we would see them again, *In'sha'Allah [If Allah wills]*."

We lived there for three months until our house on the compound was ready.

THE *SOUQ*
Jeddah, Saudi Arabia (1968)

Dad full-throttled our air-conditioned Beetle toward the *souq* with Mom in the passenger side while Dennis and I sat in the back.

Ubiquitous horn honking from cars and motorcycles deafened my ears. Vehicles weaved around traffic at crazy speeds and left me in the stir of screeching brakes from angry drivers. I gaped at the hotbed of men clothed in white traditional *thawbs* or *dishdashah*[2] (flowing white cotton robes, the most common and practical of Saudi garments according to Dad) humming past us on mopeds and bicycles, and again in new American cars or old ones from the early fifties.

Pieces of cardboard and crumpled balls of paper lay about. I wondered how people could stand all the nonstop honking and crazy driving. I plastered my face against the window and heard a *clunkety-clunk* and *hee-haw*. Dad slowed the car down.

I saw a middle-aged Arab with a beak of a nose and grayish white sideburns. His neatly coiled turban stood tall on his head. He had a prominent chin and was clothed in a T-shirt and wraparound skirt. He rode bareback with a stick in one hand and the reins in the other. His dark-skinned legs with weathered flip-flops dangled comfortably to the left side of the donkey attached to a wooden cart. He masterfully manipulated the cart, which transported a double-strapped cylindrical tank. Didn't the man mind this mayhem? How did his donkey remain calm? I rolled down my window. Then I turned my head hoping to catch a better glimpse of the donkey pulling the wooden cart. A big black fly buzzed around me; I shooed it away.

"*Yallah, Yallah!*" This expression constantly filtered through the downtown's vast hovering cloud of sticky hot air.

"Come on, roll up the window, will ya?" Dennis grumbled. "Now it's all hot and sticky again."

"All right, I get it, Dennis, it was only for a quick second." I heaved a sigh and slowly rolled up my window, making sure the fly got out.

I leaned my head forward. "Look, guys, see that man steering a donkey in the middle of the traffic? What's inside the tank?" I asked, glancing at Dad.

"I think it's full of gasoline," Dad said, brushing a loose black hair from his face.

"Seeing that donkey scene, it's as if we've traveled back in time," Mom said.

Dad smiled. "Du, I thought the same thing when I first saw that very scene. Guys, how about I teach you a few Arabic words for men's and women's clothing? You're going to think it sounds funny, and it's extremely different from English."

"Yeah, that's for sure," I said from the backseat. "Words sound like they come out of the throat."

"Yes, Carina, you got that right," Dad said while he switched lanes to loud honking, "but it's a poetic language. They also read and write from the right-hand side to the left-hand side—opposite from us. Oh, and before I forget," he added, smiling, "there will be a quiz at the end of the day."

"Yeah, right, Dad," Dennis and I imitated each other.

I watched a tall Arab with a long gray beard dressed in the traditional white-cotton *thawb* stroll briskly along the road using a bamboo walking stick. He carried a small brown package on his head. I soon learned from my Arab friend Hussein, that in Saudi Arabia the *taqiyyah* and *kofiyyah* are the same: a small white skullcap. It keeps the *ghutrah*, an expansive cotton wrapped material, from falling off the head. The *ghutrah* is usually all white and the *shumagh* is white and red-checkered.[3] In Syria, Lebanon, and Palestine, *kofiyyah* refers to the head scarf-like cover. The *shumagh* is black-checkered and is called *taqiyyah*. Camel's hair twine, called *iqal*, is worn over the *ghutrah* to secure it.[4] Some Saudi men wear a *bisht* or *mishlah*, a loose robe over the *thawb*. The *bisht* or *mishlah* is usually worn by men during formal events, such as official meetings, social ceremonies and weddings. Below the *thawb*, men are clothed in either long or short comfortable white pants referred to as *sirwal*. *Madas* is the classic leather sandal that men wear.

"I bet you'd want to own a pair for sure," Dad said, raising his eyebrows at Dennis, who pretended not to hear him.

I rolled the car window back down. Every so often I caught the perfumed fragrance of abundant pink and white oleanders in full bloom. Their soft honeyed, vanilla aroma caressed my cheek like a floating feather. Across from our villa, I often picked their aromatic petals. I listened to Jeddah's lively buzz: a mutt barking; an occasional camel roar or the mopeds hooting over the common shouted Arabic greeting *Al Salamu Alaikum*, "Peace be upon you." Then I heard the common shouted response *Wa Alaikum Al Salam*, "Upon you be peace." Assorted shades of white or beige mud/stone houses rose three, four, and five stories above the city. Some of them were falling apart, a corner of the side wall in rubble, but the rest of the houses appeared maintained. I wondered if anyone lived inside.

Overhanging balconies in turquoise, various shades of green, dark brown, or bleached wood color looked like they were made of lace. They covered half a facade or an entire floor. Some arched or square doorways were made of ornately carved wood and painted blue or light green.

While Dad parked the car, children ran and danced behind us in an improvised welcome ceremony. We began our long walk down the dirt road in the intense morning heat, careful not to step into cracks, potholes, rubbish, or rotting food piles. Repulsive odors nipped at my nose, undercut by constant sweet and sour smells.

I noticed that banks displayed signs in English and Arabic. Pepsi signs were everywhere. Sometimes the Pepsi sign boasted a picture of a red, white, and blue bottle cap with a blue "PEPSI" in the center.

Men in traditional clothes strolled casually wearing either sandals or flip-flops. A boy, who held a large straw basket over his shoulders, approached Dad from behind. He looked about twelve years old.

"Why does that boy keep following us, Dad?"

"These boys come from Yemen, and we call them basket boys. He wants to earn some money, or *riyals* is what the Arabs call it. They come from Yemen in hopes to earn a lot of money carrying groceries. He would balance a customer's basket of goods on his head from the small indent at the bottom of the basket. Their Yemeni dress is colorful plaid-colored skirts and a T-shirt."

"They wear dresses?" I asked.

"No, Carina. These young men wear pieces of cloth wrapped around their waist that look like a skirt. Dress is another way of saying clothing," Dad reassured me.

Dad turned to the boy and spoke in Arabic.

"What did you tell him, Dad?" Dennis asked, eyeing the boy with curiosity.

"I told him 'no thank you,'" Dad said.

I inhaled a refreshing citrusy smell from a nearby juice vendor. He displayed an assortment of bananas and grapes drooping from string over gigantic pyramid-shaped mounds of oranges and lemons separated by round silver platters.

"Dad, can I get an orange drink from this place, please?" I pleaded.

"Great idea, Carina. Du and Dennis, how would you like some freshly squeezed orange juice?" Dad said.

I loved listening to Dad speak Arabic. I watched the vendor lower the juicer's handle to fill up my glass with freshly pumped orange juice. Dad handed him some money and gave me my glass. I gratefully let my drink rejuvenate me.

Dad squinted at the Nasif House, situated in the old *souq* of Jeddah, which belonged to a family of wealthy merchants.[5] While my young self had no idea about the Nasif House, I now appreciate how Dad stood in front of the house lecturing us on the following:

"I've heard people refer to this house as being the 'House with the Tree.' Listen up kiddies, Du; this very old house has many floors. Muhammad Nasif was born in Jeddah in 1884. He was well educated due to his love of books, and he worked as a proofreader for newspapers. He assembled a six-thousand-book Arabic library. This community library possesses a lot of irreplaceable documents, an accumulation of regional newspapers *(from 1924 on),* and rare printed books. He was also well known as a gracious host to eminent guests arriving in Jeddah. Two honorable guests, King Abdulaziz and Lawrence of Arabia, stayed here."

"Du, those antique balconies are beautiful," Mom said, glancing at Dad.

"Yes, they are. Those wooden balconies are called *rawashin* [bay windows].[6] The greater number of terraces in Jeddah are created from an East Indian redwood. The humid air and bugs have difficulty entering such tough wood. So, Du, guys, got any questions?" Dad grinned at each one of us.

"It's like traveling back to the days of *The Arabian Nights*," Mom said.

Dad nodded. "It is indeed."

"That is definitely a big tree," I said, eyeing Dad.

"Yes, it most certainly is, Carina."

Each bay window resembled marvelously embroidered chocolate lace over a five-story white cake. The main entrance, according to Dad, existed as Jeddah's Al-Balad, the historical center, the old city.

According to my friend Hussein, "Al-Balad literally means the town, downtown. It refers to historic Jeddah in this case because it used to be down town."

Memories of the *souq* make me feel that not too far off a seductive cone-like heap of oranges, apples, mangoes, bananas, pomegranates, and grapes lay neatly displayed along the vendor's countertop. Amidst the hustle and bustle, passersby clogged narrow alleyways, examined the wares, socialized, or just strolled to take in what to buy. Above some of the shops, particularly on this street, sand-colored houses embellished the scene. Agape turquoise shutters led onto small porches. Friendly craftsmen of every type worked in their stalls and spread out every product imaginable for us: shiny brass coffeepots, colorful hookah pipes, sandals, copper trays, elaborate stone bowls. Something inside this giant maze might just enchant me.

Merchants stood outside their shops calling "Please, Amreecan." Some lured us into their shops with a cup of *Shai* (pronounced shy), a sweet mint tea. This would become one of my favorite Arabic treats.

At times a sour reeking scent bit at my nose and made me queasy. Goats and donkeys wandered unattended in the unpaved alleys hoping to find edible scraps from heaps of foul-smelling rotten garbage. The mere sight of food, a combination of *shawermahs* and roasted chickens, helped alleviate my upset stomach.

Sometimes Saudi women gracefully roamed, covered from their shoulders down, in their black *abayahs*.[7] According to Dad, a woman wore a black floor-length garment over her clothing when she left the protection of her home; she protected her head with a black shroud or *āijab*, and a black shroud or *niqab* also protected her face.

Recalling that scene, I wonder if I found it strange that women completely covered themselves—*after all, we don't have to do this in America.* I guessed that women all over the world could dress however they desired. I could see none of the women's bodies; they glided through the streets like moving dolls. Sometimes their entire garb flowed like a pendulum lost in time for a moment in the desert. I stared at them and wondered what beauty lay hidden behind the veils.

I wasn't expecting the sudden burst of bizarreness on this particular day. A woman in haste rushed forward in her black *abayah*, exposing her beautiful red dress. She carried remnants of a green bush on her head and a small white lamb in her left hand, reminding me of a walking tree. I covered my mouth and stared at this foreign thing. Why would a woman have to do this? Where was her husband? He should be right behind her assisting her, I reasoned. I stood still and stopped to watch her pass, wondering what she was going to do with the green bush and cute lamb. A Yemeni basket boy followed hastily behind her in his skirt and gray jacket. He effortlessly balanced a huge straw basket filled with packages on his head while holding a white lamb in each arm. It was better than any circus tightrope act I'd ever seen.

I felt bad for the woman. I just didn't understand why she had to do this. I felt as though this country's laws were antiquated. I would never do this, nor would my husband expect this of me, I remember thinking. In America, we don't carry bushes on our heads.

I sauntered under the tin awning of a shop, which sheltered me from the piercing sun. On either side of me, a continuous passageway stretched out into a maze of alleys bordered with small open stalls selling countless items. Donkey-drawn carts roamed everywhere.

"Dad, why is that Saudi man carrying a metal rod over his shoulder with hanging tin buckets?" I asked.

"They're acting as water porters, Carina," Dad said.

The entrance of the *souq* catered to household items. I followed the labyrinth out into the open hot and humid air where most of the stalls consisted of only a raised level of cement that spanned several feet of floor space.

I stepped out of the glare of the sun, under a wooden awning with openings, and entered the fabric *souq*. Fabric from every spectrum of the color wheel thrived here. In the spice *souq*, six tin buckets filled with colorful mounds of spices sat atop wooden crates. Thick aromas of Arabic incense and spices captivated me. Hints of cardamom, cinnamon, and many other herbs I didn't recognize enchanted me. The sweet and sour aroma stung my nose.

Part of Jeddah's downtown mystique included the exotic perfume of frankincense that permeated deep into the *souqs*. It reminded me of church incense. Shops full of magnificent natural oils and fragrances bewitched me with musk and patchouli undertones amidst a mélange of aromatic Arabic incense. I sank into a deep reverie, anticipating Aladdin awaiting me around the corner. He would then douse me with rosewater and take me on a magic carpet ride to a henna lounge where a local artisan contrived ornate reddish brown peacocks.

We strolled along dirty streets dotted with shops where vendors sold glittering gold, sparkling silver, richly decorated chests, fabric, clothing, and toys—anything one could want.

"If you wanted to buy gold, you would go to the illuminated gold *souq*; if you wanted to buy fabric, you would go to the fabric *souq*," Dad said. My eyes widened at the mention of gold.

I recollected gazing at these ornate and colorful *hookas*[8] or waterpipes displayed in the *souq*. I know now that their hoses reach almost ten feet long. Craftsmen from Yemen devised this bizarre smoking apparatus. Red and blue coils hung from nails high above numerous-sized boxes of tobacco. I soon learned from my Arab friend Hussein, that "the coils are called *sheeshahs*."

Up to now I only saw men selling goods. Here I saw four women, young and old, whose dresses covered their arms and legs. They wore straw hats over white shawls wrapped around their heads, exposing their faces. They sat, wearing flip-flops, next to round tin pans propped on boxes, selling small round flatbread.

Mom frowned and shook her head in frustration. "Joe, why are those women crying so loud? And what are they doing balancing tins on their heads?"

"Good question, Du. These women are selling water."

Their shrill cries disturbed me too.

Beneath the owner's cement house, stalls contained rounds of Arabic breads neatly stacked like pancakes on glass shelves behind windowpanes. These aromatic common Arabic rounds fresh out of the oven reminded me of Mom's freshly made white bread back in America. The smell of bread rising in the oven combined with the mouthwatering taste of freshly made bread out of the oven transmitted me to my heavenly childhood memories. A vintage retro white kitchen scale caught my eyes. I soaked up the bread's delectable hovering aroma followed by ripening bananas.

Frequently, shops displayed two to ten rows of bunched up bananas dangling on a string from a metal rod. Below, round tin trays held pyramid-shaped mounds of a variety of dried fruits and nuts; most of them I had never seen before. I soon grew accustomed to their peculiar smell and eventually inhaled their pungency with eagerness. Sometimes wooden benches or cardboard boxes supported mounds of lemons and oranges, which lay one on top of another in neat rows above the street. A citrus sweetness filled the air. Dad carried an Arabic dictionary with him. He gestured with his fingers whenever it involved paying.

Exposed under the sun, men sold various raw meats and sausages displayed over a paper cloth that covered the top of a wooden table. Down the street, someone sat hunched over Indian style on the gravel, covered by an orange/

white shawl next to several plates of food scraps, a bowl with a spatula, and a straw basket.

"What is this person selling?" I asked Dad.

"Guys, this person is a poor person who can't feed himself, and sometimes people give him food or a little money."

"And doesn't anyone ever steal anything?" I asked. "Everything is out in the open"

"Never," Dad said. "If you did, your hand would be chopped off."

I cringed and kept my hands to myself. Goose bumps covered my arms as I thought about such oppressive and harsh punishment. I wouldn't think of straying away from Mom and Dad. And yet I found myself feeling empathetic for the poor person.

We continued our exotic journey through the *souq*. Watermelons resembling white and green soccer balls lay in heaps on the sidewalk. I heard an Arab dressed in a white *thawb*, with a gleaming grin, calling, "Please, Amreecan," while he sliced the watermelon in half, offering Dennis and me a wedge. I welcomed the taste of sweet water, a quick reprieve from this heat. Dad offered him some *riyals* for a whole watermelon.

A pungent garlic aroma teased my nostrils and made my stomach growl. I'd never smelled anything so delicious.

"Hey, guys, I could eat a *shawermah*." Dad turned to Mom. "Would you like one, Du?"

Shaking her head, she barely cracked a smile at Dad's offer. "No thanks."

"Guys, the shopkeeper marinates stacked lamb, mutton, or chicken on that long metal rod." Dad pointed. "It turns and cooks for hours and hours. Watch how he shaves paper-thin slices of meat from the surface. See how he serves it tucked inside the Arabic round bread."

My stomach growled. I couldn't wait to taste these creations.

After Dad handed Dennis a bite and an opened bottle of 7-Up, he turned to me.

"Here, Carina, you can have the last bite with your own 7-Up."

I took a bite and let the meat basted in fat and its own juices combined with onions enrapture me. I wanted more.

We neared stalls with glass containers of sizzling, crispy chickens rotating on skewers. Their delicious aroma, combined with the fatty *shawermah* fragrance, made me crazy with hunger.

"Dad, can we pick up some roasted chickens for dinner?" I pleaded.

"Great idea," Dad said to me, his face creased in a wide grin.

True to Jeddah's contrasts, we rounded a corner to a sudden assault of the nauseating stench of filthy sanitation and rubbish.

"Dad, that basket boy is shouting at us," Dennis said.

"Yes, Dennis. He offered to carry our items. If we need help finding something, he'll direct us."

He must have been about fourteen. I watched him surreptitiously when he placed our watermelon into a large straw basket with tightly woven rows of straw and a raised rim. He lifted it up off the ground and placed it onto his shoulder. There happened to be an indent at the bottom of the basket, where he placed it snugly on his head. Our basket boy wore his red-checkered *shumagh* similar to a turban around his head. He then glided gracefully across the dirt road. His left hand swayed freely by his side as he effortlessly balanced the basket with his right hand. He wore a butterscotch short-sleeved shirt over a black-and-white-checkered skirt wrapped around his waist and flip-flops on his dark feet. He faithfully followed us while uttering an occasional "*A salam alaykum.*"

"What is he saying, Dad?" I asked.

"It means *Peace be upon you*. You will hear this common greeting all around you."

In our plethora of trips to the *souq* we didn't always make it before prayer time, and I fondly remember one of Dad's many educational lectures: "Listen up, guys, so don't be alarmed when you hear a man's voice over the loudspeaker. In the religion of Islam, a mosque's attendant or *muezzin*[9] performs the chant to prayer or *adhan* on Friday for an everyday prayer or *ṣalat*. Prayer occurs five times a day: at daybreak, at twelve o'clock, during the middle part of the afternoon, after the sun goes down, and at the beginning of darkness."

In my most recent research,[10] I learned that a lot of mosques have implemented computerized versions of this chant to prayer, and speakers have cleared away the *muezzin*.

Across the way bunches of bananas and green and dark grapes dangled from rods above huge cone-shaped mounds of oranges and lemons partitioned by round silver plates. I got thirsty just looking at this colorful array as a sweet citrus fragrance filled my nostrils.

"Joe, what is going on with that crowd of men over there in the middle of the road?" Mom asked.

I gazed to where Mom pointed, down the dusty road to a cluster of men huddled like a pyramid in animated discussion.

He frowned. "I'm not sure. I saw something similar another time—turned out it was a beating." His frown turned dark. "Another time when I visited downtown I saw a beheading." After a pause, he continued. "The name of this square is 'Chop-Chop.' The punishment for killing someone would result in a man in charge called an executioner chopping off the offender's head with a sword. I know for a fact that if you steal, depending upon the seriousness of what you steal, you might lose a hand." Dad raised his voice in warning. "So remember to always stay close by and never *ever* take anything."

I caught my breath and swallowed, certain that I would never dream of stealing.

"This just might be one of those situations," Mom said with a weary sigh.

"Let's ignore it and continue on," Dad urged.

"Aw, Dad, I want to see someone get their finger cut off," Dennis begged. Dad ignored him.

I cringed and couldn't believe what I had just heard; at the same time I thought of all these horrible punishments for crimes. This country had a pretty backward way of living, very abrupt and unforgiving. I buried my dark thoughts as we visited Eve's tomb.

I reminded Dad years later that when we visited Eve's tomb, nothing remained. Throughout the course of our conversation, Dad mentioned that her tomb abided back in the oldest neighborhood in Jeddah near the *souq*. He confirmed that nothing existed. Dad continued to explain how the Arabic word *jaddah* means grandmother, which is akin to Jeddah.

According to Dr. Angelo Pesce, about the existing condition of the tomb of Eve, if you gaze above the barricade, only hills and bushes appear.[11] I also discovered that Jeddah derives its name conveying "ancestress" or "grandmother" arising out of the place here regarding Eve's alleged burial place, which the Saudi authorities demolished in 1928 because it stimulated superstition.[12]

I later learned how a few Arab teachers, namely Tabari, Masudi, and others, declared that in line with established practice, Eve is entombed in Jeddah; however, these citations fall short in offering any aspects regarding her burial place.[13]

On the way home, we picked up huge watermelons sitting on the side of the hot asphalt and paid the watermelon boy three *riyal*. I happily anticipated an ice-cold drink refreshing my taste buds. For a fleeting moment I forgot the 100-degree self-perpetuating heat.

I shook my head. Everything was so different from America. I constantly stole flighty glances because I knew I shouldn't stare.

Suddenly I heard the familiar man's voice, which vibrated through the still air from the top of a three-tier white minaret with two circular porches, narrow windows, and a conical top that rose above the city.[14] "*Allahu Akbar, Allahu Akbar.*"

"He chants four times the beginning of the chant to prayer, '*Allah is most great,*'" Dad told us.

Looking back upon it, I always welcomed and rejoiced in listening to his harmonious and peaceful chant.

Geckos scurried everywhere. They climbed cement walls and glared at us. They were extremely hard to catch because they were quick and nimble. When we returned to the villa, Dad cut up the watermelon and froze the pieces.

"You promised that Dennis and I could sleep on the roof tonight," I reminded Dad.

Perplexed, he tilted his head sideways in my direction. "Did I say that, Carina?"

"Come on, Dad!" Dennis amplified his voice, to which Dad winked.

"Okay, but let's get dinner first."

"I'll make cucumber salad, and we can serve the two skewered chickens alongside Arabic bread rounds," Mom said, suppressing a yawn. I understood; the walk and the heat had tired her.

"Mom, Dennis and I are going outside," I called over the sound of her chopping cucumbers on the board.

"Dinner will be ready in five minutes," Mom said.

Dennis and I played hide-n-seek out back while thinking of food.

It wasn't soon enough when we heard Dad holler, "Dinner's ready, guys. Come on in and wash your hands."

Mom set out roasted chickens, cucumber salad, watermelon, and big Arabic bread rounds. Arabic rounds, *shawermahs,* and roasted chicken were my favorite foods so far—the final topping off of an awesome day at the *souq.* After dinner, we sucked on watermelon popsicles and then brought our cots onto the open-air roof.

Summertime befell us in Jeddah, and still at nightfall the temperature remained sweltering hot. But I was way too excited in anticipation of our sleep adventure on the open-air roof. Up to now we had never slept outside of our beds.

"Dennis, look at how close the Milky Way is—it's like we can touch it," I said, drowsy after my first day in this magical land. But he was already asleep. I yawned, wondering what tomorrow would bring.

I tried to find the Southern Cross, a series of stars resembling a cross which Dad had told me about. Then I fell asleep in the twinkling of the night, dreaming of ornately decorated camels, *sheeshahs,* and a harem of basket boys that held my glittering stash while I zigzagged from one "hole in the wall" to another.

I remained an unabashed, boundless queen roaming in an untamed land—always ready for intrigue. The *souq's* mystique lured me through infinite alleyways. Waves of the desert dunes sang through me in haunting notes of genies and magic carpet rides.

RAYTHEON
COMPOUND
Jeddah, Saudi Arabia (1968)

D
ad's boss finally gave us the go-ahead to move from our temporary villa in the city to the Raytheon Housing Compound, located on a peninsula that jutted into the Red Sea. The compound lay adjacent to the Saudi Arabian Air Defense Complex and consisted of an air defense school, central maintenance point, and support facilities.

As we drove through the underdeveloped outskirts of Jeddah, I wondered what adventure lay before me; the three-month cultural experience of downtown Jeddah had roused in me a curiosity for the exotic. It was a ten-mile drive down a lonely desert road as sun, sand, and sea converged under an azure sky. We were foreigners here, yet I sensed a kind of belonging. To my left, the Red Sea glistened like aquamarine and sapphire jewels that stretched to the horizon. To my right there was only sand. It seemed to go on forever. And it caught me in its allure. I had a whimsical thought: I was the jewel of the Arabian desert.

Fortunately, the youthful mind conjures up infinite possibilities in which the ingredients of life continually simmer, bringing forth an elixir from which we sip. Little did I know that what lay ahead would provide the foundation, keystones, and building blocks of my life. Mom and Dad answered yes to a once-in-a-lifetime invitation. They lovingly presented us with an adventure that would bring so many new friends and happy memories. And great discovery.

Two insects splattered against the windshield. Dad pushed the button for the windshield liquid to clean away their remains. Our Beetle's engine came to a purring stop to the left of the guard's gate. We pasted our faces against the windowpane, eyeing two massive white stone walls shielding us on either side. What were these walls protecting? Or keeping out? Horse flies noisily buzzed around a young dark-skinned Saudi soldier in a green army uniform and a black beret. Ignoring the flies, he welcomed us with a huge smile of white teeth. I stole nervous glances at the soldier's darkly handsome face.

"*Al Salamu Alaikum*," he said, looking at Dad.

"*Wa Alaikum Al Salam*, we're the Rourke family," Dad replied.

The soldier glanced at the brown clipboard that he clutched and nodded then waved us in. Dad started up the Beetle's engine and we slowly drove down the main dirt road until we stopped at a second checkpoint, which provided entrance into the Raytheon Company employee housing compound. Dad stopped the car and a Raytheon guard dressed in typical white *thawb* and red-checkered *shumagh* approached us. He lifted the barrier and motioned us to pass through. Sometimes when they got to know us, they waved us through. There were over a hundred one-story rectangular houses with flat roofs arranged in six rows parallel to the shore of the Red Sea. Despite my excitement, I couldn't help thinking: had we become the compound's newly captivated prisoners? I hastily rolled up the window, shooing a pesky horsefly into the hot and muggy salt air.

"Guys, we're in house number fifty, and it's right on the shore of the Red Sea." Dad's eyes twinkled with excitement.

In high spirits, Mom turned her head to the left and took in her surroundings. "Du, what's that stage for?" She pointed to an open cement area and little booth surrounded by a wall.

"That's the outdoor movie theater," he said, then threw a glance at us over his shoulder. "You know how in America weekends are on Saturday and Sunday?"

We nodded.

"Well, here in Saudi Arabia, Wednesday starts the weekend and movie night on the compound at the open-air stage. Thursday and Friday is the same as our Saturday and Sunday."

I looked at Dennis in surprise. Thursday and Friday sounded weird; not like a weekend. It would take some getting used to, just like this steamy weather.

"Where is everyone?" I scrunched my nose.

"Great question, Carina," Dad said. "Almost everyone returned back home to America for their vacation. In a few weeks they'll be back, ready for school like you two. Now, look over by the tall booth centered at the rear of the cement floor. On movie nights, a projector rests on the top floor and a parent volunteers to run a two- or three-reel movie on the stage's white wall."

"What day is it today?" My voice rose at the prospect of getting to watch a movie.

"Believe it or not it's Wednesday."

Dennis's eyes lit up. "So can we go to the movies tonight?"

I wondered what movie we'd see.

"We'll see. I'm not even sure they're starting yet. We'll check it out later."

"Neat isn't it, Dennis?" I grinned at him, bouncing in his seat.

There were no paved roads; dirt roads separated the array of white shoebox houses. The occasional date palm added majesty to the compound. I spotted them in sandy gaps between every fifth house or so. Crows circled overhead, endlessly cawing.

"Check out the cement building near those palm trees," Dad said, pointing into the distance. "You're all going to love this place. That's the snack bar next to an Olympic-size swimming pool with lounge chairs and a kiddie pool. Moosa, the snack bar cook, is a Somali. He's part of the cooking crew, and they sell French fries, hot dogs, hamburgers, soda, popcorn, Mars bars, M&Ms, and other goodies."

French fries! The thought of familiar American food set my stomach to growling in anticipation.

"We just passed the recreation center; everyone here calls it the Rec Center. It's right across from the movie theatre." Dad smiled like a boy.

Excited, I glanced at Dennis; his mouth gaped.

"You can play ping-pong, even shoot pool. And at the far end of the building is an empty room used for afternoon movies or what's called a matinee," Dad continued.

I hoped to see every movie.

"What's ping-pong, Dad?" Dennis asked.

"It's a game with a table and net in the middle. Each player gets a paddle coated with green rubber on each side. You whack the tiny white ball, bouncing it on the table back and forth across the little net," Dad said, chuckling.

"I can do that," Dennis boasted.

"Yeah, right, Dennis." I grimaced.

"Wanna bet? Wanna bet, Carina?"

"How do you play pool?" I said to Dad.

"Wouldn't it be more fun to learn with your new friends?" Dad suggested with an impish grin.

"I bet I could beat you…" I teased Dennis.

"Guys!" Dad's voice rose.

"You were right, Schatzi—this is certainly one giant playground for the children." Mom had been quietly absorbing everything.

"Dad, I'm gonna have fun here," Dennis said.

"Yeah," I agreed. "I love this place."

As we continued down the dirt road, I saw four green clay tennis courts.

"I want to get out and look around for a minute," I begged.

Dad stopped the car.

Dennis and I flung the doors open and raced outside with Dad and Mom trailing behind us. A large cement house stood adjacent to the tennis court, standing out from the other carbon-copy ones.

"This is the Grubbs's house. Glen Grubbs is the in-country Saudi Arabian HAWK program manager for Raytheon," Dad said.

The Grubbs's house was much bigger than the other compound houses and closer to the Red Sea. It had an open-air patio on each side and a small carport attached to the side of the patio. *That's not fair,* I thought to myself. Dad then told us that the Grubbs's house had to be specially constructed to accommodate the family's nine children.

A large gazebo in the yard caught my eye.

"Dad, can we have one of those at our house?" I asked.

"His house isn't like the others," Dennis noted.

"When you're the boss, you get to have a bigger house," Dad said. "That's the way it is. But guess what, guys? All the houses have air-conditioned rooms. I promise, you guys are going to love your new home."

"*Das ist schön*," Mom said, smiling contentedly.

"Yes, it is nice, Schatzi. Now let's head for our house. It's on the other side of the compound." Dad pointed his tanned arm toward the pool. "Hey, guys, look over there. Let's check out the snack bar and pool."

We all piled out of the car and I raced in front of Dennis. I felt the first wave of heat engulf my body. Horseflies buzzed about. Everything shimmered in the heat. Geckos scurried. Huge black carpenter ants danced across the pool's concrete areas and then hid behind the fence's neatly groomed tall shrubs.

A pair of date palms towered over the fence's red, white, blue, and yellow billboards, which shielded us from any onlookers. Their long arched leaves pointed to the pier and swayed in the humid breeze. I could smell the salt air. Several chirping birds darted in and out of the pink and white oleander blooms that adorned the far side of the fence opposite the pool's main entrance. They were a colorful contrast from the never-ending white sand and desert grasses that extended to the shore of the Red Sea. White plastic patio chairs and yellow lounge chairs dotted the grounds. Nearby, a tall lifeguard chair watched over the pool's six lanes. *I might just want to become a lifeguard,* I thought to myself.

When I approached the pool, I smelled chlorine and the glistening turquoise water enticed me; I wanted to jump in.

"I want to go for a swim!" I begged.

"I'm hungry," Dennis whined.

"Yeah, me too," I agreed, suddenly diverted.

"I'll tell you what. We can eat dinner at the snack bar, I promise, after we finish touring the compound. And the best part is yet to come!" Dad winked at us all, looking pleased with himself.

Dad herded us back into the Beetle and continued on to our house.

"How many families live here, Du?" Mom asked.

"About 110 or so."

"I can see a huge field—wait, it looks like a softball field!" Dennis bounced in his seat.

"We're getting close to our house now," Dad said and nodded in the direction of our new home.

"Wow, what's that huge field next to the softball area, Dad?" I said, leaning into the window.

"I've been told that PCS, the Parents' Cooperative School, *your* school, holds races on this track and field."

With the field behind us, we made a right-hand turn between two houses and Dad proudly announced "Number 50, guys. This is it. Welcome to your new home."

I stepped out of the car into an endless expanse of white desert sand.

"Look at all the sand! There must be enough to fill a giant bulldozer!" Dennis exclaimed.

"We're living in the desert," Mom said gently. "So I see there's at least a screen door to keep out the bugs."

"That's right, Du. OK, let's go around back," Dad announced.

"Look, Dennis, there's that long road again going into the water!"

"That long dirt road is called a jetty," Dad said. "It goes out to the Red Sea. When we arrive at the end of the jetty, we'll be on a huge concrete platform and a place to park the Beetle. It's called a pier. There's even a ladder to climb down to swim in the waves! And don't even think of going near that ladder. So if you promise me, then we can take a quick drive out there, OK?" Dad made direct contact with our eyes.

We cheerfully agreed, and Dad drove a short distance to the shore. Two lonely palms embellished the Red Sea's panorama. They swayed peacefully in the muggy breeze.

Clusters of whitecaps interrupted the Red Sea's deep blue. The jetty extended about a quarter of a mile from the original shoreline to the end of the reef.

"Du, let's get out for a minute. Carina and Dennis, you both will be careful," Mom warned us with a stern face.

Dad parked on the dirt side of the jetty. We raced outside.

"Stop running, guys, you'll slip and hurt yourself!" Mom hollered.

I stayed next to Dennis, watching him carefully until Mom and Dad arrived. Mom grabbed Dennis by the shoulders, making sure that he steered clear of the pier's edge and wouldn't slip in his white sneakers.

"Aw, Mom, but I want to see those huge waves," he said, pouting.

We headed toward the pier. Mom made immediate eye contact with Dennis. "Now hold my hand, then you can watch them from here."

"Dennis, cooperate with your mother," Dad said sternly. "It's slippery from the waves."

At the reef end, the pier widened. On the left, the pier was half dirt; however to the right side, a long narrow slab of slick weathered cement supported by various-sized boulders created a wall that plunged deep into the sea. Twelve white stakes with red tips prevented cars from entering. Toward the end of the pier, a huge rusty handrail extended from the depths of the Red Sea to about three feet above ground.

Further down, the pier gave way to a large rocky jetty peppered with whitewashed rocks. The Red Sea's turbulent waves engulfed its calm jade water in white froth. The waves smashed against bulging boulders, spattering us. My T-shirt clung to me in the heat, relieved occasionally by the salty breeze. I was giddy to check out our new home. I noticed that Mom looked very pleased too and eager to get on to the house.

"Ok, Du, I'm ready for the grand finale tour," she said.

We drove along the jetty to our new house. Milky white waves bashed the rocks that flanked the road. We neared the front door of our new house, and Dad swerved a sharp left and then right, taking us to the rear of our home.

We grabbed our stuff and followed Dad to the blue-trimmed screened back door, then waited while he unlocked the kitchen door. Our house sat in the last row, and the back faced the sea. Dank air wafted past us with a mineral-spiked salty smell. As I entered our new home, cool air relieved me. The three-walled U-shaped galley kitchen wasted no space. I spread out my arms on either side of me, and to my left I touched the porcelain sink next to an ivory laminate countertop and mission white cupboard. To my right, a four-burner gas stove snuggled in between two ivory laminate countertops and two cupboards also in mission white, above.

"What's this, Du?" Mom pursed her lips and pointed to a white box.

"That's a radar range, where we can quickly reheat our meals," Dad answered.

"*Das ist gut.*" Mom beamed.

The double side-door refrigerator intrigued me; ours in America had two doors on top of each other. A washer and dryer fit neatly on another wall at counter level. We turned right, into the dining room, adorned with five butterscotch vinyl-covered chairs around a square oak table. The white-walled living room complemented an open floor plan with two sets of French doors that led out to the patio. We continued toward the front door down a short narrow hallway, which led into a bedroom.

"Who gets this huge bedroom across from the small bathroom?" Dennis asked. Before Dad could answer, he said, "Look, Mom and Dad, you guys get doors to the patio too."

"Who do you think this room belongs to, guys?" Dad chortled.

We shrugged; we knew it was theirs.

"Don't worry. Each of your rooms has a set of patio doors like ours."

Dennis raced ahead to the next room and yelled back, "This room is mine!"

I quickly caught up in time to see a light pine desk and twin teak bed in a medium-sized bedroom with—sure enough—French patio doors. I guessed that mine was at the end of the long narrow hallway next to the bathroom with a white tub, toilet, and sink. *Not a bad view onto the patio. I could be comfy here.* The room looked antique, resembling a cameo goddess face painted in blue, pink, and beige with surrounding pink roses. I instantly fell in love with my room. A welcome feeling filled the air and gave me goose bumps.

"Guys, I think it's best to go to bed on time tonight," Mom announced.

Dennis didn't respond. Neither did I.

Dad entered the room at that moment. "Why don't we all go for a swim instead?"

"We'll get our swimsuits on!" I said, not waiting to see what the others did.

"I'll grab a towel for everyone," Dad announced over his shoulder, heading to the other room.

We rushed to our respective bedrooms. Opening my suitcase, I fished for my favorite bathing suit, a two-piece, sky-blue seersucker suit, and quickly changed. Dennis leaped out of his bedroom in his white T-shirt and red bathing suit.

"We all have to apply suntan lotion," Mom called from the master bedroom.

"This is a must," Dad added, as Dennis and I crowded the doorway of their room. "Always put it on before going outside."

After lathering ourselves in the white cream, we left the house and headed down the long dirt road to the pool. Dennis and I wrapped our towels around our bodies. Our adventure took on a new beginning just as we passed by date palms and the basketball court, arriving at the huge pool. The sparkling aquamarine water enticed me and Dennis to jump in.

"Can we dive off the diving board?"

"Sure, just be careful not to slip, and look to make sure nobody is in the water beneath you," Mom advised when she and Dad took up spots on a grouping of yellow lounge chairs next to the pool. She'd put on a yellow two-piece bikini and Dad wore black boxers.

"Dennis, wanna see who can hold their breath the longest?" I challenged.

"Nah, you'll probably win anyway."

"We'll race with you and Dennis," Mom said.

Dad jumped in followed by Mom, who dove in gracefully.

I thought Mom and Dad slowed down a bit to let me win.

After our swim race, we followed the lingering greasy fry aroma to the opposite side of the pool where a white lattice-covered patio with round white tables and chairs provided a shaded dining area.

"I'm definitely ordering a cheeseburger and fries, Dad," Dennis said, dripping water onto the patio cement.

"Me too," I added.

"Du, how about you?"

"I'll order the same," Mom replied.

After fetching our food, we found a free table while Dad paid the cashier.

"Wow, this stuff is really good," Dennis said.

"Just don't get too used to eating out," Mom reminded us.

"Well, it is handy, with it down the street," I said, hoping to sway her into doing this again.

"When we're all done we're going to head back home and get an early night's rest," Mom said.

Dad nodded. "Get your stuff and I'll meet you at the gate."

<hr>

Ramadan (1968)

One day in December of 1968, Dad arrived home from work early with Mom.

"Guys, let's go listen to the cannon go off in downtown. It'll be a blast since these cannons look like those used in the Civil War. Cannon fire was part of the Ramadan celebration."

"Cool, I definitely want to see a cannon!" Dennis stood on his toes.

"I'll need to plug my ears." I scrunched my nose.

"What does *Ramadan* mean?" Mom asked.

"Du, I'll explain to you on the way. Come on, guys, I think you really will get a kick out of this. Ready? Climb fast into the Beetle!"

Once in the car Dad lectured us on *Ramadan*: "Each year Muslims worldwide are not allowed to eat, drink, or smoke throughout the day for the entire month of *Ramadan*.[15] Someone told me about this cannon which goes off at sunrise, signaling to Muslims that they must refrain from eating or drinking all day long. Then at sunset the cannon goes off again. This signals to Muslims that they are allowed to resume eating and drinking until sunrise. *Ramadan* is a time to cleanse the body and soul from contamination and to think about God. Muslims think about Allah, the one and only God in the Islamic religion."

That evening brought adventure to my new life in Jeddah. Within minutes of our arrival on a desolate desert field near Prince Sultan Street, I saw a Civil War-like four-wheeled cannon.[16] I stood safely across from two brown tents, staring at a uniformed man who gracefully fired the cannon–ending in a *kaboom*. I covered my ears and felt the air vibrate while trying to avoid breathing in the stinging whiffs of gunpowder. Huge clouds of smoke rose up then slowly disappeared.

According to Encyclopedia Britannica, *Ramadan* in Islam is the ninth month of the Muslim calendar and the religious month of abstinence.[17] It commences and terminates upon sighting a fresh moon. Throughout the day Muslims abstain from edibles, beverages, and intercourse. They celebrate evening dinners or *iftars* with companions and widespread family.

Looking at one of Dad's many photographs reminded me of the intrigue of why the Saudis used a cannon. Fascinated, I detected that we had been fortunate enough to step back for a moment in time. According to Bizzie Frost's article in *The Saudi Gazette*, two contrasting anecdotes crop up concerning the inception of this ritual.[18] One anecdote occurred throughout the early era of Islam just as another anecdote occurred during the *Mamluk* period of Egyptian past events—both anecdotes involved the firing of a cannon. I unearthed that Ms. Frost also witnessed the cannon's *ka-boom,* and my revelation today confirmed why this scene had this effect on me.

Ms. Frost explained that somehow this ritual traveled to Jeddah. Throughout the eighties and early nineties, yearly, for the whole month, someone clothed in khaki uniform resided in a brown tent positioned near the field by Prince Sultan Street. His sole duty was to fire the cannon morning and evening.[19]

I was apprehensive about the cannon's position, which measured roughly fifteen feet away from one of the tents. Although I never fasted for an entire month, later in my life throughout my two-day fast, I enjoyed the purity that I experienced alongside an absolute agility of presence.

On our return ride, Ramadan's hullabaloo felt like Christmas. I thought about our lengthy Christmas vacation since Ramadan fell in December that year. I felt firmly connected to this wonderful playground which would be our new home.

"*Gute Nacht,* Mom and Dad," I said once I was firmly settled in my bed an hour later.

"*Gute Nacht;* sleep tight and don't let the bed bugs bite," Mom and Dad sang.

As I lay there in bed I wondered if Dennis recited the German prayer every night before he went to sleep. I would have to remember to ask him someday, but right now I was too sleepy so I turned over and closed my eyes.

"I am small, my heart is pure; so nobody lives inside except Jesus alone."

THE *HAJJ*
Jeddah, Saudi Arabia (February 1969)

A t the time of the annual *Hajj*, I was one month shy of turning nine. I jumped out of bed, slipped into my bathrobe, and headed into the kitchen for breakfast when I heard those two words, "Mada'in Saleh," again. Mom and Dad were sitting in the living room carrying on a lively conversation about how to spend the non-work days of the *Hajj*, when all companies shut down operations. They were admiring the patio's desert plants visible through the French doors while they sipped their morning coffee. I joined them. Dad told me that he and the Grahams were planning a camping trip to Mada'in Saleh and Petra.

"Wow, with the Grahams, for real!" I squealed.

Dennis arrived, yawning.

"Hey, Dennis, we're going camping with the Grahams to—what's the name of that place?" I asked, grinning.

"Mada'in Saleh," Dad said with a laugh.

"Now I remember, that's right, Medsala." I nodded.

"Mada'in Saleh is a city about eight hours away with monstrous rock-carved temples. Nick Graham would drive the jeep. Mom and I would drive the Beetle loaded up with camping gear and our personal stuff. Yeah, it would be a blast to camp in the middle of the desert." Dad's eyes sparkled deep blue with excitement. I loved seeing him this way.

"Dennis, do you want some jam on toast?" I said to him cheerfully.

"Sure," Dennis said.

I imagined sleeping in my cozy sleeping bag gazing at all those faraway stars. I heard the toast pop up and hurried to retrieve it. I grabbed two plates, knives, and jam then placed all of it on the dining room table.

"By the way," said Mom, "we were also thinking of doing our shopping this morning at the PX to pick up camping food. Remember all those scrumptious American goodies that I brought home the last time I shopped there."

"I sure hope I can get some Bazookas," Dennis said.

"Sure, they probably have some, Dennis," Mom said.

Talking about American goodies kindled fond memories of eating hot dogs at Friendly's.

"What about some Oscar Meyers in a bun?" I said.

"Anything you can find in America, you can be sure that the PX carries. So let's rock and roll and head out to beat the crowds," Dad said with verve.

Wow, it'll be just like the good old days shopping back in the States with those shiny white slippery floors and aisle after aisle of my favorite foods. I hope it has everything I wish for, I thought to myself.

We piled into the Beetle and headed downtown. We passed by Jeddah's airport. Today the airport is known as King Abdulaziz International Airport (KAIA) and is located a good distance from the city.

Dad pulled into a parking spot alongside the entrance to the airport near a stretch of small open-fronted shops that displayed countless items. We got out and walked lazily on the sidewalks under green or white awnings shielding us from the gleaming sun.

Fascinated, Mom asked, "Du, so what's the *Hajj* all about?"

Dad responded with an ear-to-ear grin. "In the religion of Islam, all Muslims during one occasion in their life are required to perform the *Hajj* or pilgrimage traveling to the sacred city of Mecca. The *Hajj* is the fifth of the crucial Muslim disciplines and establishments acknowledged as the Five Pillars of Islam. Jeddah is a huge gathering area for pilgrims from around the world. Before modern transportation, the pilgrims arrived by land and sea. Then they walked or rode camels or animal-drawn wagons to Mecca." [20]

I don't precisely recall how my juvenile self reacted to this *Hajj* scene; however admiring Dad's numerous photos excited my imaginative memory. Thoughts swirled in my head like a desert storm. Where were all the women? I tried hard to be the obedient daughter with diesel fuel wafting under my nose. Mom told Dad that she was impressed by all of these pilgrims dressed in their native attire. I stared at the maelstrom of pilgrims crowding the shops just at the noon rush hour.

"Why do some Arabs have their bare shoulders showing with white cloth tightly wrapped around their body?" I asked Dad, dumbfounded at the site of these strangely clad men.

"And some of them have shaved heads and they're carrying suitcases on their heads," Dennis added.

"These pilgrims carry all of their baggage to Mecca, the Holy City, to pray there to their God, Allah," Dad informed us.

That didn't explain the "Band-aids" stretched across their bare chests. Could it have been part of some ritual? There wasn't much Dad didn't know, I contemplated. But perhaps this happened to be one of them.

Vendors sold clothing, cigarettes, drinks, fruit, newspapers, and magazines. We stepped off the sidewalk onto a dirt road nearing airport construction. Dark-skinned men in colorful robes lounged outside stalls, which displayed a black sign with "Riyad Bank" written in big white letters. Foreign currencies could be exchanged here. I recognized the picture of the universally displayed red, white, and blue Pepsi logo.

I felt the heat draw out beads of sweat on my forehead. Trash lay everywhere amid remnants of rolled-up paper and pieces of cardboard. I inhaled the smell of rotting garbage and kept shooing away pesky buzzing flies. I welcomed the mouth-watering fragrance of hot *shawermahs* and spices that mingled with the pungent odors of garbage. I would soon grow genuinely fond of *shawermahs*.

We hustled across the street toward a shop displaying rugs. The splash of vibrant hand-woven rugs in bright patterns burst out with expressive color. Rugs hung from stretched ropes above an expanse of them flatly rolled out along the sidewalk. Others were folded in heaps or neatly rolled up inside the shop. Now and again a rug merchant demonstrated his commodity by spreading it out over the white-and-black-checkered curbs. Dad said many of these rugs were brought in by the pilgrims to help pay their travel expenses. Young and old carpet merchants from every corner of the world—to name a few countries, Iran, Turkey, and Afghanistan—perched crossed-legged on their wares hoping to get enough money to pay for their *Hajj* to Mecca.

A plump elderly Arab, cloaked in his white *thawb*, sat contentedly in front of a round brass tray that displayed four tiny glasses filled with a golden liquid. I leaned forward, intrigued. I turned eagerly to Dad, who was talking with another Arab. The lanky middle-aged man wore a traditional red-checkered *shumagh* and long gray robe. The Arab held a rug secure under his right arm.

I tugged at Dad's arm. "What are those men drinking?"

"*Shai*, the local sweet mint tea," Dad explained.

"Sounds like the word *shy*?"

"That's right, Carina." Dad winked.

"That's a weird word for tea," I said, and wondered if it tasted as good as it appeared. I would soon acquire a love for it.

"*Yallah! Yallah!*" men yelled, gathered in what seemed to be a friendly conversation.

"Did you hear that, guys? That means *Come on! Let's go!* You'll be hearing that a lot." Dad threw us a slanted smile.

"That's a fun word." I chuckled to myself.

————————

The airport's rug scene now reminds me of a crowded museum, with people marveling at paintings and tapestries, but here men marveled at beautifully handcrafted rugs. Today I delight over the different rugs I proudly display in my home. I own several magnificent Afghan Belouch Tribal rugs and Persian rugs, both a Baktiari Persian and one from northwestern Persia. My favorite rug is an impressive silk Persian Nain, which my mother cherishes in her apartment. Walking on a Nain carpet is comparable to walking on shimmering sand.

We made our way back to the car by a different route. I noticed a policeman in his beige uniform patrolling the airport's oncoming traffic and donkey-carts. Dark men dressed in colorful robes congregated ahead of us. Beyond them, I saw two large "WELCOME TO JEDDAH" banners in English and Arabic script hovering twenty feet above the divided airport road. American cars crowded the place, as well as vans, buses, taxis, and mopeds. Parked vehicles choked the airport entrance. Jeddah existed not entirely like a welcoming city. By this time, the high-noon sun baked down on us.

Ornamental date palms, oleander shrubs with pink blossoms, and other plants dotted the divide of the asphalt road. A dank breeze brought with it a hint of sweet vanilla perfume. When the coast appeared clear, we nimbly crossed the road.

A sea of pilgrims and their colorful patterned dress streamed in and out of the airport. Tall ebony-skinned men with ear-to-ear grins sauntered gracefully alongside the road. I searched for any women and found none, to my amazement.

I gazed up at the airport's tri-level building. It reminded me of a huge above-ground parking building. Men stood on the second-level balcony in front of colorful garments hanging over the balustrade. They must have gone inside the washroom and washed their clothes. The handrail copycatted an extended clothesline with various draped clothing flapping in a muggy breeze.

I later learned that pilgrims from around the world use Jeddah's terminal where they clothe themselves with a white robe called *Irham* (pilgrim's garment) en route to Mecca.[21] The *Irham* is made up of two layers of uninterrupted material apart from silk.

I passed by a long line of cars waiti`ng to get to the airport. Then—finally!— in the middle of this ocean of men, I caught a glimpse of a girl my age standing next to two younger boys. A man in a traditional white *thawb* and coiled white turban—probably her father—leaned down to help her close a suitcase. Her pink tightly fitted dress gleamed under the bright sun. Her shoulder-length jet-black hair was neatly pulled back in a ponytail and secured by a white elastic band. She seemed relaxed, dressed in periwinkle below-the-knee tights and white sneakers. I glided by her, brushing her shoulder. We winked at each other. I felt an instantaneous connection. Was this a good omen that all would be well here in this foreign land?

A sea of tall dark men, wearing gold-colored *fezes* on their heads and draped in colorful robes, strolled pompously. I stole glimpses at the men, who all wore a white cloth that covered the body from the waist down. Another cloth gathered around the shoulder. Pilgrims grasped colorful trunks or balanced packages over their heads. Others carried black umbrellas. Memories of this make me feel that I'm at the opera being entertained by Giuseppe Verdi's Triumphal March from *Aida*. Intermittently, like slow-moving mannequins, a black-shrouded woman or two popped through the crowds. Exploring hard enough, and in the thick of this beat of life, I noted women promenading behind their men in multicolored headscarves and vibrant-patterned dresses.

Swarthy men hunkered over their luggage and conversed with rug merchants situated beyond the rug display. Arabs in traditional white robes sat talking on the sidewalk's edge while admiring the red rug exhibition. Pilgrims with their exposed shoulders rushed over to a series of parked red Volkswagen buses with luggage overflowing the roof racks.

"Is that a policeman?" Dennis asked, pointing toward a man in a beige uniform with a dark beret.

"That's right, Dennis," Dad said, putting an arm around his shoulders. "You know that their job is to protect people and make them feel safe."

"Yeah, Dad, I know that," Dennis responded.

"Here they also have the religious police called *Mutawwa'un*, but they don't get to wear a uniform.[22] These men apply Islamic rules of behavior by making sure that women are properly covered, merchants don't open shops at prayer time, and during *Ramadan* nobody is allowed to eat or drink throughout the day until after sunset. Otherwise these men have the authority to physically punish you."

"Mmm…wh-what you say, Dad?" he mumbled, distracted by the crowd.

"Like regular policemen, the religious police carry a stick too."

"Dad, I remember at the *souq* when the women in long tight pants were stopped by the police carrying a stick," I added.

"Wow, you remember that, Carina? You monitor everything," said Dad with an amused chuckle. "I know, Dennis, I soon got used to how different life is here."

"Yes, Du," Mom said. "So we'll always stick close together in this foreign land. OK, Dennis and Carina?"

"Don't you worry about a thing," Dad said, delivering an "I love you expression" to us all. "Nothing will happen to you, I promise."

"Schatzi, we'd better head to the PX before they close," Mom said.

Journeying with Dad in the Beetle was pure adventure. We always experienced something new and different in the magical desert, even if it was only to drive to the *souq* fifteen minutes away. We picked up two large rounds of fresh warm Arabic bread and two sizzling rotisserie chickens for dinner.

I now know that Mecca is the most sacred Muslim city. [23] Muhammad created Islam, and this was his city of birth; Muslims face Mecca during supplication. Non-Muslims do not have permission to enter Mecca because it is a religious city.

I also learned the following: The *Hajj* [24] lasts five days. The long journey's celebration commences the seventh day of *Dhu al-Hijjah* (the last month of the Islamic year); it finishes during day twelve. If the pilgrimage is burdensome for a Muslim's family, he or she may designate a relation or confidant who intends to complete the *Hajj* for him or her. Once the pilgrim nears Mecca, he or she is considered in divine environment or *ihram*, and wears the *ihram* dress, which is made up of two flawless white cloths surrounding the body. The pilgrim is not allowed to trim his hair or nails until the end of the journey. He or she arrives in Mecca and performs *seven* tours encircling the divine altar, the *Ka'bah,* inside of the Great Mosque; kisses or touches the Black Stone; and runs seven times from the hills of Safa and Marwah. During the second ceremonial phase, occurring within day eight through day twelve of the month, the pilgrim stops by the religious cities beyond Mecca—Jabal al-Rahmah, Muzdalifah, and Mina—to give up an *animal* celebrating Abraham's sacrifice. The pilgrim propels seven rocks at each of the three columns in Mina and comes back to Mecca, where he or she carries out rotating the *Ka'bah* prior to departure.

I'm so glad I experienced the airport's *Hajj* scene, even though at the time, as a child, I wasn't aware of its effect on me. Today I have a better understanding of the *Hajj* significance reflected in Mansour's beautiful reminiscence regarding his *Hajj* experience: "These pilgrims left their home and loved ones thousands of miles away to be with Allah; rich and poor, young and old—they all carry their luggage to a foreign land to be with the one and only Allah their creator."

The pilgrims performing the *Hajj* reminded me of the pilgrims coming over on the Mayflower to Plymouth, Massachusetts, in 1620. Although these pilgrims sought a more bountiful life, they also sought religious freedom. The *Hajj* pilgrimage defines an individual's holiest passage, known to purify and cleanse the soul.

Commissary (PX) (1969)

I walked up and down the PX's lengthy aisles with shiny white linoleum floors, ogling the variety of meats, fresh produce, and dairy and baked goods. The shelf space stocked canned and packaged goods.

"Carina, why don't you grab ten of those crispy La Choy chow mein noodles," Mom said.

"Du, I think we should probably grab a crate of them since they will be so convenient to eat while camping," Dad added. "Keep an eye out for what you want to buy."

"Why are we stocking up on all these snap-open cans of crispy La Choy chow mein noodles?" I asked with a confused face.

"We can pour them over cans of either Dinty Moore's Beef Stew or Campbell's Chunky Beef for our camping dinner—everything tastes great when you're camping…just wait and see!" Dad chuckled. "We need to find the soup aisle. Check for Campbell's Chunky Beef and Dinty Moore's Beef Stew!" he hollered.

"Can we roast marshmallows over the fire?" I begged.

"Of course, Carina," Dad said.

"Can we bring a box of Pepsi-Cola?" Dennis added.

"The local gas stations always carry them ice-cold, Dennis. Why don't we stock up on a ton of Tang instead?" Dad asked. "Here's aisle two, guys. Each of you grab ten cans and I'll grab the rest."

Between Dinty Moore and Campbell's, our cart stood almost filled to the brim.

"Du, I'll grab bacon for your favorite BLT sandwiches," Mom said.

"*Dankeschön, Schatzi.*" Dad smiled.

"Hey, Mom, in aisle three they have Hershey's Milk Chocolate Bars in a box—can we pretty please get some boxes?" I begged.

"Only one box, Carina," Mom said firmly.

"Where's the bubble gum, Dad?" Dennis asked again.

"Keep looking. I'm sure that we'll see them. If not, remind me. OK, Dennis?" Dad winked.

"You bet!" Dennis shouted excitedly.

"Over here, I'm in number three, Dennis!" I hollered.

"I'm coming!" Dennis shouted back.

"OK, guys, our cart is full and we need to get home to finish packing," Dad announced.

We cruised at outrageous speeds down the long winding road back to the compound. Vendors enticed us to stop, and we picked out a giant watermelon from an endless supply of roadside vendors along the hot asphalt.

MADA'IN SALEH
Saudi Arabia (1969)

6

I woke up excited the next morning. An ornate mahogany dresser met my eyes from across my bedroom. I studied the cameo goddess carving of the dresser surrounded by pink roses. I felt special. Reflecting back upon this image makes me feel like Aphrodite, the Greek goddess of love. I'm ever so grateful for my parents' ability to love and cherish me. I gave a deep joyous sigh in anticipation of today's adventure.

At eight o'clock, Mom and Dad climbed into the front of our 1968 white Beetle while Dennis and I took our places in the back. An army green-colored tarp, reminiscent of a giant Christmas package, lay tightly roped and sealed on the roof rack filled with our gear and our best friends' (the Grahams) camping gear. Our suitcases were stuffed in the front trunk. Dad's buddy Nick, an amicable and slender man of medium height with jet-black hair, led our procession in their red jeep. His wife, Renate, a friendly woman with long beautiful brown hair, sat up front. Their kids, Michael and Philip, sat in the rear seats.

We drove along the Red Sea coast through a vast plateau of sand and rocks, scattered with mountains diverse in size and height. Dad later told me that we passed through Al Kura, Rabigh, and around Medina on the non-Muslim bypass road north to Khaybar, Safajah, and Al-Ula. We were heading to the awe-inspiring ruins of Mada'in Saleh and finally Tabuk. According to my good friend Hussein, Mada'in means "cities or towns of Saleh in Arabic."

The desert sprouted assorted spiky sun-baked shrubs. An occasional acacia dotted the sweeping stretches of fine white sand. I also glimpsed patches of blackened sand. Whenever I rolled down my window, the hot arid air poured in with the fragrance of sagebrush. I felt like I belonged.

Dad told us later that the Hejaz Railway was constructed by the Ottomans between 1900 and 1908, primarily to transport pilgrims from Damascus to Medina.[25] We were following the path of Lawrence of Arabia. He led the Arab revolt here. I spotted the remains of the Hejaz Railway, buried here and there by white, black, or reddish-pink sand. Various-sized chunks of railway lay scattered throughout the desert, remnants of this rebel leader's handiwork. According to my father, the blackened sand appeared to be the residual ash from the volcanic activity eons ago.

As I reflect upon my father's library of photographs, the magic of the desert returns. I recall those never-ending drives en route to what loomed under a scorching high-noon sun. An ominous emptiness engulfed me until Mada'in Saleh's enchanting monumental ruins popped up out of the mystical white powder. My father was a magician with a camera. He'd captured time and set it into an image. I don't clearly remember how my young self responded to every stop along this historical route of fascinating archeological sites, but I know I felt grateful for them just as a young girl would with anything new and exotic.

"Stop the car, Dad! Stop!" Dennis screamed. "I want to catch that huge lizard!"

Dad stuck his left hand out the window for Nick to see and gestured toward the dirt road and slowed down. We came to a stop and Dennis tore off behind the lizard, which scampered down a hole. Dennis caught the lizard's tail, pulled it out, and yelled, "Dad! See! I caught it!"

I jumped and gawked. I stood next to Michael with raised brows. Philip, a slender boy with freckles and dark brown hair, came beside me.

Dad stood with his hands on his hips and said abruptly, "Put it down, Dennis. It's poisonous." Dennis dropped it. Where did he think we would put this prehistoric looking animal anyway? It must have been at least a foot long and scaly. Dad informed us afterward that it was a poisonous Gila monster.

After hours of driving, Dad finally announced close to suppertime, "We're almost there, guys. We're almost in Mada'in Saleh, but first we have to drive through the city of Al-Ula oasis."

"What's an oasis?" I asked impatiently.

"A fertile green area where there's water," Dad said.

The sun set over Al-Ula. Tawny-pink sandstone cliffs rose out of the desert's white sand. An earthy incense-scented oasis nestled against the backdrop of massive rose-colored cliffs. Their silhouettes seemed to protect the city. A minaret rose up behind Al-Ula's ruins. In the midday sun, the parched cliffs resembled snow that settled around their base like a fan. I learned much later from Dad that Al-Ula's old city consisted of fields of abandoned square mud houses. I tried to relive that scene. A faint image brought back memories of me playing hide-and-seek in the thick of Al-Ula's arid ghost town.

"Guys, let's get a move on to our next adventure," Dad said excitedly.

"I'll be right there, Dad," I called back from my explorations amid the abandoned ruins.

Dad drove behind Nick to the remains of a rusted-out caboose. I climbed up the rusty ladder of the caboose and its empty cargo carriages parked in front of several station houses. I've since compared my Dad's photos with other photos that I found during my Google search, and I've concluded that we stood on or near several of Al-Ula's station houses.[26] Dennis followed suit. Dad pretended to be the train's conductor wearing his white cap, or *taqiyyah*. He later explained to us that this caboose belonged to the Hejaz Railway. Mom, Dennis, and Nick posed by my side while I stood on the top step of a parched and dusty station house across from the caboose. I grinned over the history of Lawrence of Arabia.

I now know that the Hejaz Railway operated amid Damascus, Syria, and Medina, Saudi Arabia, and passed through Ma'an, Transjordan, entering Saudi Arabia onward to Al-Ula and Medina.[27]

Thomas Edward Lawrence (he favored the initials T.E.) came from Oxford, England.[28] He had an initial fondness for archaic militant construction. After obtaining a scholarship from university, he accompanied an exploration dig of the Hittite community of Carchemish on the Euphrates, where he worked from 1911 to 1914. Whenever he had a spare moment, he roamed, acquainting himself with his surroundings. By 1914, he earned the rank of lieutenant in Cairo. Lawrence worked on secret information for over a year in the Arab country controlled by the Turks.

I'm grateful for T.E. Lawrence's fascination with the Middle East and the Arab people. Alongside his ability to befriend and fit in with the Arabs, he assisted in the Arab Revolt. Beyond the rising shimmering heat, I can only imagine the hardship these brave Arab fighters endured when attempting to decipher a mirage or an enemy.

On our way to Mada'in Saleh, the desert valley abruptly opened up to a vista of sands dotted with mesas the height of several buildings. Glancing back at Dad's photographs, I recognize similarities with the desert landscapes of Utah and Arizona.

The Holy Qur'an states that the Thamudic people previously settled in Al Hijr.[29] Around 25 BC the Nabataean dynasty developed (al-'Ula) the oasis of Dedan and nearby Al Hijr (Hegra') coming out of the north.[30] Mada'in Saleh's greatest educational aspect belongs to the first two centuries BC and first century AD, that is, at the time of the prospering Nabataean community and prior to its absorption into the Roman Empire in 106 AD. [31]

Dad later revealed that those massive mountain walls stood several hundred feet in height and were sculpted by wind and sand over time. He then pointed out that the Nabataeans settled there over a thousand years ago. These people carved decorative tombs out of the surrounding huge rocks to bury their families.

The valley stretched out into a sea of extra fine white sand and sun-bleached shrubs. Mesas soared up with flared buttresses, graced by old castle ruins.

I can't recall exactly how my child-self reacted to our camping escapade, but I know it remained an adventure for me.

"We'd better set camp before night falls here in Mada'in Saleh," Dad said.

Once again Dad signaled his hand down toward the dirt road for Nick to see, and we slowed to a stop. I was tired from sitting so long and relieved to at long last get out. We joined the Grahams, who had stopped behind us.

Arching his back with a deep sigh of relief, Dad proposed, "What you say we get off these tracks and camp on the sand here near that huge rock?"

"Sounds like a good plan to me, Joe," Nick agreed.

What did I feel then? I'm not sure; I just know how it affects me now. We drove from Al-Ula to Mada'in Saleh. We climbed back into our respective cars and forged our own tracks onto the dusty white sand. We headed toward a mushroom-shaped rock with twin rock coffins carved into its façade. This rock probably measured one hundred feet; so it seemed at the time.

The rock's pitted exterior reminded me of the surface of the moon. When Dad stopped the car, we spilled out and beads of sweat formed on my forehead. I couldn't take my eyes off the intricately carved door designs that boasted a crown-like top. Tall Roman pillars on either side protected its tiny crowned doorway. It beckoned with thoughts of adventure and hidden riches of sparkling jewels. The sun highlighted the tomb's yellow sandstone along its base.

Nick and Dad headed toward the huge package on top of the Beetle. While they untied the rope, they looked like they were opening a huge Christmas present. They hauled it to an open flat area and there unraveled the package, which contained all of our camping gear, and laid everything out over the giant tarp. Dad reminded us, "Watch out for scorpions. Whatever you do, don't touch them. They're poisonous."

I ran over. "Yes. I promise I won't touch them," I answered with a frown. *Why would I anyway? They're so ugly*, I thought to myself.

Dad emphasized, "Mada'in Saleh has over one hundred tombs. We're in the thick of them. We're headed to visit these tombs in the morning after a good night's rest. Does that sound fun?" He grinned, obviously pleased with himself.

I agreed with a yawn. I realized that I felt too tired to investigate and gave in to my exhaustion from the hot day's drive. I watched the last luminous rays disappear in the western horizon at the same time that cool relief set in for the night. The Arabian sun's glow emblazoned the desert's saltbushes. What my child-self didn't know but intuitively felt abided in the desert's eeriness and magic that flowed from its symphony of whistling winds, night birds cooing, and insects crawling.

"When are we going to eat?" Dennis cried out.

"Soon, I'm setting up the gas propane grill," Dad replied.

Michael, Philip, Dennis, and I found our spots on the giant tarp. I restlessly watched the grownups prepare dinner. I ate from a plastic spoon scooping Dinty Moore beef stew topped with crispy La Choy chow mein noodles out of its can and sipping Tang from a paper cup. The refreshing orange flavor soothed my parched throat. We transported all of our trash in a garbage bag and disposed of it at the next town.

We could have roasted marshmallows, but feeling the desert's chill, I curled up inside my sleeping bag in my jacket. The cold nighttime temperatures contrasted with the hundred-degree temperature of the day. As I lay there, mesmerized by the fuzzy Milky Way and the countless bright stars, I patiently watched for a shooting star. Dad had told me that if I saw one it would bring me good luck. I thought I saw one. Was it real or did I dream it? Because I fell asleep.

Others were busily collecting their camping gear as the chill of a sunny morning awoke me. I rolled up my sleeping bag and watched Dad unrolling them and pressing his knees down to secure them in the act of tightly rolling them together. After a breakfast of Arabic round bread and cheese, I pitched in to help everyone accumulate the plastic utensils, the Coleman jugs, pots, and pans, and a pile of waxed paper cups. Dad and Nick lifted the huge khaki-colored tarp bundle onto the Beetle's roof rack.

I don't clearly remember how my young self responded to the Bedouin clothed in his traditional *thawb* and red-checkered headdress who approached us on his camel. Dad later told me that he and Nick headed over to greet the amiable Bedouin and spoke in Arabic.

"The Bedouin told us that we would have to return to the main road because it was impossible to take a shortcut or for either of us to pass through the red dunes."

Whenever I heard Arabic spoken, I always detected a harsh and pronounced "A" "H" guttural sound coming from the back of the throat, which added accents to their otherwise melodic speech. Arabs speak loudly and forcefully. The Arab men constantly stared at me, making me uncomfortable with thoughts of vulnerability. Dad explained that Arabs rarely see women with blonde hair and blue eyes. I stole glances at their traditional attire and replayed what Mom said to me about her unforgettable experience: "a lonely Bedouin in traditional white *thawb* and red-checkered *shumagh* propped on his trusty camel gracefully surfaced from behind a rippled dune."

Bedouin is an Arabic-speaking wandering community of the Middle Eastern deserts, exceptionally of North Africa, the Arabian Peninsula, Egypt, Israel, Iraq, Syria, and Jordan.[32] The Bedouins comprise a tiny portion of the entire Middle Eastern culture, but they occupy a sweeping section of the country. The majority of Bedouins are shepherds who travel into the desert during the damp winter. In the dry summer months, they return to the cultured districts. The classic Bedouin holds true nomads in high esteem. Camel wanderers lead in stature. They inhabit extensive regions and establish abundant clans in the Sahara, Syrian, and Arabian deserts. Lower in class would be the *sheep and goat* wanderers, remaining next to the sophisticated areas of Jordan, Syria, and Iraq. Cattle wanderers are established in South Arabia and in Sudan, named Baqqarah (Baggara).

What did I feel then toward the Bedouin? I'm not sure; it now provides me with a deep admiration for the Bedouins of Saudi Arabia. During another one of our many camping events by the Red Sea, we camped near a huge black Bedouin tent. I later learned that these tents consist of black goat hair. One of the young Bedouins demonstrated his artistic ability as he produced a striking image of another clan member. The Bedouins offered to sell us an ornate blue velvet dress embroidered in gold and intricate designs of vibrant colors. Some of the small round designs resembled rubies. Mom bargained and purchased it. Our genuinely hospitable Bedouin neighbors zealously offered us a cup of *qahwa* (coffee) or *shai*. They prepared their traditional succulent rice and a goat dish. I felt welcomed and safe next to them, and I enjoyed watching their sheep and camels graze freely under the surrounding acacia trees.

Two wonderfully affable Bedouins freed us from tire-deep sand near the outskirts of Jeddah. And Dad tipped them each a generous $23 at that time. These Bedouins remain heroes etched in my memory. I recall how frightened I felt in the vast arid desert.

A few years back, Dad's good friend Ziad shared what my father told him: "The desert is

beautifully unique and magical. There's a lot of natural undisturbed treasure out there."

I realize how fortunate I am to have experienced these events firsthand. What I witnessed was possibly what the Prophet Muhammad, Sir Lawrence of Arabia, and countless other explorers witnessed: to appreciate and understand the Arabian Desert's immortal mystique and beauty. I envision the Rub' al-Khali painted in a sky of irregular red and yellow-orange streaks. A fiery sun sets behind a sea of rippled dunes. The Arabic word Rub' al-Khali, known in English as the "Empty Quarter," is the earth's largest region of unending sand and has invaded over a quarter of Saudi Arabia.[33]

<hr>

Throughout Mada'in Saleh, we continued our sweeping trail through a perpetual sea of multicolored sand.

Recently I asked my dad, "Since the Beetle always got stuck, what did we do?"

"Nick and I dreamed up a scheme. Nick led the Hejaz tracks in his jeep. He attached a rope to his jeep and had to tie it to the front bumper of the Beetle, constantly having to rescue us out of the fine white sand."

My younger self was oblivious to these distressed occurrences. Nick and Renate later added more detail, including the fulcrum idea. I have no clue about fulcrums. Nonetheless, I enthusiastically listened to Nick's explanation of how we followed the Hejaz Railway tracks.

Suddenly, Nick's jeep began tipping. Nick jumped out, followed by Renate, Philip, and Michael.

"Everyone get out of the car immediately!" Dad shouted.

We all jumped out of the Beetle.

"One hell of a close call for sure, Nick—you're lucky you didn't roll over," Dad hollered.

"You can say that again, Joe."

Whenever I was afraid, Dad always consoled me.

"Nick, that was way too hairy, and we certainly don't want to slide sideways. Let's tie the vehicles together with a rope so that they balance each other," Dad said, rubbing his forehead.

"My thoughts exactly, Joe," Nick said with a grin of relief.

The others stood still and watched in the thick of this sultry heat. I paced back and forth. Sweat ran down my face. I couldn't help it. Whenever we got stuck, a deserted stillness overwhelmed me. I wondered what we'd do if we became stranded. Would the other party abandon us to find help, or would we send up an S.O.S. flare?

Nick and Dad carefully drove the jeep to one side of the embankment so that its front pointed up. I imagined that they kept rubbing beads of sweat from their faces. They drove the Beetle along the other side of the embankment, parking it next to the jeep until both cars sat opposite each other pointing in the same direction on either side of the blackened embankment. Nick took one end of the rope and attached it to the side of the jeep as Dad took the other end of the rope and attached it to the side of the Beetle.

"This should do it, Nick." Dad faced him, pleased.

"I think we've got a nice balancing act here." Nick nodded in agreement.

Dad hollered, "OK everyone, let's get a move on!"

"That's right, gang. Let's check out some ruins," Nick shouted.

"Yay, we're finally done!" Dennis cried out happily.

Mom and Renate smiled discreetly at each other. We all returned to the vehicles.

We forged ahead side by side along the Hejaz Railway to Mada'in Saleh's massive sandstone bulge. Formations rose out of the desert like towering giants. Sometimes I envisioned a face in the mountainside. I learned about these two huge rocks from my research on Google and the Saudi Tourism website.[34] This region is called Mount Athleb. Comparable to Petra, Jordan, this part also contains a thin gorge or *siq*. Large pillars flanked the huge carved-out entrance, described as a *diwan*. We parked near two goliath mushroom-shaped sandstone rocks, towering side by side and separated by a narrow gorge. Large skeleton-like grooves made the rocks resemble giant shaggy mushrooms. Mom sauntered toward the entrance ten times my height. I frolicked in the sand, apprehensive of these mushroom-shaped rocks ready to swallow me up like The Blob. I followed safely behind Mom, but then she left me standing still in this huge room. I gazed around at the stone benches in the huge silence and pretended I was an archeologist investigating the undiscovered. And in a sudden moment, my tremulous apprehension dissolved to wonder. The place seemed timeless.

Then, catching myself, I scurried back to the others. We piled back into the Beetle, ready to unravel more of Mada'in Saleh's wondrous treasures. After a short drive, Dad parked near a cliff. Reviewing these memorable photos reminds me that from a distance the cliff's color developed a mixture of white—similar to the ubiquitous fine white sand—and ash, mixed in with yellow sandstone. Depending on the position of the sun and how it hit these massive tombs, they reflected in various hues of pink, gold, butterscotch, and a caramel desert color.

Sifting through Dad's photos, I now understand why he took this shot: the sun's reflection off the middle and base sections of its knobby surface painted a mesmerizing 18-karat gold shine akin to the gold *souq*. What I only subconsciously felt then, I now keenly feel about this burial place: that I most likely never wished to remain alone inside these ancient dusky chambers. I recalled strange odors that stung my nose. Was it the smell of camel urine that forced me to bolt out into the desert heat?

According to Saudi Tourism, the burial site Al Fareed Palace acquired the title *Fareed* (Arabic for unique) given that it exists on an individual *rock* dissimilar to the rest of the area.[35] We walked several hundred steps over fine white sand mixed with rocks, and then I knew we'd reached our destination. I gaped up at a majestic three-story desert-colored tomb carved out of rock washed in a tawny-pink hue from the high-noon sun. Moon-like craters riddled much of the rock's surface. This isolated yet majestic tomb exposed from the vast desert plain overwhelmed me. *Did the Nabataean people erect this imperial tomb for a warrior who defended his battlefield?*

In addition to its massive height, four Roman columns wonderfully engraved into its smooth façade protected a small opening. As I romped inside, I couldn't help glancing at the intricately carved door design. It was roughly two feet higher than my small size. I forced myself to enter the cramped and dark chambers, feeling goose bumps rise on my skin. While I rounded the bend, Dennis shouted "Boo!" A creepy darkness enveloped me just as I bolted into the beaming sunlight.

Dad's soothing voice relieved me: "Kids, are you ready to explore some of this unique landscape?" He had the energy of a kid himself. I so appreciated Dad's childlike eagerness for adventure. The Grahams were always within earshot.

We piled into the Beetle, and the Grahams packed into their jeep. Dad drove behind Nick over a blend of white sand and blackened dirt then parked the car in front of an imposing mountain. I'm so glad that I experienced this, even though being a child I wasn't overtly aware of its significance. According to Sandra L. Olsen, this huge ridge of Nabataean tombs is called Qasr al Bint from the first century BCE.[36] Admiring this image today suggests to me that it was the biggest of Mada'in Saleh's burial places. My friend Hussein mentioned that "Qasr al Bint means 'The Place of the Girl (or the Daughter).'" What I only subconsciously felt then, I now keenly realize: we explored a truly spooky area. Its pale cream-colored exterior displayed never-ending moon-like craters forming skulls or full-bodied skeletons. Glowing yellow sandstone loomed around its baseline.

We all got out and listened to one of Dad's history lessons. "Well," he said, eyes twinkling, "a few thousand years ago, wind and sand sculpted these strange shapes, and the people who lived here were the Nabataeans all the way back to the sixth century BC. They became wealthy by controlling the spice trade. Sometimes a caravan of twenty-five hundred camels, five miles long, rode through the desert."

"Really neat," I said in deep thought, wondering about what jewels lay buried inside the tombs.

Mom tucked her hair around her ear. "Du, these monuments are spectacular. It's astonishing what nature produced in the middle of the desert."

"This is only the beginning!" Dad said, embracing her. "So you're having fun?"

"Of course." Mom glanced over contentedly.

I sat down on a sandy ledge not far from a tall opening and studied a green acacia tree towering over the low-lying shrubs under a scorching sun. I grew accustomed to the hot air and admired the permeating peace and stillness.

"That dark entrance with columns in front resembles a door!" I exclaimed. But I refused to go inside another dark chamber after Dennis had spooked me last time.

"The front is sandstone," Dad said. "It's carved out of a cliff wall several hundred feet high. The Nabataeans probably used it to hide their fortunes or as a burial tomb."

According to Dr. Angelo Pesce, human effort is evident throughout these impressive memorials chiseled from the edge of a cliff.[37] A plethora of Nabataean engravings indicate that these burial places date back to Haretas IV dynasty. Additional engravings exist in Minaean, Lihyanite, Thamudic, and Greek, plus others, created in contemporary days, in Turkish and Arabic.

These wonderful photos evoked dreams of a lost desert kingdom and made me wonder how the Nabataean folk produced elaborately carved-out sky-high burial places and shrines. I entered into a reverie and imagined how ancient spice merchants traveled by camel:

I step back in time escorting my trusty camel, Saffron, to a nearby well and fill a bucket of water. I mount Saffron with dreams of market bargaining and the never-ending buzz of a four-thousand-camel caravan trudging from the Orient carrying riches. I summon images of treasures containing exotic spices, foodstuffs, perfumes, and incense. My family descended from the Hejaz Bedouins, and we prospered by trading rare frankincense from Yemen. We worship the abundance goddess, her yellow sandstone shrine, which rises to heaven. A giant genie bursts onto the road, summoning me to rub his magic lamp. I am Scheherazade, Queen of the Desert living.

I had no idea then how Mada'in Saleh affected me; I now know that it provided me with alluring evidence of a seemingly advanced masonry which I couldn't ever fathom possible so long ago. Mada'in Saleh's allure derives from adept craftsmen who chiseled steps into an enlargement of sandstone rocks and produced exquisitely adorned high-placed burial chambers.

According to UNESCO, the excavation location of Al-Hijr (Mada'in Saleh) exists essentially as the first World Heritage attribute to occur in Saudi Arabia.[38] Mada'in Saleh was inscribed in 2008.

Years later, after admiring the thousands of slides that Dad had taken, I noticed figurines, some with human heads attached to animals' bodies. I recognized the intricate detail of thin Roman columns with double rows of figurines within panels; a warrior on a horse with a person kneeling down worshiping him appeared to be only some of the artwork meticulously carved in stone. Great wealth abounded from the incense trade that Dad had mentioned earlier. Now, when I burn patchouli incense, I think of this place, seductive and soothing.

Poring over Dad's photos brings back memories of climbing gingerly on the higher ledges of this gigantic plateau. I wonder if while my feet thumped over the ruin, Dad had pointed at a graceful gray hawk in flight. I recollected sweltering breezes caressing me and gazing at a hawk's acrobatic agility over its piercing screech.

As I overlooked steep crevices with breathtaking views of goliath mushrooms, I felt like the queen of the incense trade. Did Ali Baba's forty thieves lurk around these massive walls? Delighted, Mom smiled at Dad, who took our picture. I made sure that I wouldn't slip climbing down.

"We need to be on our way back to Al-Ula to be sure to find a gas station to check and fix the Beetle," Dad announced. My only memory of our return trip was reaching a lonely blackened dirt road. Again, remains of the Hejaz Railway tracks emerged from under reddish-pink sand. The dirt road stretched out before us toward pointy hills. Pristine red sand dunes rose like smooth velvet to a perfect point, in curved knife-edge tops.

We left Al-Ula and drove toward Tabuk. Mesas and mountains shrank and eventually sank into the horizon. I noticed huge chunks of the locomotive and the rail bed semi-buried under desert sand and gravel. We'd entered a vast desert plateau. Nothing existed here but endless sand and rolling dunes. We were the only inhabitants—if we ran out of gas, I wondered if we would shrivel up and die, leaving our bodies to the desert hawks. We eventually reached a large white sign supported by two posts on the side of the dirt road. On the left side of the sign black print read in English, "THE KINGDOM OF SAUDI ARABIA WELCOMES ALL PILGRIMS. TO MAIN ROAD 22 KM. TO TABUK 112 KM. FIRE HAZARDS IN THE WAY." The Arabic version could be seen to the right.[39]

Tabuk is one of the considerable military bases situated in northwestern Saudi Arabia next to Jordan.[40] The now-defunct Hejaz Railway ran through Tabuk. During the period 630-631 AD, delegations throughout the Arabian Peninsula reached Medina to embrace Islam; already nearly all of Arabia, except the northern areas, had banned together under the religion's flag.[41] As a result, Muhammad and a massive battalion paraded north to Tabuk, although he wouldn't attack. Still, the Jews and Christians from the area complied with his command. Muhammad assured them individual protection from harm and the right to undertake their set of beliefs just as he had done with the Zoroastrians from eastern Arabia.

Dad rolled down the window and gave the slow-down signal. I was relieved to stretch my legs, even though it was under the heat of the baking sun. I walked toward the white board where Michael and Philip leaned against the sign. Dad grouped us for another one of his picture sessions.

Celebrating that moment, I wonder if the adults felt like "pilgrims" discovering a foreign land. Had everyone's soul been "cleansed" throughout our adventure? One can't help but acquire a fascination and appreciation for this spellbinding desert. Did we feel closer to God?

We arrived in Tabuk at sunset. Recently, Renate informed me that we slept in the Raytheon HAWK Battery Army barracks full of filth and cockroaches—dead or alive, I shall never know. We unloaded the Beetle and shifted some equipment from the jeep into storage. Then we all crowded into the jeep to travel through the black desert sand, according to Dad's map, through Al Bir and Al Mudawarah into Jordan. We left the Beetle temporarily parked at the barracks. Nick drove with Dad in the passenger seat. The rest of us crammed together on the back vinyl padded seats—separated by a huge spare tire. We had been barreling along the lone main dirt road to Jordan for an hour when Nick yelled, "Dip in the road—hold on, guys."

I didn't hold on tight enough to the metal frame above and hit my head on the jeep's roof.

Alarmed, I wondered if I was the only one nervous while driving so fast.

"Slow down next time, Dad!" Philip screamed from the back.

"Sorry, guys. I didn't have time to slow down," Nick said, trying to comfort us.

To make matters worse, Dad and Nick had removed the canvas top so it always felt like one hundred-plus degrees. Hot air whipped through my hair and slapped my face. The jeep blasted through the desert, flinging dust up from the tires and stinging my eyes.

I vaguely recall crossing the border into Jordan. Nick later shared that it had been an ordeal. Nick and Dad spoke with the customs control guard, who instructed us to turn back en route to Petra and Amman. The only visible route that existed would be to follow desert tracks. However, Dad and Nick insisted that we must travel to Petra and Amman. The Jordanian customs guard finally relented. He stopped a truck driver and asked him to escort us. Dad paid the truck driver fifty SAR ($10). The driver obliged. We followed him across the black sand, ruts scraping the bottom of the jeep, until we reached Ma'an, where an actual road existed. We turned into Wadi Musa, which is the village before entering Petra and, exhausted, settled in anticipation of the next great adventure.

PETRA, JORDAN
(1969)

I t was dark when we stopped. We parked the jeep at Wadi Musa. As I got out of the jeep I saw a colossal rock cave with the occasional rock carving. A massive full moon lit up the night sky. I've always loved gazing up at the mysterious and beautiful moon. What did I feel then? I'm not sure. I just know how it affects me now.

Wadi Musa (the Valley of Moses) is located next to bygone Petra or in Arabic Baārā, which was the heart of an Arab dynasty during the Hellenistic and Roman periods.[42] These relics are located in southwest Jordan. This ancient metropolis was originally constructed on a plateau cut from east to west by Wadi Musa. According to belief, Moses struck stone here and water flooded outward.

We were met by a party of guides near a huge acacia tree. A dark-skinned man in a sweatshirt and jeans helped me mount a dark brown horse with jet-black mane. Smiling, he offered me the reins. I had no problem riding since I'd learned to ride bareback in Jeddah; we owned a horse, Hashim, at the Bin Laden stables outside of Jeddah. After ensuring that I was safely on my horse, the guide hurried over to Dennis and mounted him securely onto a saddled white horse. Dennis's horse looked a bit like Hashim. I found out later that these men belonged to the Palestinian Liberation Organization (PLO).

We rode single file through a steep and cramped gorge, or *siq* (Wadi Al-Sīq),[43] at times according to Dad only ten feet wide and about a mile long. We navigated the commonly accessed route from the east via this precarious *siq*.[44] The site diggings since 1958 by the British School of Archaeology in Jerusalem and, later, the American Center of Oriental Research contributed immensely to awareness of Petra's historical importance.[45]

According to Dad, nature created this deep split several hundred feet high in the sandstone rock. Luckily I wore my jacket to protect me from the brisk night. Never-ending twists and turns led us past several cramped and dripping wet carved rocks. Sometimes the gorge appeared too precarious to enter, or it felt as if the dark and frightful rocks would squish me to death. An eerie mystique overwhelmed me. Dad wouldn't let anything befall me, though. Then I noticed a small, thin slit. Out of nowhere, a speck of light emerged followed by tiny glimpses of an unmasked marble color. I rounded the bend and a massive gorge unfolded into a wide-open plateau, revealing a treasure.

The first site visible from the *siq* is the Khazneh el Faroun, or the Treasury of the Pharaoh, a burial place chiseled meticulously from the edge of a cliff that measures over 131 feet high.[46] Immense Roman pillars with blossoming capitals rise like quiet sentinels, separated by a veranda with its crown-like roof. During 1985, Petra became a UNESCO World Heritage site.[47]

This majestic pink marble tomb, with its colonnaded entrance, rises up to meet the sky. One has to experience Petra to believe its splendor. That night as I gazed at it, a bright glow emanated from the huge temple. A grand palace fit only for kings and queens, I thought.

"Wow! Mom, look!" I pointed to the huge rose-colored rock. "Does someone live there?"

"No, Carina. Though in the days before Jesus Christ existed, human beings lived here," Dad told me.

The Nabataeans' central city, Petra, resides just over one hundred miles south of Amman in Jordan.[48] This fortified metropolis is situated in a canyon with houses of worship and burial places, stone-chiseled precisely from the sides of steep cliffs. The Nabataeans resided here around the sixth century BC. In the coming centuries, they prospered as a merchant people trading in incense and spices from South Arabia and other commodities from as far as India and China. The Nabataeans had converted Petra into one of the marvels of a bygone era. They also established a satellite community and depot at Al Hijra three hundred miles farther south in the central Hejaz, an area that competes for pure exquisiteness with Petra.

Time froze. I stood awestruck. I let this magnificent jewel enrapture me with its brilliance. I believe that each one of these alluring sites contributes a rare uniqueness to Mother Earth's legacy. I am grateful to UNESCO for recognizing these sites' raw glamour.

Amman

We drove for two hours and arrived at the five-star Intercontinental Hotel in Amman at midnight. Palm trees adorned the shimmering Hollywood-style courtyard at the front entrance. I stood next to Mom thinking of an aromatic bubble bath and impatiently anticipating Dad's and Nick's return with our room keys. In recalling this event, I wonder if our grand entrance brought me back to the exotic and glamorous setting of my all-time favorite film, *Casablanca*. I paid no mind to the black sand completely covering my body. I'm sure I looked like a hoodlum.

More curious than alarmed, I noticed soldiers hanging out on the rooftop of the hotel, conversing and staring at us. Years later, Nick confided to me that the army men on the rooftop of the Intercontinental Hotel were PLO fighters. The hotel's administration told us that they had no vacancies. The PLO fighters radioed on their walkie-talkies down to another hotel to have four rooms ready for our arrival. While my young self had no idea of how desperately we needed to find a room, I now appreciate why the hotel management didn't comply with us. If only we hadn't been covered with black sand from head to toe, imitating goons from the Arabian Desert, we might have stood a chance of obtaining a room. Nonetheless, I'm grateful to the soldiers' kindness.

My father and Nick recounted on separate occasions the following scene to me: The hotel manager in the Philadelphia Hotel checked us all in. Fully-armed Palestinian fighters pointed a gun at Dad and asked him for some Saudi Arabian *riyal* (SAR) toward a political contribution for the PLO. Nick shared that Dad swore obscenities at the soldier, refusing to hand over money. Then another fully armed Palestinian fighter approached Nick, who didn't hesitate to hand him some SAR. The soldier offered him a ticket stub.

Although my child-self did not understand at the time, my travels contributed immensely to how I thrive on meeting people of different nationalities and learning about their cultures. As we embrace and enjoy these cultures, we break through and move closer to one another. And it was as if I discovered a part of myself in each of these cultures. While I was a nomad searching for identity, more than a passion and love for discovering new cultures, they filled my void and assisted me in creating a new identity.

My memory of Amman is that of a hilly city dominated by gleaming white stone houses and green trees. I was impressed by the remains of a magnificently conserved ancient amphitheater carved deeply into the side of a hill—a half-bowl filled with rows of seats. I now know that this Roman amphitheater housed six thousand spectators.[49] Downtown *souqs* covered in white awnings ran along stone sidewalks. Men wore Western clothes; women did not always wear *abayas* and exposed quite a bit of their faces. A fun and friendly atmosphere prevailed. I felt safe there.

I gaped at the remains of columns and a great temple. Dad explained to us that the column remnants were from the Roman period, thousands of years ago, and that this happened to be the Temple of Hercules. I thought about the Greek hero pictured in front of a chariot. My thoughts revolved around my own hero, Dad—he brought me here, after all.

Subconsciously, I knew when standing atop the remnants of the archaic citadel that a great hero had resided there.[50] The Roman colony of Arabia admitted Amman during AD 106, and the Romans reconstructed Amman. Had history dating back to AD 106 unfolded in front of me? Picturing civilization dating back over eighteen hundred years was incredible; I stood on debris from the foundation of the Temple of Hercules constructed during the time of emperor Marcus Aurelius (AD 161-180).[51]

On the way to Aqaba, Nick obligingly pulled over to let a long military convoy pass. I wondered with some trepidation where this steady stream of armored tanks, hummers, and jeeps equipped with military supplies was headed. The convoy ever so slowly passed us by, and the soldiers waved at us.

Dennis shot up out of his seat. "Wow. Look at all those army tanks." He rolled down his window and waved back.

Dad grinned with glee. "Hey guys, that British military convoy traveled from the Port of Aqaba where we're heading!"

Gradually I exchanged trepidation for excitement.

"Du, I'm going to take pictures, all right?" Dad said and hopped out of the car with his camera.

Nick recently shared that an officer who was the French general manager at the Coral Beach Hotel in Aqaba had spoken with him.

Aqaba, Jordan

We drove the twisting road to the exquisite Gulf of Aqaba. We stayed one arid night at a hotel with bungalows on the beach. According to Renate, on the following day the French general manager allowed us to stay at the Coral Beach Hotel even though it hadn't yet opened.

The photograph of Mom and me standing in our bathing suits in front of fat date palmsreminds me of how upbeat and appreciative I was to end our desert odyssey with a grand splash. No matter how many cockroaches we encountered, it didn't matter. I clutched my pair of desert moccasins, one in each hand—reminding me of the scalding pink sand. Yet at the same time a steamy sea breeze wafted by me, and the refreshing salty air caressed my soul.

The backdrop of jagged four-thousand-foot Jordanian mountains protected us with their proximity—Dad made sure I knew their height and informed me that Israel lay across the Gulf of Aqaba. Gleaming white bathhouses with square holes dotted the beach. Reddish colored small pebbles sparkled intermittently across the pinkish sand. I have fond memories of spending the rest of the day swimming and climbing all over the resort. I later learned that the people living in the caves near the mountains were PLO fighters. The men and boys took a motorboat out for a spin on the Gulf of Aqaba while Mom, Renate, and I relaxed on the beach.

We left Aqaba around noon and three hours later returned back to Tabuk. The Grahams continued on to Jeddah. We stayed overnight in the gloomy barracks. I was elated to leave the dark barracks the next morning. We packed up the Beetle and began our seven-hour drive back to Jeddah the same way we came.

Somehow I ended up in my bed lulled to sleep by the humming of my air conditioner, dreaming of what other magnificent and enchanting adventures Dad could present me. All I ever wished was to stay happy with almost 365 days of sun, sand, and the Red Sea.

Petra was my grandiose wonder of the world. Once the massive gorge unfolded onto a wide open plateau and burst in front of me revealing its treasure, I became an exotic princess. I felt loved and special. I was the Jewel of the Arabian Desert. This rare moment has remained with me to this day.

I realized at that moment that this is what dreams are made of. My dream to marry my Prince Charming awaited me, and it *would* come true. He would show me the world on a magic carpet ride. I had laid eyes on the world's most glorious treasure. Determined, I would open and cherish each and every present offered me, and I learned to explore life's greatest quest—to forever be loved and happy. I'm the exotic princess happy to have arrived home.

I'm ever so grateful for Dad's keen interest in history and in escorting us on these phenomenal trips. I've had a once-in-a-lifetime opportunity to step back in time and witness a rare glimpse into our world's history as it unfolded in front of me.

SHARM OBHOR, SAUDI ARABIA
The Creek (1971)

Since our arrival in Jeddah in the late summer of 1968, we often prepared for a weekend day trip to "The Creek" as we called it. I soon learned from Mansour that the creek is called Sharm Obhor.

Because the Beetle always got stuck, Dad had bought a new Toyota jeep. Mom packed a huge watermelon—a must in hot weather—and prepared a jug of ice-cold Tang. I helped her pack bologna and roast beef into Tupperware containers along with rounds of flat Arabic bread.

"Don't forget your snorkel, mask, and fins," Dad reminded us.

"Carina and Dennis, grab your beach chairs and mats to put in the jeep," Mom added. Dad hauled out our red Persian beach rug, along with his scuba tank and spear gun, and packed them neatly into the back of our jeep. Medina Road lay to the left of the compound—I thought of "The Road to Medina"— but we took the road to the right for the creek, which led us north on an approximately twenty-five-mile undulating trek across the vast desert. Our compound's remote silhouette trailed behind us in a dust draft. In the back,

Dennis and I bounced up and down with the bumps in the road while Mom and Dad engaged in animated conversation.

The hot wind thrashed through my hair and sand scoured my face. But I didn't care; I inhaled sagebrush undertones blended with the Red Sea's fresh salty air and reveled in the thrill of Dad driving the open-air jeep at full throttle. We blazed our trail, spewing out behind us endless clouds of sand that billowed into the air. What an adrenaline rush—not a soul in sight or a cloud in the sky; we were alone and free to drive as fast as we wanted. Dad often mentioned the name Lawrence of Arabia. Did Lawrence of Arabia have a similar experience with the desert? I know that he loved the desert.

Dad eventually turned onto a winding road that hugged the creek's embankments. Joyous butterflies filled my stomach as I gazed out to my left side, where sea met land, and spotted many sand-colored coves along the meandering coastline of the Red Sea.

"How about here," Dad inquired, pulling close to a rocky ledge and slowing the car. He pointed to a huge indented rock with a flat top that rose up from the beach. "We can wade there. It looks as good as any, guys."

The rock formation reminded me of a huge mushroom rising out of the sea.

"Park the car then already," Mom said impatiently.

The smell of salt wafted from the Red Sea and stung my nostrils. I was ready for another day of fun in the sun. We unloaded our belongings onto a small beach at the edge of the creek.

Hiding in the back of the jeep, I hastily changed into my favorite two-piece suit. Dennis leaped in and out of the ocean in his T-shirt, covered in seaweed.

It dawned on me that maybe, if I filled up an empty plastic water bottle with seawater, I might be able to get that seaweed off his shirt. Pretending to lounge in my blue plastic lawn chair, I waited for the opportune moment to strike.

Dennis emerged from the Red Sea like an impish sea monster. I heard a faint voice in the back of my brain: *go for it!* I snuck up behind him and emptied the bottle over his head. He gasped and stiffened then laughed. I relaxed and was convinced that he wouldn't retaliate.

Mom lounged on the blue plastic beach chair, wearing a sunhat totally covered in towels. Dennis and I jumped off the low edge of the creek into shallow water and climbed back up. I tried not to scrape my body against the creek's sharp edges. The warm aquamarine water conspired with the hundred-degree weather to make me drowsy with joy.

"Hey, Dennis," I said, pointing. "Check out that clear mushroom-shaped jellyfish with its long tentacles washed up from shore." I smiled playfully. He hunched over it like a predator, poking it with a stick. I made a face. "Stop poking it, Dennis. That's gross."

"It won't hurt it. It's dead."

"Yeah, but they still sting. Remember the time I accidentally squished one?"

Throwing the stick, Dennis screamed, "Ouch! That stupid slimy thing stung me."

"Mom, Dennis got stung from a jellyfish!" I yelled.

"Carina, rub his hand with sand immediately. He'll be fine," Mom reassured us.

Grabbing my mask, snorkel, and flippers, I joined Mom and Dennis snorkeling while Dad prepared his gear to scuba dive. Dad reminded me of Jacques Cousteau, submerged underwater wearing his half wetsuit and oxygen tank on his back. A hose attached to a mouthpiece under his mask, and he clutched his shiny blue spear gun. He swam gracefully below us, trailing white cloudy bubbles.

Waves gently caressed my body when I dove as deep as I could, holding my breath and kicking my flippers furiously. Mom stayed on the surface, but Dennis remained right beside me, kicking out.

The bright sunlight penetrated the clear water, helping me find amazing red and peach coral reefs of various shapes and patterns. I saw grouper, parrot fish, blowfish, triggerfish, flounder, barracuda, manta ray, and even sand sharks; they twisted and turned gracefully at the bottom. There were so many other fish but I didn't know their names. The colorful reefs enticed me to seek what lived behind every nook and cranny. A long mucky brown moray eel glared at me from a green algae-covered crevice. Although they are not considered dangerous, its ugly protruding snout frightened me. Manta rays swam around us like acrobats, their triangular wings flapping elegantly. Occasionally, schools of fish accompanied us.

The masks provided no peripheral vision, so unless we turned our head right or left, we didn't know what might emerge on either side.

I suddenly realized that Mom was gesturing with her index finger to the right of my mask. I turned to look and beheld a school of long shiny barracudas. I shook with fear and my stomach churned. They eventually disappeared. I kept turning my head from the left side to the right side to make sure all of the barracudas had swum away. Dad always told me not to panic; however, deep inside of me I was still frightened.

When we got back, Dad was still on his underwater journey; Mom instructed us to pack our belongings.

A short while later, as Dad accelerated along the creek road back to the compound, I recounted my adventure. "Dad, Dad, I saw a school of barracuda. And guess what, they were really, really close to me!"

"I bet you were scared, but you did what I always reminded you to do, right? You stayed calm. Plus barracudas are only a threat if you bother them." Dad threw me a sweet smile in the rearview mirror.

The hot sticky air engulfed us and a huge cloud of dirt and sand trailed behind. Feeling the sand between my toes, and eyes stinging from the gritty wind, I embraced the wallop of the day lingering inside of me.

Mom announced, "We have some leftover cheese. Let's do grilled cheese for dinner."

Dad added, "And I still have frozen watermelon popsicles in the freezer."

It was an end to a perfect adventure, I thought.

THE GOLD *SOUQ*
& SEAMSTRESS
Jeddah, Saudi Arabia (1971)

9

I'm so glad I experienced the following, even though as a child I wasn't exactly aware of its effect on me. I soon discovered that the gold *souq* remained the highlight of my visits downtown. We returned to that familiar spot at the end of the road and entered the main *souq* under a tin awning. Sunlight filtered through occasional openings. Although my armpits grew moist, I paid no mind to the abiding hundred-degree heat. My thoughts centered on being enchanted by the gold *souq*. The strong aroma of frankincense and other rich spices like cardamom aroused my senses. I kept my eye out for my favorite illuminated gold jewelry stall—I was Queen Cleopatra awaiting her trophy. I pulled zealously on Mom's hand, pointing to one particularly bright stall.

"Joe," Mom said, "Carina and I are going to look at the jewelry."

"OK," he said. "Dennis and I will look at the watches over here."

I wondered why Mom constantly watched me out of the corner of her eye. I'm sure she didn't wish to lose me in this foreign land, but that thought never occurred to me then.

"Carina, I'm so proud of the grownup girl you've become at age eleven. You remind me of a flower waiting to bloom." Mom's eyes sparkled.

"Thanks, Mom. You're the best mom in the world. I love you tons.

"I love you too. Now hurry, I can't wait to find my gold charm." She gave me a wide smile.

We both liked jewelry. We took turns while we switched from one ring to another. Gold and silver necklaces hung neatly under a glass countertop, glinting in the sunlight. Silver necklaces—crescent- or square-shaped with beads—dangled underneath. Gold bracelets, stacked high beneath the glass, resembled large gold coins. The glistening gold offered me so many choices that I stood in a daze of indecision.

Sitting behind the counter, a man yelled at us in broken English, "Please, you come!"

We stepped inside. He pulled out a thick gold bracelet then offered it to me to try on. I frowned, not sure if I wanted to buy this one. I caught sight of an elegant gold snake ring surrounded by green enamel and a cluster of ten tiny rubies mounted on a gold rim for its head and two rubies for eyes. I tried it on my pinky carefully so that it wouldn't become stuck. Dad arrived just then.

Beaming, I said, "Dad, I love this snake ring."

Dad grinned.

He began to bargain with the man. The man mumbled something in Arabic to Dad. Mom eyed a gold band. When she tried it on, the bracelet glistened. Straight-lined grooves about one-quarter-inch thick surrounded the entire bracelet. The man brought out some *shai*. I loved its velvety smooth bittersweet taste. We all took sips out of tiny glass cups.

"Schatzi, are you interested in this gold bracelet?" Dad asked, eying the gold bangle.

"I think so. I might even buy two."

"He also sells Bedouin jewelry over here." Dad pointed to a sparkling arch-shaped necklace that hung from a silver chain. Mom leaned in close with me as the man showed me the chain. Tiny raised beadlike knobs outlined the entire silver piece. Barely visible silver-coiled beads, resembling thread with small marbles in the middle, surrounded pinhead beads that looked like clusters of grapes. Along the center of the necklace, three silver diamond-shaped designs stood out among the many scattered squares.

Beaming, Mom turned to Dad. "Du, I'll take this beautiful Bedouin piece too."

"Schatzi." Dad chortled.

Dad did his bargaining and ended with "*Shukran.*"

Mom stood radiant, eyeing the two gold bracelets on her; I proudly wore my snake ring, ogling the rubies as they glistened in the sunlight. The man wrapped the silver necklace and provided Dad with a brown paper bag.

We witnessed an exchange of words back and forth until finally Dad offered him some money.

Young and old Arab men had more striking, chiseled features than the men in America, I pondered as we threaded our way through the crowded *souq*. When I heard Arabic spoken, the words sounded heavy as they emanated out of the back of the throat.

Mom tilted her head slightly forward. "Why do you bargain?"

"Everyone bargains here, Du," Dad told her. "Never accept the price they offer. You know that haggling or negotiating is common practice here when you buy something."

Elated, we snaked onward in the thick of Jeddah's downtown, filled with a mix of camels, donkeys, and basket boys. Meanwhile, welcoming *shawermah* flavors floated around me. But then an ugly urine stench startled me. I brushed my clammy hands against my pants and gazed up at the sun gleaming through the *souq's* roof opening.

Rows of white, black, and brown sandals covered a scruffy color-striped mat inside of a store. I noticed how the mat hung over the edge of the curb with its fringes buried in sand and rubbish.

Across from the shoe place, a stall sold men's and boy's clothes, displayed on hangers below a wooden rod nailed into the concrete. There were men's and boy's shirts in dark blue, but the drab gray shirts matched the color of loose debris scattered about the dirt-covered alleys. I preferred the women's apparel that boasted refreshing bursts of orange and blue patterned with daisies and flowers. Cotton dresses swung on hangers in a rare yet steamy breeze. Some colors reminded me of my favorite red-striped hot pants from America. Pink and yellow rayon scarves complemented the scene. They hung precariously over the dirt path, infested with remnants of trash.

I felt compassion for people having to buy their clothes hanging over filthy streets. Why couldn't they keep their clothes inside nicely cleaned stores like J.C. Penney back in America?

I welcomed the sight of a small box of invigorating nectarines which lay tilted on its side. A neatly arranged mound of oranges lay on a metal platter. The sun's rays intensified their orange skin. I welcomed their thirst-quenching citrusy bouquet and the aroma of well-ripened bananas dangling in bunches from strings over the common sewage and garbage stenches. I thought it peculiar to sell fruit mixed in with the clothes.

Down the alleyway, a baldheaded young Arab poked his smiling face out of a stall. He gently unwrapped a bolt of orange fabric painted with orange daisies and unfolded it in front of his white *thawb*.

Men yelled at us, "Please *shai*," inviting us to drink and buy. Arabs appeared kind and helpful and enjoyed bargaining with Dad. They sometimes laughed when Dad stumbled in his broken Arabic. Young men and boys promenaded casually grasping their huge straw baskets over their shoulders for needy shoppers.

"You and Carina need to choose some material for your long robes to wear out in public," Dad said.

"I can hardly wait." Mom chuckled wryly.

"You both get to wear colorful ones. Lucky you," Dad teased.

"Du, Carina, here is the fabric *souq*. You might want to go on in and choose your cotton design." Dad pointed to a colorful stall lined with fabric.

A young man in a traditional white *thawb* and *taqiyyah* sat behind a desk hidden in the back of the stall among every color and pattern of fabric imaginable—the entire color spectrum. He was reading a newspaper. Upon our entrance, he welcomed us with "Please Amreecan." Then he guided us to rolls of fabric tightly wrapped around wooden rods which were piled over each other, filling up the entire place. Mom pointed to blue, yellow, gold, orange, and white cotton fabric in a flower pattern. Picking up the rod of material, he unfolded it against the measuring stick under the glass countertop. The salesman unfolded the material five more times around his arm. When he finished, he cut the fabric once with scissors and set it aside. I pointed to the pink, yellow, and orange daisy pattern fabric, also made of cotton. The man yanked the rod tucked behind the others and placed it on the glass counter. Speaking in Arabic, he measured and wrapped our material in brown paper. Dad exchanged a few words with him, presenting the man a bill, and finished with "*Shukran.*"

Nearby, I noticed a man in a beige uniform standing at the counter of a stall. He appeared to be in friendly conversation with a man who sat behind the counter wearing dark glasses, also in a *taqiyyah* and white *thawb*. "Are those men in uniforms policemen like the ones at the airport?" Dennis asked.

"Good memory, Dennis." Dad winked.

"Let's go find that seamstress that I heard about from work," Dad said, leading us past more of the same dirty zigzagging alleys.

In recalling our search for the seamstress's house, I wonder how Dad actually found it. In hindsight I remember strolling down a lonely side road. An occasional scooter buzzed by. I welcomed the bubbly chattering of a few young children playing in the dirt road. Here and there women shrouded in black reminded me of moving dolls. Dad finally led us to a sand-colored stone building. We followed behind while he opened the door to a set of stairs.

Dad glanced at Mom with a confident nod. "This is the place. So all you have to do is climb to the top of the stairs and ring the doorbell. Dennis and I will be at the watch *souq*, and I'll return in a half hour."

We entered a somber hallway and climbed up a steep set of stairs to the top entrance.

Mom rang the doorbell and we heard "*Al Salamu Alaikum.*" The wooden door opened and a petite woman beamed at us with her ebony eyes. She had short dark hair and wore a skirt and blouse. The middle-aged seamstress escorted us into a rectangular room with bare and bumpy white walls. Loosely scattered and colored fabric lay strewn about the otherwise bare room. A combination of mustiness and spray starch lingered in the air. I glimpsed the worn white sewing machine with the pedal on the floor; it reminded me of my grandmother's.

My young self took in the scene with curiosity. I heard a scooter buzz and a horn honk from outside beyond a lonely window fan. The damp air hovered over pungent-smelling fabric. A wooden ruler lay over mounds of brightly colored fabric on the plastic laminate table. A red pincushion filled with pins and plastic containers sat on a pile of spools of colorful thread, scissors, and a red tape measure. A pleated bluish-gray curtain hung from a ceiling rod near a naked brown mannequin.

The woman smiled gently at us with ebony eyes. One hand supported her other arm, raised to her chin with fingers stroking her chin. She looked as curious about us as we were about her and this place, I thought. We presented her our brown paper package. In turn, she opened its contents with pursed lips and a furrowed forehead. Smiling at me, she motioned her right hand toward the grayish curtain.

Once I emerged, embarrassed in my underclothes, the woman wrapped me in my daisy pattern material from neck to below my ankles, and pinned a bottom hem. She then wrapped material around my arms for sleeves down to my wrists. She circled her right index finger, motioning me to turn and raise my arms as she poked, pulled, and pinned my material. Once finished, she disappeared then returned with a round brass platter and two tiny clear glasses filled with *shai*. The seamstress placed it down on a small wooden table in front of a wheelbarrow green-colored couch. Grinning, she pointed to the glasses then to us. We both took a cup of *shai* and drank the sweet drink. Then it was Mom's turn. As Mom disappeared behind the curtain, the seamstress carefully disrobed me without pricking. I giggled at Mom in her bra and slip. Our seamstress enveloped her with material, pinning away. Mom and I each drank a glass of *shai*, letting it cool our throats.

Raising five fingers, the woman said in broken English, "You come *Khamsa* days."

We nodded, not understanding what she meant, then left with our thanks. We met Dad and Dennis outside.

A week later we returned to pick up our new robes. Mom tried on her new robe one last time for safe measure. The robes covered us down to our wrists and down to our ankles, exposing only the skin on our hands and feet. Once Mom appeared, I chuckled seeing her in her tent-like dress. So I stepped behind the grayish curtain, excited as I tried on my new outfit. They each fit perfectly, roomy like a tent. I felt like one of the locals. The seamstress tightly packed our four robes in brown paper—we each had two from our chosen pattern—and Mom offered her several *riyal* notes for all four robes.

Dad took us to a store that sold household goods and food that needed refrigeration. The shop maintained about ten crates of 7-Up bottles stacked high on top of each other.

"Du, let's all get a soda," Mom said.

"All right, Mom!" I agreed, licking my lips.

"Yeah, Dad, I'm thirsty," Dennis whined.

"I got it, I got it." Dad winked at us.

We entered the air-conditioned store, and I enjoyed a rare cool break from the heat. The tiny store was cramped with narrow aisles. I recognized some items: boxes of Tide detergent and Tang with Arabic script. Dad offered the man in his white *thawb* a bill. Then Dad handed us each an opened 7-Up, which I readily gulped down.

Today, the pieces of alluring gold jewelry that I own include a magnificent gold pendant that spells out the word *Allah* in Arabic calligraphy, a pair of Arabic sandal gold-charm earrings, and a gold and white gold four-band puzzle ring—all nicely tucked inside of my jewelry box. These lovely souvenirs of my childhood in Jeddah transport me there, and I rejoice in assembling my ring and puzzle over Jeddah's celebrated traditional *souq*.

THE EMBASSY BOAT
Jeddah, Saudi Arabia (1972)

W hen we were not at the creek, or driving to the mountains of Taif for a cool retreat, we cruised the Red Sea on the embassy boat for an afternoon treat.

"Some of the guys in Mom's office are renting the embassy boat to take out to the deep reefs," Dad said, grinning at us engagingly. "Do you guys want to go with him? Maybe we can even fish on the boat."

"We're up for it," I said, delighted.

Wow. It's Wednesday evening already? Whoopee, the weekend's begun again, I told myself. We packed food and gear and prepared a jug of Tang the previous evening so that we could get up at 6 a.m. the next morning to meet at the dock in downtown Jeddah by 8 a.m. In the morning, I made everyone cinnamon toast with sugar. This remained Dad's, Dennis's, and my favorite breakfast. We all helped load our items into the jeep. As usual, Dad zoomed along dirt roads and the windy asphalt road parallel to the Red Sea. It didn't take long to get to Jeddah's rocky dock. The fresh fishy smell of the Red Sea wafted around me while I gazed up at the white sun already nearing the middle of a cloudless blue sky. Dad parked next to a 1972 black Mercedes sedan and we piled out.

"That must be Mahmoud Nasif's car," Mom said.

"Who?" I said.

"Mahmoud is the liaison officer between the United States Army Corps of Engineers and the Ministry of Defense. He works with me in the office along with John Mulholland. It's Mahmoud's job to make sure that everything runs smoothly between the Americans and Saudis. His combination of fluent Arabic and English, understanding of the American mentality and Western ways, plus his technical knowledge as an engineer rendered him invaluable to both the Army Corps of Engineers and the Ministry of Defense," she said.

"He is also a descendant of the Nasif family," Dad added. "Remember when we visited that huge house next to the tree?"

"Yeah, it had a ton of windows that reminded me of chocolate," I said, making Dad smile.

A twenty-five-foot white rusty boat swayed back and forth against the rocky dock with a dirty white canopy and American flag—the only American flag in this sea of yachts, tugboats, tankers, and fishing boats. I enjoyed the cacophony of chirping sea birds and the never-ending cawing of crows and gulls. They created a welcoming ceremony for our seaward journey.

Dennis fidgeted with excitement. "Dad, is that white boat ours, the one with the American flag?"

"You got it."

We picked our way over the rocky dock toward the boat. Dad escorted Mom onto the boat and Dennis leapt aboard.

Gagging on the diesel fumes, I clambered aboard, slipping on the gunwale.

Mom and Dad greeted the two men who stood under the open white canopy, talking and drinking from white paper cups. I gazed out at the calm blue water with the rising white sun and wondered nervously how we would maneuver past the tanker and tugboat to my right and another yacht to my left. I scanned the boat with rapt anticipation looking for a comfy spot to relax and enjoy this enchanting sea journey. The top deck next to the American flag enticed me. A dark-skinned young man, probably around twenty, stood at the helm. He wore regular clothes like me.

"Dad, who's that young man?" I asked, intrigued.

"He's the captain, Carina. Let me introduce you to him. Dennis, come here and meet your captain," Dad said with a playful smile.

"Coming, Dad!"

We followed Dad to greet the captain.

The captain seemed an amicable man with short black hair and dressed in beige pants and a gray shirt. He chuckled upon our approach.

"You Amreecan?" he said in a thick Arabic accent.

I smiled cheerfully and responded, "Yes."

Dennis grinned and said "Hi."

Dad took over the conversation in Arabic. I heard the word "*Shukran.*"

I found myself leaning over the boat's edge, wondering what lurked beneath the windswept blue-green Red Sea, only to discover murky water. A stocky, medium-sized man with black-rimmed glasses stood next to me. He turned toward Mom and smiled. He wore the traditional white *thawb* and white *ghutrah.*

"Hello, Renate," he said. "Nice to see you again. Are you ready for a fabulous Red Sea experience?"

"Yes, Mahmoud," my mother said. "I can hardly wait. These are my two children, Carina and Dennis, and you remember my husband, Joe."

"Hello, Carina." Mahmoud gave me a large grin. "Have you been out on a boat like this before?"

"No."

"So, Dennis, are you ready for some real fun?"

"Sure." Dennis beamed.

"Nice to see you again, Joe."

"And you too, Mahmoud. We'll see what kind of deep-sea fishing we can do later," Dad said.

I recognized John Mulholland sitting and drinking coffee. He looked up at me with an endearing expression. Dennis and I had met John years ago. He loved exploring Jeddah's adventurous environs, just like Dad. This was why he and Dad were such great friends. John was a fun, amiable man with black hair, freckles, and a reddish-brown mustache, tanned and of medium height.

"It's time to rock and roll," John announced.

Like a kid in a candy shop, Dennis yelled, "Yippee!"

I chuckled, anxious to depart Jeddah's shoreline and explore the Red Sea's reefs.

I found a free spot by the boat's gunwale and stood next to Mom, who grasped the canopy's rod. Hearing the start of the engine delighted me because it beckoned the onset of an adventure. Our jovial captain kept the engine idling while he approached Dennis and pointed to the rope. "Please," he said, proudly gesturing for Dennis to begin unwinding it.

Dennis slowly kicked off his shoes and jumped ashore. He nervously uncoiled the thick brown rope, attached to a huge nail sticking out of the rock, and threw it toward the captain, who then hoisted the anchor out of the water. Dennis jumped aboard next to Dad and the other men. I heard our captain cry from behind me, "*Yallah!*"

Dad and his two male friends responded with "*Yallah!*"

Our skillful captain returned to the helm and navigated the boat off the dock. Whiffs of fresh diesel bit at my nose, suggesting yet another grand outing. Dennis and I climbed to the top deck with the American flag sailing in the wind at the helm. I leaned against the rusty mast, feeling like a movie star in my green sundress with white circle designs. Dennis relaxed opposite me on the other side of the mast. He made a peace sign at Dad. Then Dad pulled out his camera and took our picture. John sat in a beach chair staring out into the sea. Dad kept snapping pictures. Mom looked content leaning against the rear railing. She held a white paper cup sipping some beverage.

I turned and gazed out at the sapphire sea, lulled by the boat's swaying. We'd left Jeddah's Corniche, its white city under a scorching sun, and languidly passed tankers, tugboats, and anchored sailboats. Frothy whitecaps appeared at the edge of the boat's foaming wake and then slowly dissipated under the choppy waters. I stood ready to sail with the wind.

The captain announced in broken English, "We go maybe far away for fish and beautiful swim."

John Mulholland added, "Where some reefs most likely have not been visited."

Dad constantly snapped pictures. He called to us, "Hey kids, look over here, only one more, smile, say cheese!" I wished Dad would simply take the picture. Sometimes Mom replied with a frown, "Du, I wasn't ready."

Dad and John Mulholland each grabbed a fishing pole resting against the side of the boat and attached a shiny stainless steel hook and cast it far out into the whitecaps trailing behind us.

"Carina, do you want to hold the line?" Dad asked me.

"Sure," I said, fascinated.

Dad handed me the pole and I sat in the white plastic chair, praying I would catch a huge fish. While I stared out into the wake, I remained a gratified soul. The side-to-side motion lulled me into tranquility just when I yearned to catch a huge fish. I realized that Dad momentarily abandoned me to get a cool drink and socialize; I nervously placed the pole into the holder and stared off into the foamy wake, hoping to glimpse a grouper or some other big fish. I felt grown up because Dad trusted me to fish alone, but I also wanted him beside me to share the experience. I settled, knowing fully that he'd be back. I caught a glimpse of a school of silvery fish whizzing by. I wondered how long it would be before I would finally catch one. I hoped to catch a fish so that Dad would be proud of me. I didn't want to sit there forever, though. After endlessly watching my straight pole without any activity, I turned around to see what the others were doing. They were relaxing.

Just as I was starting to get bored, the pole tugged suddenly and formed an arch, became straight, and then bent again. My heart pounded and goose bumps covered me. I clutched the pole's handle and felt a huge jerking tug of the pole as it arched, shivered, then arched again. *Could it be a big one?* I thought as I felt another hard tug. My heart pounded. I began to sweat, trying ever so hard not to let go of the heavy pole.

"Dad! Dad!" I shrieked, keeping my eyes on the pole and the foamy water. He raced over, leaned in close, and pulled the pole out of its holder. Then he turned to me and said, "Carina, grab the pole, place your hand above mine. Let's catch this together." I grabbed hold and we alternated between straightening and bending. At the sound of his high-pitched tone, the rest of the gang gathered around us. The captain slowed the engine and appeared instantly, observing enthusiastically. An ear-to-ear grin stole onto Dad's face as he tried to reel in the big fish that I hoped for.

"Wow, this is impressive. You just might have caught a biggy, Carina," he said. I felt myself puff out in pride. I thought about us in the act of the A-Team—father and daughter catching a Red Sea fish together. He struggled to reel in the line. My heart raced. Those goose bumps returned all over my body. "Maybe even a tuna!" Dad beamed at me.

"I know, Dad, I think it's going to be a grouper!"

"Hey, everyone!" Dennis yelled. "Carina caught a fish!"

"Holy mackerel! You might possibly have a red snapper," Dad said. He never let go of the handle, and soon a reddish-colored fish emerged out of the water, flapping its body.

"Hey guys, look what Dad caught, a red snapper fish!" I said, beaming at the others.

"Congratulations, Carina," Dad said.

"Nicely done, Carina." Mom smiled at me, delighted.

"Hey, did you really catch it all by yourself?" Dennis said.

"Well, Carina, you actually hooked it first," Dad said. "It's a nice-sized red snapper." I was content with my accomplishment.

"Indeed, a good foot and a half," John said, scooping it up with a black net. Dad tried to release the hook from its mouth. Seeing that Dad had some difficulty, the captain bonked the fish's head with a fish club to stop it from thrashing—essentially knocking it out. Dad removed the hook entirely. We all followed Dad to the center of the boat, and he placed it down on a bench away from the food and chopped off its head. He held its body down and used a long fat-bladed knife. He threw the head into the sea and cut its body in half, then placed it in the ice bucket in the chest.

I sat beside Dennis next to the white mast on the top deck and stared out to sea. I reminisced about how heroically Dad stepped in at the time of my fishing adventure to help a damsel in distress. The ocean revealed three distinct colors: a sudden shade of aquamarine, sapphire blue farther out, and closer to the horizon a dark sapphire.

After an hour and a half of cruising out to sea the boat's engine died down.

"We now stop. For fishing and swimming!" our captain announced.

Dennis and I watched him release the rusted bronze anchor attached to the thick brown rope. It plummeted to the bottom of the clear water. Occasional dark, rich, and velvety sapphire-colored patches reflected the reefs below.

"Joe, let's take the tanks and try to spear some more red snapper for dinner," John suggested.

"You got it, John," Dad said eagerly.

The noon sun lured me to the deep cool water.

Pointing to the flag, I suggested to Dennis, "Let's jump off the top." I scrambled into the head below to change into my two-piece seersucker suit and Dennis eagerly stripped to his bathing suit.

"Mom, can we jump off the side of the boat from up top?" I asked, already in my bathing suit.

Mom looked up from conversing with John, Dad, and Mahmoud. "Make sure you jump away from the edge, and don't splash too much. We don't want any sharks around!"

"OK!" we both hollered.

"Put suntan lotion on your face and wear a T-shirt on your back, Carina and Dennis, right now," Dad commanded.

We grabbed our T-shirts out of the orange plastic beach bag and doused our faces with white cream. Dennis raced in front of me and jumped into the sea with a splash. I first climbed down the rusty white ladder into the sea, holding onto my blue flippers.

My heart thundered in the process of climbing the ladder out of the water and propped myself up to the top deck. Making sure that Dennis was swimming toward the boat, out of my way, I yelled, "Here I come!"

From the water, I watched Dennis do a cannonball into the sea.

I climbed up to the American flag and copied him, hoping to make a huge splash.

Gratification and serenity come to mind as I reflect back upon those audacious Red Sea excursions, snorkeling and spending the afternoon flipping, jumping, and diving toward the reefs below. The warm surface water caressed our backs, instantly relieving us from the cold water when we surfaced. Colorful fish surrounded us while we snorkeled. The yellow and black striped angelfish were my favorites. They appeared so bright. I was reminded of an underwater tropical forest. Often my body collided with a clear white mushroom jellyfish and its tentacles. I was so busy having fun that I got used to it. It was almost impossible not to get stung.

I wasn't always in the mood to put on a gleeful face when Dad swept in for a photo. I recall that in many ways Dad and I were similar. Kids have a knack for exhibiting their natural and carefree spontaneity. Dad's *joie-de vivre* and his passion for photography allowed him to be fully present in the moment. He appreciated what he had around him and thrived on capturing the beauty through his trusty Pentax—refusing to bypass life's opportunities. I remember how he delighted in showing us our movies. We sat on the living room floor, rapt with joyous memories, and gaped at home slideshows of our adventures.

I loaded my gear and followed Dennis and Mom, already snorkeling, and swam among the fish, coral reefs, eels, stingrays, and sand sharks. The Red Sea was alive with fish. A reef reared up like a lurking monster underneath us while we snorkeled. Curious, I dove down to investigate the mysteries behind every nook, cranny, and peek hole.

At times I was a bit frightened to uncover what prowled below the colder, darker waters of the reefs. I felt exposed and alone in this vast sea, especially when long fat eels with their big heads reared out of a reef's hole. I stared spellbound by graceful manta rays performing their acrobatic and dazzling dance. Then a sense of peace enveloped me. Frequently, huge schools of tiny silver fish accompanied us. I glanced at Dad—the heroic hunter with his prey. Fifteen feet below us, Dad and John swept in beneath a cloud of bubbles. Each had a tank on his back and held a spear gun. Dad gallantly returned with a red snapper, which we kept on ice next to the one I'd caught.

By late midday we headed back inland. The boat swayed against huge waves. They appeared to be eight- or nine-foot swells above my head while the boat tilted on its side. The waves threatened to engulf us, but the captain confidently steered our boat. I sat on the edge of the boat, braving the ocean. It reminded me of a rollercoaster ride. I marveled at Jeddah's Corniche and the city behind it.

After docking, Dad thanked the captain. We said our goodbyes and grabbed our red snappers. My eyes stung and I constantly tasted salt on my lips from swimming all day. I wanted to sleep but it was impossible in the jeep as Dad steered over several dips in the bumpy dirt road.

Once home, Dennis and I stood by the straw bench. We attentively watched Dad skin the red snapper and remove the entrails, throwing them into a white bucket. My appetite went wild as I inhaled the buttery smell as Mom tossed and turned the sizzling snapper in the pan. A sweet nutty aroma wafted by me as Mom placed the fish platter in the center of the solid pine table. Dennis and I delivered two bowls of cucumber salad to the table. Dad sat down in one of the captain's chairs, and we all hurriedly followed suit. We enjoyed the fresh red snapper and sucked down Dad's watermelon popsicles for dessert. After supper we gaped, always in awe, through our picture window at the sun falling into the Red Sea. It created a fiery sky of irregular lines across the downy clouds. Today was once again another joyous day.

Many years later, Dad confided in me, "Living in Saudi Arabia was like a paid vacation of never-ending adventures."

Carina's Dad, Joseph C. Rourke, age twenty-two, circa 1955.

Carina, age nine, in a *souq*, 1969.

Carina's brother, Dennis, age seven, in the mountain city of Taif, two-and-a-half-hour drive from Jeddah, 1969.

King Abdulaziz International Airport in Jeddah during *Hajj*, 1969.

Rock-hewn churches in Göreme, Cappadocia, Turkey, 1975.

Carina, age fifteen, at the Temple of Hadrian, Ephesus, Turkey, 1975.

Right: Mada'in Saleh, Al-Fareed Palace, 1969.

Below: Carina, age nine, with her brother, Dennis, age seven, climbing on a locomotive that belonged to the Hejaz Railway; one of several of Al-Ula's station houses, 1969.

Hagia Sophia,
Istanbul, Turkey,
1975.

Right: Southern region
of Saudi Arabia, 1969.

Below: Aleppo Citadel,
Aleppo, Syria, 1975.

Above: Dome of the Rock,
Jerusalem, Israel, 1975.

Right: The Church of the Holy Sepulchre,
Jerusalem, Israel, 1975.

Left: Jeddah, 1969.

Right: The Nasif House in
Jeddah's Al-Balad,
the historical center,
the old city, 1969.

Below: Carina, age nine,
in a *souq*, 1969.

Covered *souq*,
Jeddah, 1969.

Clothes section of
Jeddah's *souq*, 1969.

Carina, age nine, with
her brother, Dennis,
age seven, in Taif, 1969.

Matthias Church,
Budapest, Hungary, 1975.

A gold *souq*, 1971.

Carina, age eleven, in a gold *souq* behind two Arabian women with vendor, 1971.

Carina's dad, Joseph C. Rourke, age seventy-three, in Bremen, Germany, 2006.

THE PARENTS'
COOPERATIVE SCHOOL
Jeddah, Saudi Arabia (1972)

ennis and I sprinted to catch one of the two red and white
school buses parked across from the open-air movie theatre.
An Arab in his white *thawb* and red-checkered headdresses
sat patiently in the driver's seat. He showed off his pearly whites while I
boarded the bus. I always hoped to get a window seat so I could admire
the sun, sand, and Red Sea. Otherwise I sat with one of my friends for a
chat, or next to a younger kid, anywhere I could find an empty seat. The
drivers delivered us to the Parents' Cooperative School (PCS), grades K-9,
in downtown Jeddah. Just after I walked to the school building, I fell into a
happy reverie.

I was the happiest kid alive. I thought about the breakfast I placed
on the table ready for Dad—my hero. Ever since I turned old enough to
cook, and when I had time, I alternated between poached eggs, cinnamon
toast with butter and sugar sprinkled on top, or eggs sunny-side up with
two slices of toast. His favorite was cinnamon toast with sugar—he always
winked and smiled at me after I placed the plate in front of him. If he was

still in the shower or I was running late, I'd yell excitedly, "Dad, your eggs are ready!"

"Thanks…have a great day at school," Dad always yelled back.

I was proud Dad was happy, but mostly I felt so grownup.

Mom already left for work, and you wouldn't catch Dad in the kitchen… well, maybe to boil an egg. I knew he liked me serving him. Mom's driver for the Army Corps of Engineers honked precisely at 7:30, chauffeuring her downtown (women were not allowed to drive) where she worked as office manager to the lieutenant colonel. Mom's hard work for the Army Corps of Engineers allowed us many special benefits including access to the PX. After we left for school, Dad drove to Raytheon in downtown Jeddah.

Our school bus ride lasted around fifteen minutes. The bus entered the sandy school grounds and parked double-file along with all the other school buses from the other compounds. A ten-foot cement wall enclosed PCS. A gate secured both the front and rear entrances. Sometimes I spotted Arab youths peeking curiously around the corner of these immense walls. Sweat beaded on my forehead in the ninety-degree heat. It was only 8:30!

Desert sand-colored bricks complemented PCS's exterior, while protruding white cement ledges supported four rows of V-shaped bricks, creating a lace-like filigree on the walls. White oleander trees and un-groomed hedges resembled tamarisks. Steamy sweet air permeated the grounds. Everywhere I went I spotted huge black ants, beetles, and flighty geckos. House sparrows chirped sporadically while crows cawed and strutting pigeons cooed.

PCS's simple square architecture dominated the school. Wide columns constructed of red and beige bricks with square holes formed both horizontal and vertical patterns and adorned the walls outside of the classrooms.

I yelled over to Michael, whose family camped with us. He wore his sandy blond hair in a crew cut, which exposed his big ears, tons of freckles, and endearing expression; he was always nice to me.

"I hoped to challenge you at tetherball before the bell rings. I really want to show you a move I learned."

"OK, Carina, I'll catch up with you once I get past the wee guys; but make it fast. I don't want to be late today. We're beginning a new chapter in Social Studies, and remember the teacher doesn't like it when we're late."

I chuckled. "OK, I'll make it fast."

In the process of a mass pandemonium of students from K-9 swarming into school, Michael and I sprinted to one of the two orange tetherball sets stuck in sandy ground away from all the parked buses. I'd developed a love for this game. I never saw a tetherball before arriving in Saudi Arabia. If I was upset about something, smashing this hard ball helped. Hurting the bottom of my fist did not deter me. It definitely helped to be tall.

"Michael, look at how fast and hard I can fling it over your head. Cool, huh?"

"Yeah, well that's only cuz you're taller." He thumbed his nose at my winning with a sneer. "We gotta go, remember we have a test!"

We ran back toward the brick building. The cloud of sand my feet kicked up went behind me, not into my face.

Dring-dring went the 9 a.m. school bell. My armpits moistened from the oppressive morning air. I followed the rest of the students. We crowded into our respective air-conditioned classrooms. A huge two-toned brick courtyard inlaid with horizontal grooves improved the school's interior. Twenty-foot brick columns with tent-like arches supported the second floor and its hollow brick-layered railing. This lace-like appearance added simple elegance to PCS's design. A set of zigzagging white marble stairs with a wooden railing led me to the upper level.

Ten-foot-high tamarind trees that lined the dirt path provided meager shade from the baking sun when we played dodge ball at lunch. I always went to the courtyard during lunch, hoping to get in on the ongoing game.

"Hey guys, can I play, please?" I begged cheerfully.

"Sure, stand way in the back to get this guy out," said someone from the center. "He's a hard kicker."

I ran to fetch the wayward ball, distracted by those flighty geckos and making sure not to step on a marching carpenter ant or two.

I had PE first class. I dreaded it. I followed a herd of girls talking giddily as they rushed from their lockers, pushing to get inside the eerie locker room with a shower sectional. No sunshine existed within these confining cement walls at ground level. I became a forlorn prisoner to every girl's deodorant, powder, and perfume. A permeating unpleasant cocktail stung my nostrils. The room was a crowded ocean of fish swimming to and fro. Girls crammed together and quickly undressed and removed their uniforms from their bags. The chosen ones had flawless curves and moved swiftly, dressing in their white one-piece snap-up uniforms with the green PCS logo patch.

The next group consisted of the girls who patiently took their time. With no care in the world, they seemed immune to the chaotic scurrying all around them. Then the modest group tended to trickle out just in time. I remained in a group of my own. I safely hid under my towel and let my hawk-like eyes scan the room to be sure that nobody stared at me. Could I be the only girl with such obsessive thoughts? Was it every woman for herself? I can still hear Dad telling me that I had my mother's beauty. I never believed him because I always had a tummy pouch and long legs.

One morning, relief arrived; our teacher allowed us to wear normal everyday clothes to play softball in the midmorning ninety-degree air. We sweated it out on a sweltering sand field in front of the school. (During the latter, mature PCS years, our uniforms changed to green shorts and a green-collared white top with green horizontal stripes. *Not much better,* I thought to myself.) I agonized in anticipation of having to take showers. I made sure that my towel didn't drop. I never wished to be exposed like a Rubens masterpiece in front of the girls, who were bustier and curvier in all the right areas. I anxiously waited for *that free shower* with a curtain, of course. Were these nightmarish thoughts mine alone? Where would modesty get me? I thought to myself.

I arrived safely at my organized open-front wooden desk with plastic book box. Some of the other students' desks overflowed with their books and papers. We brown-bagged our lunches and ate at our desks. No cafeteria. I usually ate with my friend Denise Ponder, who had olive-toned skin and medium-length brown hair. I admired her upbeat personality. Denise faithfully brought in homemade chocolate chip cookies along with a peanut butter and jelly sandwich and a red apple. Whenever she didn't want to eat her cookies, she held the bag up for grabs, seated at her desk, and shouted, "Who wants my chocolate chip cookies today?"

I wondered why she gave up eating those delicious cookies. Her mother couldn't have known what she did. Had she known, why would she continue to bake them for Denise? She often chose me over others, which gratified me. Mom never put cookies in my lunch. I only had them as a rare treat at home. I was so grateful for Mrs. Ponder's chocolate chip cookies.

The three o'clock bell rang. Refreshed from being in the air-conditioned classrooms, I headed to my bus in a stream of students, hanging onto our school supplies. Some carried musical instruments. Students opened lockers and slammed them shut; they walked up or ran down stairs, laughing and screaming over cacophonous chatter; the fidgety few pushed and shoved, rushing to the buses.

The dank and pungent smells of pure life alongside camel or donkey sweat mixed in with the local vegetation and *sissing* of insects. The whispered presence of acacia sap and sun-drenched grasses mixed with the lingering odor of henna and frankincense with which the Arab women doused their hair.

My fondest memories came from life in the PCS—we were like an extended family outside of my home.

We encountered a rare torrential rain on the way to school one morning. We were the first bus and our driver decided to gun it through the pond. I peered out the window and noticed that I couldn't make out the tires. They'd disappeared in the rain. We all screamed and stood up, looking around, scared. The driver yelled in English with his thick Arabic accent, "Seet down!"

After several rocky attempts to try and head to school, the driver backed the bus out of the pond and delivered us to the compound, a load of contented, shouting children singing "99 bottles of beer on the wall, 99 bottles of beer, take one down and pass it around, 98 bottles of beer on the wall."

Monday, after school and before leaving the house, I replaced the key in our secret hideaway, a hole in the cement patio wall, so that Dennis could find it when he got home and skipped down the long dirt road past all of my friends' houses toward the Rec Center. The date palms with their pineapple-like trunks rose out of eight-inch-high dirt mounds. I felt like I was in nirvana. I was free like the wind. I stopped to dig my toes deep into the fine white sand on the top layer, digging deeper to discover yet another color and letting the granules massage my toes. It was like hot sand therapy. If I listened attentively, the desert guided me in whispers. I had no fear. I was the desert's precious stone.

I passed our neighbors, the Grahams and then the Websters, who lived across from the basketball court. I slowed to investigate their vegetable garden, surrounded by a white picket fence. At the Rec Center I saw Michael shooting pool.

"Hey, Michael, want to shoot a game?"

"Sure."

After several rounds of pool we started a game of ping-pong. Michael returned spin-speed balls and got another point, making it finally ten to seven in his favor.

"How about another round?" I said.

"Oh, all right, let's go." He pasted a smile on his face. "Nice spin return, Carina."

I grinned. "Since I'm winning, let's make this the last round?"

"Fine with me."

"That makes ten to eight, my favor. Nice game, Michael."

"Yeah, nice. Gotta run!" He dashed out.

By Wednesday, I'd turned into a giddy girl. The weekend began and the open-air stage held movies at night. In addition, movies took place on Wednesday and Friday nights. I hoped to catch every movie in addition to the three-o'clock matinees on Friday in the spare room at the Rec Center. The only big rule of our house was that I had to finish my homework before I could see a movie. Dennis and I had permission to stay outside the entire day, especially since we could never leave the compound without Mom and Dad.

"BLTs for dinner tonight! Hurry while the bacon is still warm," Dad yelled from the kitchen.

"Is this Wednesday?" Dennis asked.

"Wow! You're making dinner, I can't believe it!" I said with a laugh of delight.

"Well, it's not that hard to fry bacon," Dad said with a slanted smile.

Every night around dinner, we all sat at the table to watch the sun with a golden perimeter dip behind our two palm trees into the Red Sea. Sometimes in the middle of eating, we'd run outside to the straw bench against the back wall of the house to finish gazing. A milky, bumpy line separated the far sapphire blue color from the closer teal waters of the sea. White fluffy clouds slowly drifted away, turning into peach-colored streaks while they stretched across and lit up the remnants of an azure sky. Dusk approached. A fiery explosion erupted in the horizon setting off a cone-like sphere of pink, red, and orange rising to the heavens above. They created a lasting stillness in the Red Sea's glassy reflection.

I hastily bit into my crunchy BLT, letting the bacon melt in my mouth. I had to make it to the movie on time.

"You both finished all of your homework, right, guys?" Mom inquired.

I nodded my head.

"Me too," Dennis said.

"OK, guys, then you can each have a *riyal* for your pocket money," Dad said.

Under a starry sky and the desert's humming nightlife, we sprinted down the dirt road with our small plastic beach chairs. I adjusted the chair over my shoulders, and I wondered what I would buy using the *riyal* Dad gave us—*should I get popcorn, a Mars bar, or a small yellow bag of peanut M&M's at the snack bar?* Anticipating the surprise movie gave me goose bumps and an adrenaline rush. Dennis joined his friends already comfortably nestled on blankets or chairs. Others sat in their favorite spot on the cement floor with popcorn and soda, chattering. I placed my chair in a cozy spot and parked myself in a comfy position, watching for my best friend, Heidi. The cool air emitted an earthy aroma of sun-dried moss. Heidi lived on the far right side of the compound.

Then I spotted her in a mass of tall and small black silhouettes, flocking toward me. They carried blankets or pillows and summer lawn chairs suspended over their shoulders. I waved, jumped up, and ran over to greet Heidi.

"Hey, Carina!" Heidi beamed from ear to ear.

"Hey! If we hurry we can make it to the snack bar before the movie starts."

"OK, let me put my chair next to yours. I'm ready."

We hastened to the snack bar across the cement floor, then along the dirt road toward the entrance of the pool. We turned a hairpin left and opened the swinging door to the snack bar. An intense buttery aroma greeted me. I hurriedly passed the chairs and round tables to a movie theatre-like machine spewing out popcorn at the beat of a fast drummer. Moosa, the snack bar cook, a tall Somali with jet-black hair and a round face, flashed a white smile at me. He stood behind a pair of metallic soda fountains, smart in his white shirt and apron and black bowtie. A proud and jolly expression stole over his face and he asked us in broken English, "Vat you vant?"

"I'll have two Mars bars, please."

"I'll have the same, please," Heidi added.

Waiting patiently, I saw Moosa dancing back and forth holding someone's order of a vanilla ice cream cone, laughing all the way to the cash register.

I offered him my *riyal*, said goodbye, and waited for Heidi to pay. We returned to our cozy spot next to other children in time to catch the beginning of that night's feature. My favorite film, *Wait Until Dark*, ran that evening. Although certain parts frightened me, my best friend sat next to me. That made me happy. I loved the anticipated suspense and prayed that Audrey Hepburn wouldn't get hurt while she secretly hid the heroine-filled doll from the bad guys. Audrey played a vulnerable yet self-reliant woman and gave an outstanding performance—she did exactly what I would do if I were in a similar situation, I thought.

One night in the early summer of 1970, I woke to howling winds. I was the first one up that morning and discovered a beautiful crescent-shaped sand dune in the center of the kitchen floor.

Oh my gosh! Nature has wreaked havoc at house number fifty! I quietly ogled the amazingly unblemished fine sand, which had seeped through the thin space underneath the back door. Stunned, I stared at nature's intriguing beauty. No doubt, there remained an endless supply of white desert sand outside. I opened the back door and dug my toes into more sand that had drifted by the door. I turned back to our very own dune in the kitchen and felt reluctant to ruin this creation with a broom, which is probably what Mom would have expected me to do. Suddenly inspired, I left the beautiful sand dune and yelled, "Mom, Dad, Dennis, wake up, wake up! There's a sand dune in the middle of the kitchen!"

"Carina, this better be good," Dad yelled from their bedroom.

"It is, Dad, I promise!" I grinned happily.

"Leave me alone, Carina, I want to sleep," Dennis cried back.

"I'll be up in a minute to see," Mom promised.

Dad appeared. "Wow, this is pretty wild, huh? Schatzi, Dennis, Hurry! Hurry! You'd better hurry and see this," he shouted exuberantly.

Mom appeared with wide open eyes. "*Was ist los?*"

Dennis followed.

"Careful, dummy, don't wreck the dune!" I scolded.

"What's up?" he said with a yawn.

"A sandstorm arrived overnight and left us a surprise." Dad grinned with amusement. "These parched thirty-mile-an-hour winds blast down from the north and northwest and hit most of the Arabian Peninsula.[52] These winds also appear in two other countries near here, Iraq and Iran," he explained. "The sandstorms appear out of nowhere—pretty cool, guys, huh? They call it a *shamal.*"

"I'm surprised that the sand seeped this far into the kitchen," Mom said. "Carina, would you mind sweeping it up and making sure all of the sand ends up back outside?"

"Aw, do I have to, Mom? Can't Thabit clean it up tomorrow morning when everyone is gone? He's got the key."

"Carina, we want to keep the sand outside where it belongs. Plus our houseboy has enough to worry about, washing the ceiling-high pile of dishes we always leave for him in the sink the night before. In addition to cleaning the bathrooms, vacuuming, and ironing all of your Dad's shirts."

"Carina, it's important to listen to Mom," Dad said, gazing at me.

Reluctantly, I grabbed the broom and dustpan from the back porch and sadly watched my broom's bristles dissipate nature's creation. I wasn't about to complain about my job of having to put away the air-dried dishes stacked high in the rack, which Thabit cleaned every morning. After all, I always played afterwards.

THE DISCOVERY
Jeddah, Saudi Arabia (1975)

E very family has a secret, whether it's found in dusty old letters buried in an attic chest or a precious gem tucked inside a jewelry box. I only ever wished to be happy forever, like that young girl—that was me—to have enjoyed the ultimate freedom whenever I opened the door to sun, sand, and the Red Sea. The peace that surrounded me was the peace within me—until that momentous day seven years after our arrival in 1968.

Ever since I can remember, a burning call for the truth obsessed me.

I had just turned fifteen at the end of March 1975. Now more than ever those urges manifested themselves into a full-blown obsession—a magnetic pull that fueled my heated desire to search inside Mom's jewelry box. Rhonda Byrne, author of *The Secret*, confirms here: "The Truth of Life is right here for everybody, as it has always been, but only the ones who ask questions receive the answers and discover the truth. When we ask questions, deeply wanting to know the answers, we will attract answers in a form that we can understand." [53]

Dennis and I had received a brand-new yellow mini-bike for Christmas 1974. By the spring of 1975, I became quite skilled at mini-biking; I considered myself a *pro* and could "pop a wheelie." I cruised up and down the compound's endless rows of dirt, speeding up and down the pier—skidding to a stop to avoid plunging into the Red Sea—or learning to "pop a wheelie." I rode without restriction, and I paid no mind to the hot, dank wind smacking my face. We were after all living in the desert!

I dared to go beyond the walls, learning to dune jump; but I kept my lips sealed. I would have been restricted from mini-biking had my parents found out.

This night I hoped that I would be able to go to sleep in peace. No matter how hard I tried, though, this recurring image so annoyed me. Here it came again. Dennis and I sat next to other preschoolers hunched over on top of a large round table. We looked at something—maybe a puzzle? I couldn't seem to get rid of it. Why did it vie for my attention so? I knew I simply must remember to ask Mom and Dad about it when I woke up. They'd be sure to have an explanation for me.

That did it. I couldn't stand this unsettling memory any longer.

Now more than ever I needed *my* answer.

I threw back my covers and slogged into the living room to ask Mom and Dad about this recurring image, although I wasn't sure if the image was a memory or simply a dream.

I found Dad barefoot, leaned back in his leather Eames chair, surrounded by a stack of books and his trusty two bowls at his side, one for salt and another for peanuts. Dad loved dipping peanuts into salt. Tonight he wore his favorite striped T-shirt and casual beige pants. Mom relaxed on the sofa, reading a copy of *Architectural Digest*.

"You can't get to sleep?" Dad asked.

"You're not feeling well?" Mom added in concern.

"I can't get this image out of my head," I said, annoyed.

"Oh?" Dad looked up in curiosity from thumbing through the big black book on Jeddah.

"Two-year-old Dennis and I are sitting next to other preschoolers, hunched over on top of a large round table. We're studying something—maybe a puzzle?

Sometimes I'm watching whitecaps above ocean waves, looking through a brass-rimmed porthole..." I frowned and thought that none of it made any sense to me.

Dad shot up in his chair, grinning from ear to ear, and proudly announced, "In 1964, when you were four and Dennis had just turned two, we all left Bremerhaven, Germany, to live in America. It took two weeks by ocean liner to arrive in New York City. Every morning, without fail, we ate breakfast at a small square table near a porthole."

The answer rolled off his tongue slowly and deliberately, as if he wanted to make sure I listened. My question caught Mom's attention, and in a reflective mood she turned her head toward me with a faint smile. "That's right! Then we whisked you and Dennis away to the ship's nursery school after breakfast." Mom's brows drew together in wry amusement. "I must have gained fifteen pounds on that cruise."

Dad's answer reassured me; I sensed that Mom wasn't enthralled with the trip. But I'd received the explanation for which I had hoped, and that mattered the most.

"Thanks, Mom and Dad, that helps a lot; *gute Nacht.*" Ready for bed, I stooped down to give them each a hug and rubbed my fatigued eyes.

"*Gute Nacht, gute Nacht,*" they both replied.

I returned to my bed. That scene had been one of my few earliest childhood memories: the beginning of life for me. It happened in 1964. I was born in 1960, and no matter how hard I tried, I couldn't remember much except a couple of very early childhood visits sauntering through Nürnberg with my Mom, Dad, and Omi prior to leaving for America in 1964.

Ever since Mom bought her huge turquoise opal ring, I noticed that she wore it often, but not her wedding ring. I remembered the day she proudly explained to me that the opal came from Australia. The opal stood shiny and smooth with beautiful deep blue-green hues accompanied by a background of randomly scattered soft yellow orange hues. It puzzled me; I thought that once a person got married they faithfully wore their wedding ring without ever removing it, no matter how many other rings accompanied it.

I'd never dreamed of looking inside of Mom's jewelry box—that remained private territory. But that day my curiosity gripped the best of me after Dad asked me to bring his wallet from his bedroom. Always in that same spot, the octagon-shaped Syrian mosaic pearl jewelry box lay centered atop the light pine armoire. The jewelry box's ornate beauty and what lay inside of it intrigued me. I opened the lid and heard Mom's footsteps. I slammed it shut and hurried toward the patio, grabbing Dad's wallet.

Mom glanced at me. "What are you doing, Carina?"

"I'm getting Dad's wallet," I answered, poker-faced.

"Carina, I would appreciate you not going through my things without my permission—OK?" She wrinkled her forehead.

Embarrassed, I replied with a heated face, "I understand, Mom."

After this incident, my curiosity burned unceasingly.

⁙⁙⁙⁙⁙⁙⁙⁙⁙⁙⁙⁙⁙⁙⁙⁙

One day in early May, Mom left on a midnight flight to Germany to be at her ailing mother's side. As with all the other times, I accompanied Dennis during our walk home from the school bus stop across from the open-air movie theatre.

That day, Dennis surprised me with, "See ya, I'm off to Frank's house."

"How long are you going to hang out?"

"Till suppertime."

My obsession returned in full force and stirred up butterflies in my stomach. I thought about how I often noticed Mom remove her rings and place them down on the table next to her. And each time I stared at her beautiful and different rings, the more I wanted to try them on.

I always felt that I happened to be different, that I didn't fit in. But, while I believed the pieces to my life's puzzle were fitting, those irresistible urges—to snoop inside of Mom's jewelry box—returned. Might a piece to my life's puzzle have been missing still?

I glanced out the window to be sure no one appeared. I gulped down a glass of water in the kitchen. The dishes that Thabit cleaned this morning were stacked high in the dish rack. I knew that my job included putting them away by dinnertime, but right now the dishes didn't matter. I paced up and down the living room, psyching myself up to go into my parents' bedroom. My arms crossed over my chest and I felt my heart pound. I passed by my own room. A feeling of uneasiness overwhelmed me. Should I proceed to my room? Should I read a book or change course?

Thinking about the smart thing to do didn't work. I scuffled my feet and intertwined my hands. I fidgeted with them and got cold feet. The cuckoo clock's pendulum swung twice each second, reminding me that I could turn back, but I didn't. Instead, I kept walking down the long narrow hallway toward my parents' bedroom. I watched behind and in front of me. I passed Dennis's room, kept surveillance corner to corner, acting as if I were waiting for something or someone.

When I got to the open bedroom door, my heart raced faster. The room felt forbidden to me. The cuckoo clock chimed on the hour, reminding me that it was only 4 p.m., lots of time before Dad returned from work and Dennis got back from Frank's. My body felt like it had a mind of its own. I bit my nails even though I had previously stopped. I probably would never have another chance so perfectly designed as this one—I persisted, determined to satisfy my urges.

The tightly shut patio doors kept out the intense afternoon sun. I flipped on the light switch to their dusky bedroom. Laundry detergent permeated the air. Dad's clothes, which Thabit had neatly folded, sat untouched near the edge of the bed. Mom and Dad's sleek beige armoire sat at the opposite end.

I eyed the alluring Syrian jewelry box, which sat opposite the hand-carved mirror. The mere sight of it made me breathe faster. With trembling hands and the utmost care, I lifted the lid of the jewelry box. Before I touched anything, I scanned all the pieces to be sure I didn't forget what went where. I noted four small plastic bags filled with diamond rings in each one. There were a lot of diamond rings here—I wondered if they were real or just costume jewelry. Why on earth would Mom own so many? I then recalled her telling me that she bought fake diamond rings.

I pored over the pieces. I recognized two shiny gold bracelets and concluded that she had bought them at the gold *souq*. I spotted an ornate silver necklace; it looked exactly like the Bedouin jewelry that Mom bought at the gold *souq* at the time I chose my snake ring. I pored over gold rings with rubies, emeralds, and semi-precious stones. There must have been a ring for each day of the week—these couldn't all be real too. Dismissing them, I set my gaze on a filigree silver pin encased with diamonds and three black stones. It appeared antique. I guessed this one belonged to my German grandmother, whom I call Omi. Today I own this beautiful vintage gem. Every time I wear my lovely pin, I remember Omi and her exquisite taste for art nouveau.

I noticed Mom's silver wedding band; the reflection of the silver caught my eye with its intriguing black etchings. I loved pretending to be married. I thought of my biology teacher and began to fantasize about someday being married to him. I slid the ring onto my ring finger—only halfway just in case it got stuck.

I frowned. *Why wasn't Mom wearing her wedding ring?* I twisted it around on my finger and then removed it. I stared more closely at the black etchings and read the inscription on the inner band: "1962." I held my breath. I focused on the date more closely.

"Nineteen sixty-two?" I whispered. But I was born in 1960!

I felt suddenly lightheaded. My heart slammed in my throat. I checked again just to be sure. With fumbling hands, I put everything back the way I had found it, determined to muster up enough strength to ask my parents why they had married *after* my birth. A crazy thought whirled endlessly in my head like a vast desert sandstorm. *Am I a child born out of wedlock? Yes, that must be it. If that's the case—sure, I could handle it, no problem.* I tried convincing myself that I had nothing to be suspicious about and that this was my overactive imagination. They probably just got married later on.

Minutes went by. Now the immediate shock to my new identity engulfed my whole body, followed by horrible thoughts which entered my mind. *Are my parents my real parents? Am I a mistake? Am I adopted? Who are my real parents?* I knew that I would have to ask Mom about my discovery no matter how hard it would be to hear the truth. What on earth could they be hiding from me? I just prayed that it was something I could handle.

I found myself outside. A hot, sticky wind slapped my face and the salty air snapped at my nostrils. I leapt onto my mini-bike and sped down the pier, wishing myself away. A nomad searching for an oasis. I eyed the wall near the baseball field. Nobody would catch me if I ventured outside the compound, I thought to myself.

I turned my mini-bike around the immense concrete wall, and for the first time I escaped Raytheon Compound. An exhilarating feeling filled my lungs. I was one with the sand dunes and the rocks. A crazy freedom engulfed me as I full-throttled my mini-bike alongside the Red Sea's shoreline, throwing sand behind me. The smell of the sea's humid, salty breeze accompanied me, caressing my body and filling my nostrils. I licked the saltiness off my lips.

My mini-bike and I wandered over the different-sized desert dunes, passing sun-scorched shrubs, various-sized driftwood, and scavenging beetles. I knew all too well to steer clear of scorpions.

"One poisonous bite could kill a human," Dad had warned me.

Is he my real dad?

"Don't you *ever* touch a scorpion, Carina," Mom had stated firmly, her chin pulled in. *Was she my real mom?*

No matter what the truth held for me—I knew I was different. In the act of trying ever so hard to utter those ugly three words, "I am adopted," I tried to convince myself that this wasn't the case. *I am not one of them. After all, my brother looks like me and I look like my mother. I simply must find out my truth real soon—I don't know how much longer I can go on, not knowing my story.*

Stopping for a moment, I could still make out the bend of Jeddah's Corniche, but the huge cement wall shrank in size. Two- to four-inched lizards scampered in the white sand. Flies buzzed incessantly over the calming seashore's light splashing waves. I listened to the desert speak to me. Somehow, a wonderful peace overcame me. I hopped back onto my mini-bike and wandered home through the desert ready to uncover my true identity—whatever it held for me.

I wished God would help me the way He helped the Israelites to cross the Red Sea. I would wake up to my former life. I sympathized with the people of Israel, who left Egypt for better land. I too wished for better land right now. I admired their strength and determination by staying together in hard times. It must have been hard to start a new life elsewhere. They had no choice but to flee. *I must believe in myself, in my deliverance—because I am the one who sought out this discovery. I know that God blessed me with the strength to take on this feat because He wanted me to know my true identity—a deserved right for all of us. The Israelites knew their true home awaited them elsewhere. How will I be able to face my parents again after this? Will I have to start a new life?* I knew there was a reason for everything in life. I hated secrets.

Even though I had a question—the most important question of my life—I understood that it would not be an opportune moment to ask Mom about my discovery. *What if only one of my parents adopted me? Then where is my other biological parent?*

My gut told me that I might hear something different from what I always knew to be my truth. Up until my discovery, I'd always believed that my parents wed before my birth and that I was their daughter. Now I only yearned that it would be something I preferred to hear. I prided myself on my determination that I could handle anything and everything thrown at me. As for unspoken truths, I couldn't tell Mom that I snuck into her jewelry box.

Six long days had passed by since Mom returned from Germany. Almost three weeks had passed since my discovery, and my heart burned with questions.

"Almost time for dinner!" Mom called out from the kitchen.

I had to fake all of my emotions. I wanted to ask Mom alone because my truth was inscribed on her ring. Would I be able to face the world?

"Just a sec, Mom," I hollered, emerging from my bedroom.

"Dennis, would you please help put out the dinner plates, bowls, and glasses?" Mom asked.

"OK, Mom, I'll be right there," he answered.

Minutes later Dennis headed to the kitchen and grabbed four plates, bowls, and tumblers.

Once he set the last plate on the square mahogany table, I announced, "The table's set, Mom."

"No it isn't, Carina. It's your job to get the forks and knives!" Dennis yelled at me.

"You can take care of it, Dennis. After all, I've done favors for you," I said.

"Are you OK, Carina?" Mom asked. "Is there something wrong?"

I shook my head and stared out the window.

"Mom, it's not fair that I have to do Carina's job," Dennis whined.

"Dennis, be a good sport and just let it go for now," Mom said sharply. "It's time to eat," she reminded Dad while she carried a platter of hamburgers and a bowl of cucumber salad to the table.

He replied, "I'm coming."

"Dennis, where's the Tang? Aren't you in charge of it?" I bossed.

"Carina, you're not yourself tonight. Is something bothering you?" Dad winked at me.

There he goes again with his stupid winks. I wish he would just stop once and for all.

We seated ourselves in yellow vinyl-covered chairs opposite our picture window. Drawn white-and-black-checkered drapes hung on both sides. I studied the mahogany buffet. It displayed several international artifacts: a vintage silver Russian Samovar souvenir and a delicate Lebanese moss green vase. A vintage brass Middle Eastern plate and a colorful floral ceramic plate hung over the buffet on the white wall.

"I'd like to light a candle for Omi," Mom said in a sad voice.

"I'll get the matches," Dad offered and hurried into the kitchen.

Upon returning, he lit the white pillar candle that sat on a blue plate. We sat in a moment of silence. Mom alternated between sniffling and using a Kleenex.

I heaved a sigh, ready to leave. "I'm not hungry. I'm not feeling well. I think I'll go to bed."

"Check to see if you have a temperature, Carina," Mom said with concern.

"She'll be OK," Dad added.

I wanted everyone to leave me the hell alone. I wanted to escape. "I don't have a damn temperature, Mom. I just wish you'd leave me be."

I stormed off.

I heard their conversation from my bedroom.

Dad softly broke the silence. "How was your day?"

Part of me wanted to yell, *"You want to know about my horrific day? Well, I made the most devastating discovery of my entire life. Though I don't have to tell you, Mom and Dad, since you already know about it, right?"*

I felt the toll of faking and pretending. I loved Omi, but I wondered if she was my biological grandmother. I only wanted to know the answer to my burning question about what happened when they met? *I bet if Omi were alive, she would help me.*

I opened the French patio doors and looked for the Southern Cross star, which Dad had pointed out to us. Jeddah prevailed hot as always. Sweat trickled down near my waistline. I sullenly watched a sand-colored gecko just as it scurried down the moonlit patio wall. I couldn't wait to curl up in my comfy bed; again I'd spoken to no one of the secret I uncovered. I lay in bed listening to the humming of my trusty air conditioner while the cool air caressed my body.

Several days later, Dad and Dennis went to the Bin Laden horse stables to ride our white Arabian stallion, Hashim. Mom and I were home alone, sitting across the dining room table from each other. She busily polished her nails; her rings were close by. Here was my opportunity. I felt the thrill of wanting to and dreading to bring up the question. How was I to discuss her wedding ring without giving away the fact that I snooped in her jewelry box? She looked up, satisfied to allow her nails to dry, and stared out the picture window.

I took a deep breath. "Mom, I need to ask you something." My lips quivered.

She looked surprised and then cracked a smile and said, "Yes, Carina."

Nervously twirling a strand of my long blonde hair, I leaned forward at the other end of the long mahogany table. There remained a bitter taste of bile in my mouth.

"Why does the date on your wedding ring read 1962, but I was born in 1960?"

Dead silence. Her face paled. Mom looked down at the table and then up at me. She looked anxious. After a long pause, she heaved a sigh and finally answered with a trembling voice, "We wanted to tell you when you turned eighteen."

I felt every one of my muscles tense in my body as time stood still and a pit formed inside my stomach.

Her brown brows shot up with concern just as they formed a perfect double arc, and her lips quivered. "Your father is not your biological father."

My brain understood what I just heard, but I felt overwhelmed with a sense of detachment. My foundation, everything I believed in, disappeared.

"Why didn't you tell me earlier?" I shrilled.

Mom didn't move.

Staring blankly at me, she said, "We wanted to wait until you were old enough to understand."

I needed to do something—anything; I jumped to my feet.

"What the hell is this? You can't be real? I can't believe this is happening to me. How could you do this to me?" I burst into tears. "So all these years, you had me believing Dad was my father. And now, just like that, you tell me he isn't my father and that we are not blood related. How the hell did you expect me to react? I just can't believe it!"

Dad was my hero. But now he wasn't really my dad. I wanted to throw my chair across the room, but I didn't have the guts. She looked down contritely and turned her face away.

"We thought that you were too young—" Mom stuttered.

"Don't tell me I'm not old enough—it's too late for that now!"

"We did what we thought would be best for you," she said, her voice pleading. "I wanted your father to tell you himself."

My eyes stung, holding back my tears.

"Who is my real father?"

"Your father is your real father. When he first met you it turned into love at first sight. He took you into his arms and said 'I will adopt her.'"

I wanted to scream and make it all go away.

How dare she keep the truth from me; I felt abandoned. Anger raged at my biological father—and my parents. My stomach twisted into a burning knot.

I slammed my fist onto the table. "What happened?" I demanded.

"Your biological father was never around. There is nothing else to discuss." Mom firmed her delicate lips into a purse. Her moistened eyes challenged me with one of those powerful direct looks I'd become accustomed to. She sat, tapping her fingers against the table in an annoying manner.

I knew she wouldn't tell me any more—not even his name. I stormed off to my bedroom and slammed the door behind me. When I heard her footsteps, I yelled, "Leave me alone!"

I heard her footsteps softly dissipate down the hallway.

My father is not my father. I am not biologically related to my father. Then who is my real father? I can't believe that my father is not blood-related to me. My heart hurts. I cannot fathom this. How dare my parents control my life this way! How could they have kept such a critical detail a secret from me?

Her response, "There was nothing else to discuss," angered me and arrested all the questions I had: Does he know about me? What is his name? What is his profession? What does he look like? Do I look like him? Is he good-looking? What does he like to eat? Does he like to read? Why did he leave?

Why had she kept the truth from me? I wanted to run away. I wished I had never had this conversation with her. I threw myself onto my bed and cried. How on earth was I to overcome all of these emotions? I felt ashamed. I felt lonely. I felt abandoned. No matter how hard I tried to sleep, my thoughts swirled around like a desert storm. *How can I ever be worthy of anyone else's love if my biological father rejected me? How can I ever trust and believe anyone again—if my parents kept my truth a secret from me? How can I trust my future family or my friends or myself?*

I lay in bed that night, listening to the hum of my trusty air conditioner— lulling me to sleep with its cool caresses. I hoped to find that peace which surrounded me before and to feel whole again. Through my patio doors, I watched another gecko scurry up the moonlit patio wall. I wished I could run away.

By now certainly, Dad and Dennis had returned from the Bin Laden stables. It felt weird using the word "Dad"—it felt different. How did Dad react to Mom telling him that I finally knew? Did it cause him pain? *I wonder what Mom is feeling now.* When the house continued to be quiet and I knew that everyone slept, I tiptoed to Dennis's room and just stared at him. He was snoring lightly. One arm rested gently over his head, exposing his small hand and slender fingers. He had blue eyes like me and our faces resembled each other, but he had short fingers and round hands, not narrow like mine. I wondered why I hadn't noticed this before. Although it saddened me to have learned that Dennis was only my half-brother, nothing could have ever changed my tender feelings for him. I liked to think that I was like a guardian angel to him, and I wanted life between us to go on just as usual. I wondered if it was at all possible to love someone even more because they were adopted.

The next morning I made myself cinnamon toast sprinkled with sugar for breakfast. Like every other morning for the past seven years, I wandered into our dining room and gazed around at the colorful Kandinsky photograph, a glossy black-and-orange Arabesque print, and tall East African ebony statues. They'd constantly reminded us where we had been, who we were. Who I was. In many ways, I didn't know who I was. How would I ever forgive my parents?

The thought of facing Dad embarrassed me. How would I react? What would I say? Was I supposed to be myself? What did Dad think? Would he treat me differently?

My hands glanced over the Arabic brass and copper pots and vintage radio and record player on the shelves. My gaze rested on the boxes of records, which included Antonin Dvorak, Vivaldi, Beethoven, and Brahms—any classical music my parents could get their hands on. I remembered Verdi's *Triumphal March*—Dad mimicked its processional march with his voice—a particularly moving piece. Today it brought me to tears. I stared blankly at the walls. I wanted so much to be blood-related to Dad, but that would be to deny the truth. Did my biological father have blond hair like me? Is that where I got my tall, graceful height? Was he athletic like me? Questions swirled in my head like swarming locusts. Across the room, Dennis read *The Adventures of Tom Sawyer,* totally unaware that my world had been torn apart. He relaxed in his jeans and short-sleeved shirt, one leg rested comfortably on his knee and the other on a butterscotch armchair, as if it were any other day. For him, of course, it was.

I dropped into the matching couch opposite Dennis and thumbed absentmindedly through my favorite magazine, *Architectural Digest*. Although I wore my comfortable bell-bottom jeans and a red V-neck short-sleeved shirt, I felt anything but at ease; I felt displaced. No matter how hard I tried to focus on the magazine, my gaze shifted to the house. I loved this house. I had always felt secure here. Had the house taken on a new significance for me? I remained unsure about embracing the unconditional love and stability my home had represented for seven years.

I felt lost.

I ran to my bedroom to find a couple of *riyals* that I kept underneath my underwear in the top drawer. But the pain of wanting Dad to be my biological father filled my bedroom. I doused myself with suntan lotion and made a bee-line for the snack bar along the dirt road toward the entrance of the pool. I swung open the doors and passed by white plastic chairs and round tables. Luckily for me nobody presented themselves. I wanted to hide from the world and shove any unwanted feelings down. I hoped they would go away forever and I would be over this in a matter of weeks. An intense greasy smell wafted past my nostrils. I waved to Moosa, who chuckled, showing off his pearl-white teeth. He asked me in broken English, "Vat you vant theez aftnoon?"

"I'll have two Mars bars, please."

He gave me two Mars bars.

I offered him two *riyals*.

Trying to force a smile, I said, "Keep the change, Moosa." I bolted.

"*Shukran*," he called out.

I ran over to the open-air movie theatre and sat at the top of the steps behind the door of the stage. I tore open the waxy black wrapper and bit into the soft and chewy chocolate. Once I bit into the chocolate, the caramel exploded inside my mouth. I felt my face brighten up. I let chocolate seep into my veins like poison.

THE SECRET DISCLOSED
Jeddah, Saudi Arabia (1975)

S ince age thirteen, I'd become infatuated with my favorite teacher, Sean Jacks. I couldn't wait to see him again at school tomorrow. I distracted myself by thinking of the day I wore one of Mom's zirconium rings to school, showing it to my girlfriends and mentioning that Mr. Jacks and I would be married someday.

Like every other morning, the sun glowed in the intense morning heat, and I ran to catch the red and white school bus to PCS. I felt an urgent need to tell someone my secret, but not Dennis. I chose my best friend, Lucy Pullen, even though she was three years younger than me. How on earth could I concentrate on schoolwork today?

"Hey, Carina, how's it going?" Michael smiled, climbing onto the school bus.

"Huh? Oh, hi, Michael. OK." I looked down and swung my face away. I grabbed a seat and saved a place for Lucy. She was the daughter of Dad's boss, Paul Pullen, and the Pullens were our best friends and neighbors. Lucy continued to be my best friend—my confidant. I knew that I could tell her anything and that she wouldn't spill the beans. Lucy's freckled face always radiated the warmest, friendliest, happiest expression. I needed to talk with someone my age who would listen to me and understand me and my newfound truth, to accept me for who I'd turned into. I needed someone to reassure me that I could go on—*this stuff only happens in other families, but now it's happening to me.* I just couldn't hold it in any longer. I would tell her tonight after school. I felt it in my heart that I could genuinely trust Lucy.

"Hey, Lucy! Over here!" I hollered over the screaming kids.

"Hi, Carina. How are you today?" Lucy asked.

Looking down, I said, "OK. Hey, you want to hang out after school today?"

"Sure. I'll meet you at your house, OK?" Lucy laughed.

"Great." I tried to smile and act normal as the bus arrived at PCS. "See you tonight, Lucy."

"You got it, Carina." Lucy ran off.

I hurried to my locker and grabbed my geography book along with the rest of my binders.

I wondered if we were going to have a quiz today in urbanization. I couldn't focus, no matter how hard I tried. Mr. Adams was a really neat teacher, and I believed that he'd let me retake the quiz if I failed. I also thought about Sean Jacks. His jet-black hair reminded me of the sophisticated charm of Omar Sharif.

Oh my gosh, here he comes down the hallway.

"Hi, Carina, how are you today?" He winked and smiled.

"Hi, Mr. Jacks, I'm fine and you?" I beamed, utterly drowned in happiness.

Now I think I can make it through the day.

Later that afternoon the doorbell rang at my house. I bolted from my room, tired from studying for my biology test. *I bet that's Lucy,* I thought to myself.

I opened our front door. "Hey, Lucy. Want to hang out on the front porch and talk for a bit?" I let out a deep sigh.

"Carina, how's it going?" Lucy threw me a concerned look.

"Well, actually I have something to tell you, but you have to promise me that you'll keep it a secret." I pushed my brows together and bent my head down.

I hunkered down on the warm cement at our front door. I sat Indian style and stared out into the dirt road while Lucy crouched down beside me.

"Sure, Carina, what's going on?"

My hands were clasped tightly in my lap. I harbored a tiny doubt: was it really going to be OK to tell her?

"I promise," she whispered. "I won't even tell my sister, Amy."

"You'll never guess, Lucy."

"What?"

"Well, I'm not so sure I know where to begin…"

"What do you mean?" Lucy scrunched up her nose in curiosity.

"It's not that easy to say." I tucked my chin into my chest.

"Wow, it must be important. OK. Take your time." She scooted closer to me.

"Thanks." I tried smiling but couldn't because my eyes filled with tears. I tried dabbing them with my shirt. "OK, here it goes…I'm adopted." I sighed with quivering lips and lowered my head, pressing my lips together. Tears streamed down my face. I grabbed the corner of my shirt and wiped my face.

I couldn't believe that I actually uttered those three ugly and lonely words "I am adopted." How on earth would I ever overcome this new identity? A powerful fear resided inside of me. *All I want is for someone to hold my hand, hug me and tell me that they understand what I am feeling—to love me.*

I heard her gasp. "Really?"

"I never knew my biological father. My Dad adopted me."

She wrinkled her nose and lowered her brows. "Is your mom your real mom?"

I heaved another sigh, teary-eyed and nodded.

"Does Dennis know?"

"I don't think so, but I'm pretty sure that my mom will tell him." I gave my eyes a final dab with the corner of my shirt.

We both sat close to each other for a few extra minutes in silence, trying to absorb it all. I sat in shock knowing now that my father was not my biological father, and I wondered if people would judge me or think that something amiss existed. I resorted to not telling anyone. This way I could hide all of my fearful emotions—or maybe they would go away on their own.

Lucy put her arm around me.

"Best friends, Carina. Don't you forget that!" She squeezed my shoulders.

I sobbed. "Yup." I tried to crack a smile but I couldn't. I decided to change the subject. "Wanna go see what Christy and Patsy are up to?" I didn't want to dwell on my new identity. I felt ashamed. Nobody understood these feelings inside me. Dismay. Abandonment. Anger. *How dare my parents control my life in such a way! I never will understand how they could keep my identity a secret all this time!*

We never discussed it again. She kept my secret, though, even from her sister Amy. I looked forward to the softball game that night held on Raytheon Compound. *Maybe Mr. Jacks is playing tonight?* My crush had recently intensified.

———————————

"Mom, I'm off to the game!" I announced.

I wanted to yell out my anger to the world. I often screamed at the top of my lungs. Out of respect for my mother, I never screamed at her, but I frequently answered curtly.

"Did you finish your homework?"

"Of course I did. Otherwise I wouldn't be asking," I snapped.

"Carina, I don't appreciate the way you're speaking to me. Be home at nine sharp."

"Whatever," I muttered.

Mr. Jacks played outfielder on the baseball team. Lucky for me, I lived near the field at the far end of the compound. My heart throbbed as I ran to the baseball field, hopeful that Mr. Jacks would be playing tonight. Suddenly, in the distance, I spotted his silhouette running to catch a pop fly—I never saw him drop the ball. I owned my love for Mr. Jacks. Nobody could take that away from me. He would never abandon me. Elated, I felt those familiar goose bumps taking over my body. I sat on the first row of bleachers. Sometime later I got up and stood near the baseball net, behind the catcher. I melted at his every move.

The game started at seven and sometimes didn't finish until ten o'clock. I checked my watch; it read a few minutes before nine. I sprinted home and made sure Mom and Dad knew that I had gone to bed. Then I snuck out through my bedroom door onto the patio. A squeaky gate next to my parents' bedroom presented the only way out. Instead, I climbed the cement holes in the wall, jumped down, and dashed to watch the rest of the game. *Ever since my discovery, my infatuation grew stronger and stronger. I felt a yearning to be loved. My biological father had rejected me—Mr. Jacks never rejected me. His endearing smile and winks confirmed his love for me. I had nobody else to help me. My parents chose to control my life, and now I was controlling it.*

The next day, we had a substitute teacher for biology.

"Mr. Jacks had to return suddenly to America to visit his sick mother-in-law. The school does not know when he will be coming back," the sub announced.

"Oh, and before I forget, Carina, he left something for you." The entire class let out an "Ooh-la-la."

She handed me a small piece of paper wrapped around a thin object. I knew I blushed as I headed back to my desk. I quickly read his note wrapped around a Hershey chocolate bar: "For Carina Rourke, 3rd period."

Lightheaded and saddened that I might never see him again, I felt that familiar ache in the back of my throat as I fought back tears. The classroom noise became a blur—the only thing that mattered existed in my heart; I knew he understood that I had a crush on him.

Dad bestowed the same amount of love and care toward me—exactly as he always had. A week later, he asked, "Carina, want to drive with me downtown to the *souq* to pick up fresh roasted chickens and a watermelon for dinner?"

"Aw, do I have to?" I complained.

Constantly embarrassed, I felt awkward calling him Dad. It felt different. I had difficulty being myself. I didn't know how to act.

"Come on, it'll be fun, just you and me, kid—OK? We won't be gone that long."

"All right, I'll be a minute. I only need to change into my *thawb*." The long cotton dress flowing down to my ankles had a pink and yellow flowery pattern. The wonderful seamstress made my second robe much longer so that I would have one for later on.

I sauntered vaguely to the jeep. I felt fairly certain that Mom had told Dad about our conversation. I knew that I couldn't go behind Mom's back and ask Dad all of my impending questions. I understood that my discovery rested between Mom and me. Her response that there was nothing further to discuss did not invite me to ask questions.

Would Dad even be able to answer any questions about my biological father? My newfound truth made it embarrassing to talk to him. Dad remained my hero, though.

I watched him furtively out of the corner of my eye while he turned on the ignition and put the open-air jeep into gear, and then jettisoned us into evening traffic. I scrutinized his oval face that nowhere near resembled my long face. Halfway there, Dad pulled to the side of the road, shifted his head toward me, and said, "It isn't so bad after all, is it?"

I continued to sit in silence, staring out the window, heart now slamming. I couldn't face him or else I would burst into tears. I simply wanted everyone to leave me alone. I wanted so badly to jump out of the jeep, but I plainly sat there.

"I guess not," I murmured and stared toward the infinite, dark, and distant Red Sea. It boiled with violent choppy waves.

Apparently satisfied, he started the engine and put the jeep back in gear. He drove along a lonely dirt road. On the point of nearing the *souq*, I studied Dad's handsome features. Why hadn't I ever noticed that his nose had a bump? It wasn't pointy like mine. I stole glances at men in their white traditional *thawbs* in the act of buzzing alongside us on mopeds and bicycles, or driving old American cars from the early fifties. Beside us, alleyways were lined with shops where vendors sold pots and pans, gold, clothes, fabric, footwear, shirts, and toys. I peeked fleetingly at Dad and realized that his ears stuck out. Plus his chin pointed out more than mine. We walked side by side toward stalls with glass containers of sizzling, crispy, wonderfully aromatic chickens rotating on skewers. Mom and I looked so much alike. It never occurred to me to wonder why I didn't look at all like Dad. Dennis and I had similar round faces.

Dad ordered two chickens and paid the vendor a few *riyals*. We were both extroverts. But you don't need to be blood-related for that. Then we headed toward the stall with rounds of fresh Arabic bread. On the way back, we picked up a huge watermelon alongside the asphalt road. The fact that we all had blue eyes made it even harder to suspect anything. However, my height towered over both Mom and Dad. And still I had never questioned anything.

All passed by in a fuzzy blur. I found it impossible to have believed, let alone accepted, that Dad was not my biological father. If I couldn't have trusted my parents, who could I trust?

That night, the same ten-mile drive toward the outskirts of Jeddah which I knew so well seemed never to end as I stared out the window trying not to burst into tears. The desert road that once conjured wild thoughts of adventure and freedom now only reminded me of how vast and lonely the world was.

I'd become the lost nomad of the Arabian Desert.

Dad eyed me with concern. "How's it going...it's not so bad after all, is it?"

I didn't answer. I stared out into the vast and unknowable Red Sea.

Leave it to Dad to check up on me, like he always did. Dad was being...Dad.

Tears pooled in my eyes. I tried so hard to maintain my composure. I continued to stare out the window at the burning sunset. My thoughts drifted in the silence, and I wondered what my biological father looked like. Did I get my lankiness from him? Did he have blond hair and blue eyes? An intense yellow-orange fusion settled over the Red Sea just as the sun slowly sank behind two lonely sailboats.

Dad parked the car at the back door.

He said, "I enjoyed our ride together, Carina. Are you ready?"

I didn't meet his eyes. "You go ahead. I'll be a moment," I said.

He nodded and went inside, leaving me alone with the evening.

The palms swayed gracefully in the hot summer wind. The sun was setting. It painted the sky in different shades of blue. The sky's shadowy flames blazed intermittently between slow-burning embers like those that burned in my heart.

The evening came and went. I was soon safe and curled up in my bed. I recalled my German prayer, one I had recited nightly ever since I was little. I always heard Mom's voice reciting it. I sought solace in it this night:

Ich bin klein, mein Herz ist rein. Soll niemand drin wohnen, als Jesus allein.

"I am small, my heart is pure, and nobody shall live in it than Jesus alone."

It didn't help this time. I felt abandoned.

DRIVING FROM
JEDDAH TO PARIS (1975)
(Middle East: Part 1)

14

The summer of '75 was blistering. My family drove from Jeddah to Paris. I'll never forget King Faisal's assassination earlier that year. For three endless days, the desert's silent stillness hung over all of Saudi Arabia like a thick mourning cloud.

I hoped to find Lucy or any of my buddies to shoot pool with, grab an ice cream cone, or even swim a few laps. Where had she gone? There was no one in the compound. I could smell the scent of sagebrush as I watched a gecko zip through the fine white sand. I reveled in those tiny moments that took me away from my sadness. So much truth enveloped me and settled heavy on my shoulders.

Our five-thousand-mile drive provided me an opportune distraction to help me escape from the shock, anger, and fear that continued to threaten me after my discovery. After learning that my father adopted me, I decided it would be easier to deny that my father wasn't blood-related to me. This defense mechanism numbed my internal pain. However, I learned that it remained only a temporary "fix." I was faking it. Ugly feelings and emotions surfaced without warning. Although my mind knew the truth, my heart couldn't accept it—no matter how hard I tried. Your heart beats daily to keep you alive—but still, my heart and I closed the door to every unwanted sensation or emotion.

"I hope the Thomas family is unhurt by this war," Dad said, betraying fear and concern for his friends in his downturned eyes. The Thomases lived in Beirut; civil war had broken out there in April.

We had visited their home last Christmas in Lebanon. I remember the mountains surrounded by snow and tall sweet-smelling cedar trees. I too hoped that Mr. Thomas would survive and guide his family to safety.

Are we the only Americans crazy enough to drive from Jeddah to Paris? I asked myself. *Who is my biological father? This kind of thing only happens in movies, and now I'm watching my own movie.*

A few days before our trip, Dad mentioned that the body shop owner told him that our white Mercedes 230 sedan arrived from Europe, ready for pickup. Dad withdrew thirty thousand *riyals* from the local downtown bank and then placed them into a brown paper bag, folding it tightly under his arm, ready to buy and pick up our car. He arrived at the weathered cement shack at five o'clock, where he discovered that everyone had left. Dad returned to the office, placing the bag on his desk. He would pick it up in the morning. Then Dad came home that evening driving the jeep.

"I thought you were picking up our new Mercedes?" Mom asked, bewildered.

Dad nodded. "Me too, but the shop was closed, so I'll have to pick it up tomorrow—but we're definitely leaving in two days."

Early the next morning Dad spotted the brown paper bag in the middle of his desk. He realized that he'd forgotten to lock the door overnight. He snatched the bag and in a panic searched inside. The one hundred riyal notes were in the exact position, all three hundred of them. He sighed. No one in Saudi would dare to have touched it.

The day before our departure, a shiny white Mercedes appeared in the driveway. Running outside to check out our fancy new car, I yelled, "Mom and Dennis, Dad is out back with our new car."

"Wow, Dad, I love our huge car."

"Pretty nice, eh, especially since I only paid thirty thousand riyals for it." He grinned, obviously pleased with himself.

"What happened to the jeep?" Dennis asked.

"I sold it to a coworker." Dad heaved a sigh of relief.

After our favorite Arabic rounds, roasted skewered chicken, cucumber salad, and watermelon dinner, I fell asleep in my sleeping bag. The humming of the air conditioner lulled me to sleep one last time. I felt sad to leave my loving home of seven years. It had contributed to who I was. Or who I thought I was. Anger came back. How would I ever overcome my parents' betrayal? Then an impression of freedom burst and awakened my senses. I contemplated who I would soon become. *A beautiful flower waiting to bloom,* Mom had once shared with me. But this time I would reflect a different flower—a magnificent hybrid metamorphosed. I daydreamed about the magnificent Eiffel Tower and my new life in Paris—Dad revealed that he and Mom chose an apartment overlooking the Eiffel Tower. Whenever I thought of Paris, I succumbed and became hopeful.

In the usual hot and humid morning heat, Dad loaded the last suitcase, slammed the trunk of our glossy white Mercedes, and shouted, "Guys, ready to roll?"

Mom got in front, Dennis jumped in behind Mom, and I sat behind Dad. I felt the onset of butterflies in my stomach and a yearning for an exhilarating journey.

Dad had introduced the notion of moving to Paris over a year ago. I couldn't believe that we were finally on our way. Paris conjured up images of culture, couture, and cuisine. Having studied French for a couple of years, I became familiar with all the famous tourist attractions. Yet to soon have the real Parisian experience would be dreamlike. I once heard Paris referred to as the "city for lovers." I quietly giggled at the thought of meeting a handsome lover and found the thought invigorating. Dad had told Dennis and me that he wanted us to attend a private French school for a couple of years. I would soon become fluent in French.

I looked at the guard's gate one last time. A lump formed in my throat, but I didn't cry. Although I said goodbye to Jeddah, she will forever remain my true home. This is the city where I unlocked my true identity. In reliving that scene, I wonder if I ever thought about the fact that Eve, the mother of humanity, was buried in Jeddah—and I visited her burial site.

If my sadness overtook me, I tried to imagine recent photos of the Eiffel Tower, Notre-Dame, and the Arc de Triomphe off the Champs-Élysées. I pictured myself sauntering down chic boulevards, sipping a cappuccino, ogling the expensive boutiques, and indulging in French pastries.

Dennis read *The Hobbit*. I leaned my head against the left window to stare at the black slickness that suddenly appeared in front of us on the asphalt and then disappeared. I bugged Dennis: "Let's have a contest to see who can count the most mirages."

Dad switched on the A/C. The fan whirred on then hesitated and stopped. I thought new cars were problem free!

"Damn it all. Sorry, guys, but we're going to have to go back to the auto body shop and have this checked out." Dad sighed wearily and mumbled something under his breath. Would my biological father have reacted the same way?

"I just don't understand it. He installed the new A/C when the car arrived," I said.

"We certainly didn't need this." Mom shook her head.

I looked at Dennis.

"This is serious, huh?" he said to me. "Does this mean we're not leaving?"

I couldn't help thinking that this might be a bad sign for the beginning of a journey. "Who knows?" I replied, aloof. We headed for downtown Jeddah to the man who sold Dad the car. I hoped that the shop was still open. I sighed impatiently and began to sweat. It hovered already over eighty-five degrees.

I knew not to fuss if Dad got angry. After all, I hated to hear him raise his voice at us. I gazed peevishly out the open window. A combination of hot aromatic meats and pungent spices drifted toward me on the steamy breeze. The auto body shop stood near the center of Jeddah's downtown. Jeddah's national date palm ornamented the streets. Dad parked near a couple of dilapidated Mercedes and a white tow truck. Used and new tires lay sprawled about. Trash lay scattered amid crumpled paper and large pieces of cardboard. I inhaled the familiar sweet cloying smell of uncollected garbage left by a passerby.

Dad jumped out and hurried toward an opening in a weathered, small cement building. A man in his white *thawb* approached Dad. We got out of the car, and I leaned against our Mercedes on Dad's side. Meanwhile Dad spoke to him in Arabic. The man nodded vigorously. Dad later told us that all Mercedes arrive in Jeddah without an A/C. So the man installed an A/C simply as Dad requested. "But he never mentioned that on the point of going uphill, we must shut off the A/C!"

"*Shukran*," Dad replied.

A younger man approached us by our car. He stood in front of us balancing a round brass plate with four thin clear tea glasses and matching tea saucers.

He exposed all of his teeth grinning. "Please, *shai*."

I took a small glass and offered him my thanks. Cooling my parched throat, I drank my tea, hoping that we would soon be on our way. Dennis and Mom drank theirs in silence.

"Hey, Dennis, when you're done with yours will you also give them mine, pretty please?" I said.

"Why can't you do it yourself?"

Mom threw Dennis a look. "Stop being mean to your sister."

Flaring his nostrils, Dennis brought back my empty glass along with Mom's to the amicable young man. Thirty minutes later we left Jeddah with the A/C on full blast.

We forged ahead, according to Dad en route to Badr through the valleys of the Hejaz Mountains. An expectation for adventure and discovery once again rebounded. Umbrella-shaped acacia trees and brown saltbushes emerged from the sides of hills, covered in sand the color of yellow pound cake.

Mom, Dad, and Dennis ventured into their new life. I ventured into my own life of pretending to be happy.

Two hours into driving in desert scrub, Dad sighed and said, "Guys, it's time to turn off the air conditioner for a little bit. I also need to take a break."

"I would stay on this road," Mom counseled him. "This is not the Toyota jeep."

Dad ignored Mom and left the asphalt road to the right and parked in the sand. Dad stretched out and closed his eyes. Dennis and I bolted out of the car to stretch our legs.

I wandered, lulled by the desert's whispers. I gaped at the expanse of solitude. I felt small. Would my own truth set me free? In the desert I had no contact with the outside world. No phones, no TV, no materialistic amenities, no guiding hand to parade me on the right path. I glanced at the distant asphalt road we'd abandoned, hoping to spot yet another mirage; they stirred up images I thought never existed. Did I have what it would take to be a deserted nomad? I ran to check the jug of water in the trunk next to an army green Jerry can and funnel; we never left home without these three indispensible items. *Had we plenty of water?* I thought to myself. I watched my footprints soon be lost in timeless sand. The desert did not betray.

Mom's shout from the car jolted me out of my reverie. I felt refreshed. She still rested in the same reclined position in the front seat of the car. *Was I gone that long?* I wondered.

"We're leaving, guys," Mom called.

"We'll be right there," I yelled across the hot desert.

"Don't get in yet, guys. Go behind the car and start pushing. Schatzi, you'll need to momentarily get out and help the kids push us to safety," Dad said, red-faced.

As Dad stepped on the gas, the car's tires spun furiously and dug us deeper into the hot sand.

Nervous, I squinted. "Dad, are we OK?"

"Quiet! We're stuck!" he yelled. "Get out of the car and go find pieces of asphalt and carry them over here, right now!"

Dad rarely got mad. Dennis and I gaped in silence at the deep groove of sand covering the bottom half of the tires. I gawked at our car stuck in the parched desert sand, wondering how on earth we would get out of this mess.

Two apparitions approached us about fifty meters away. Two swarthy men dressed in *thawbs* and white *taqiyah* covered by red-checkered *shumaghs* neared.

"Two Bedouins heading our way!" I yelled, pointing with urgency.

Dad ignored me and kept shoving more chunks of asphalt under the tires.

"Joe, be careful. Don't let them touch the car," Mom shouted from behind the car.

The two Bedouins waved to us.

"*Al Salamu Alaikum*," one of the young Bedouins called out as they approached.

Agitated, Dad looked up and tilted his head back, responding, "*Wa Alaikum Al Salam.*" Dad stayed still near the tire. I stared at the strangers. The Bedouins walked toward Dad and shook hands. In the meantime, they studied our Mercedes. After conferring between themselves they proceeded to remove the asphalt chunks Dad had just put there. Agitated, Mom stood next to me and Dennis. I bit my lip, alternating my gaze between the deep hole and Dad. Dad stared, baffled. The Bedouins hastily collected twigs from nearby and placed them where the asphalt had been secured behind each tire.

"*Yallah, Yallah.*"

The Bedouins pointed to the twigs in the distance, gesturing for Dennis and me to collect them. We scurried about, returning with our arms full of twigs and dropping them next to the Bedouins. When they were satisfied that the holes of sand were covered with twigs and secured under the tires, they asked Dad to get behind the steering wheel. Dad shot up and sat behind the wheel. Meanwhile the Bedouins signaled him to accelerate forward at full throttle. Stunned, we stared in silence. Without hesitation, the car soared out of the sand.

Euphoric, Dad shook both the Bedouins' hands. "*Shukran.*"

He offered each Bedouin one hundred riyals (equivalent to about twenty-nine dollars). The Bedouins grinned with gratitude and left.

We went back to the main road, the only road to Tabuk. I leaned my head against the left window and studied the road, trying to decipher the black slickness that suddenly appeared in front of us on the asphalt. Sand covered the rocky hills; the towering Hejaz Mountains lay beyond. Remote villages with secluded white mosques and desolate petrol stations appeared here and there. Lonely stations comprised a flat cement roof over a few gas pumps. I thought about the dusty American Westerns: a lonely gaucho arriving in a ghost town. Soon the Hejaz Mountains surrounded us; their rugged surface rose to gigantic peaks. I spotted intermittent rocky hills enveloped with my favorite yellow-colored sand. It looked like a sand dune.

Not long ago, I looked at a photograph from this trip, and examining Dad's map, which his secretary, Caroline, produced, I read "Badr" in bold black letters. I remember that after several hours of driving we stopped to tour a reclusive pile of rubble. After a Google search, several particular photographs brought me back to that precise moment.[54] I found myself gawking at a similar Mercedes sedan making that exact turn, just as we did, entering the white city of Badr. I had never in my life experienced a déjà-vu like this one. We turned the corner at a weathered cement wall to the right of us. Dad continued along an asphalt road lined with abundant green trees and glimmering white houses, white minarets, and a luscious oasis. We stopped the car not far from a pile of rubble enclosed in several squares. There lay the lonesome loose rubble in a square. I remember Dad telling us about a famous medieval battle that occurred here. After researching *Encyclopedia Britannica*, I confirmed that the legendary battle which took place was called the "Battle of Badr (624 CE) during Islamic past events, the earliest combatant success of the Prophet Muhammad.[55] The Muslims stuffed sand down water holes along the convoy's road next to Medina and seduced Abu Sufyan's troops to fight at Badr in the spring of 624."

Back then I fought my own first battle for greener pastures.

We were alone on the road, save the few and far between trucks and assorted American cars whizzing by us. Until the contrast of beauty and the beast arose—two brown camels and a Bedouin emerged crossing the highway. The Bedouin wore a white *thawb* with a red-checkered *shumagh* draped over his head and shoulders.[56] He swatted his camel with a long stick, making the camels run. Dad slammed the brakes and we all jolted forward. I gaped at the graceful creatures. Later that evening we arrived in Tabuk, then departed the next morning for Amman, Jordan.

I missed the freedom of innocence, the freedom of ignorance and "knowing" who I was. I missed the joy of simple childhood cares and pleasures, of the good life on Raytheon Compound. I now felt burdened with impending womanhood. Yesterday I belonged to my parents. Today I didn't know where I fit in. I felt uprooted. I was a nomad in pursuit of self. I did not regret my new knowledge. I embraced my new identity with trepidation—fearful of the unknown—and anticipation of an exciting journey.

The oldest and strongest emotion of mankind is fear, and the oldest and strongest kind of fear is fear of the unknown. – H.P. Lovecraft

I'd left behind a place I could never retrieve except in memory. That place no longer existed. I acted differently now. My time at Raytheon lived in my memory. An exotic dream of a place where the sun—a hybrid of yellow and orange—created an incandescent sky of irregular streaks. Of a place where the harvest moon resembled a fiery setting sun, intense yet smooth like velvet.

I missed Jeddah. Was it its mystical aura that came to light from its illuminated gold *souqs* full of pure eighteen-carat gold treasures? Or its three-tier white minarets that rose above the city whose shapely date palms swayed in an occasional sultry breeze and lined the roads? Or was it something more elusive?

I could still see in my mind the four- or five-story buildings with radiant turquoise, green, and brown wooden window coverings and balconies that dominated Jeddah's characteristic 's ancient architecture.

I could still smell the sweet and pungent odors, a rich aromatic smoke that lingered like a long-forgotten poem—the ubiquitous scent of frankincense.

To be forever happy, like that innocent young girl, is all I ever wanted.

Amman, Jordan

"Wake up! Wake up!" Dad urged. "We're at the border of Saudi Arabia and Jordan, guys."

At the Al Mudawwara border crossing, we came upon two guards bent over red carpets, praying, on the side of the road. Their machine guns rested nearby them. We politely waited. The guards rose off their knees, placing their machine guns over their shoulders. *"Al Salamu Alaikum,"* they said.

"*Wa Alaikum Al Salam*," Dad replied, handing them our passports. Once Dad explained something in Arabic, they motioned us through.

"How long are we staying here, Dad?" Dennis mumbled, yawning.

"I figure overnight should be fine." Dad tilted his head toward Mom. "And, Du, you certainly remember some of the sights from our trip in 1969."

Mom heaved a sigh of relief, gratified because we had crossed the border. "Well, I'm glad we made it into Jordan without a problem." She stared out her window. "Yes, I recall Amman was extremely hilly, an avant-garde city."

We approached Amman's white stone houses in the surrounding mountains. How could I forget the abundant white houses sprouting up out of the hill? After registering at the Intercontinental Hotel, we freshened up.

"What do you say we visit the important spots such as the Roman amphitheater and the remnants of the ancient Citadel," Dad suggested.[57]

Eager to engage in my journey of self-discovery, I said I was ready.

We walked up the hill among green trees to the remnants of an impressive amphitheater. Carved deeply into the side of a hill, the amphitheater formed a half-bowl filled with rows. I eventually stood on top of the hill, braced by the view over Amman. Loose rubble lay over portions of fallen columns.

"This debris of stone columns is from the Roman period thousands of years ago,[58] and this is what's left of the Temple of Hercules,"[59] Dad said.

I imagined myself an Olympic runner. I saw myself challenging my parents and their paradigm of deceit. I thought back to the moment when Mom related that she wanted Dad to tell me the truth himself. I wondered why he never told me.

I glanced over at my father who wasn't blood-related to me. Had Dad been my Hercules? And still? What did I think of him now? I couldn't be sure.

According to my research on Google, "The celebrated house of worship of Hercules (Herakles) was constructed from 162-166 AD. The house of worship's portico is enclosed via six 33-foot high pillars."[60] I noticed that the picture of the Temple of Hercules displayed some intact columns.

I wonder now if Jordan's archaeological society unearthed more artifacts, or had they endeavored to construct columns over the ensuing years since 1975?

Descended from the hill, we entered the downtown *souq*, teeming with independent stalls, clean and orderly and protected by their weathered white cloth canopies. Brightly colored umbrellas shaded fruits and vegetables, displayed in orderly pyramids on square wooden trays. Vendors and people surrounded me.

I heard lots of "Madam, Madam, please you look here my shop. Please, you like jewelry?" I grinned at how the men dressed like Westerners. I felt a kinship to the women, who did not always wear an *abaya*—they exposed their beautiful faces.

I sauntered through the clean *souq*, inhaling the sensual aromas of cardamom coffee, pungent spices, and roasting kebab meat. This city had a modern and ancient and safe feel to it. I'd arrived closer to home away from home with fond memories and gratitude.

Jerusalem, Israel

I bolted awake and shook. My head floated in the stupor of a scary dream. I sat up in my bed and rubbed the sleep out of my eyes. A touch of sunlight from the corner window bathed my face. I cleared the tousled hair from my face and hugged my knees. My mind lingered on my dream, my ongoing nightmare. In it two shadow faces eyeballed me for eternity, but I couldn't recognize them. I screamed "Please don't abandon me." I knew that I had to choose one of the shadow images over the other; yet I couldn't do it. I shook my head hoping to clear it. I forced the disturbing images from my mind by pondering the coming day. *For God's sake, today I'm alive and well and going to tour Jerusalem—the oldest and holiest city of the world. Maybe today will be the first day of the beginning of my new life.*

I looked across the room and noticed that Dennis had already left. I jumped out of bed, grabbed my red shirt, blue jumper, and a pair of sandals and quickly dressed to meet the others. After pulling back my hair and securing it into a ponytail, I strung my elegant gold Allah pendant around my neck. I never left home without it. Grabbing my Agfamatic pocket camera, I rushed downstairs to the breakfast area. Surprised, I saw that everyone had already finished eating.

The Wailing Wall measured the size of a one-hundred-story house in an enclosed large courtyard. I wondered if I would find everyone crying at the wall. An air of serenity permeated the courtyard. Young and old men, dressed in either Western clothes or black suits with black hats or yarmulkes, walked around or stood in line with reverent looks either to kiss the wall or to pray. Women found their spot almost three quarters of the way across, segregated by barbed-wire fence and panels for privacy. Some women wore either a hat or shawl over their heads and were dressed in Western clothes. They stood tall or hunched over and struggled to stick a piece of paper into the cracks of the wall. Others sat tall on a bench near the wall, praying and sobbing.

I approached the wall where remains of pieces of paper stuck out between the bricks of this massive stone wall. Tilting my head upward, I spotted a full bush of grass growing out of the cement cracks. *Is someone listening to every prayer spoken here?* I thought to myself. I took the piece of paper out of my pocket where I'd written asking God for compassion and strength to help me find and redefine my identity. I looked back upon my nightly German prayer, hoping it would comfort me.

Ich bin klein, mein Herz ist rein. Soll niemand drin wohnen, als Jesus allein.

"I am small, my heart is pure, and nobody shall live in it than Jesus alone."

Dad reminded us that the Dome of the Rock, Al-Aqsa Mosque on the Temple Mount, was nearby as well as the location of Solomon's house of worship and its heirs, which the Muslims acknowledge as Al-Haram al-Sharif.[61]

"Du, why do you always carry that heavy bag around?" Mom said softly.

"Schatzi, then how would I be able to show you the world?" Dad gazed lovingly at Mom.

On top of the world, Mom tilted her head sideways toward Dad and nodded.

Dad always carried either his green Michelin Guide in his back pocket or one of us carried the black bag with his trusty Lonely Planet guidebook. He stood relaxed, proudly reciting with his Pentax hanging over his right shoulder.

"Guys, this magnificent holy place is called Dome of the Rock, constructed during the late seventh century CE by the Umayyad caliph [or ruler] Abd al-Malik ibn Marwān. The Dome of the Rock is the earliest Islamic memorial in existence. The stone, above which this holy place was constructed, is cherished by both Muslims and Jews. On this spot, it is of common belief that the Prophet Muhammad, founder of Islam, rose to heaven. And, in Jewish culture, it is here that Abraham, the forebear and founder of the Hebrew people, is said to have arranged to sacrifice his son Isaac," Dad lectured, grinning with slightly raised brows.[62]

I stood still, gawking at the gold dome set against an azure sky and luring me to my humbleness. It mimicked a vast eternal sun, shielding a celestial masterpiece. Nothing felt real here. The magnificent architecture included an octagonal arcade with a façade of intricate tile work. Rich blue mosaics, splashed in green, yellow, and white, produced latticed arched windows. Graceful white Arabic calligraphy adorned the exterior. A lavish arched entrance boasted two grand wooden doors, guarded by marble pillars.

I pondered whether someone watched over me, sending me a message that all would be fine.

We skirted around the magical city of Jerusalem, past colossal stone walls and narrow alleyways, and neared the lofty tower of a medieval-looking church. We entered the serene cobblestoned courtyard and lingered to listen to what other sensational sights we might yet explore on this warm and arid day. An ancient dust permeated the air from the piles of rubble I intermittently encountered. *Are they repairing the cobblestoned courtyard?* I thought to myself. *Or is this another archaeological finding?* Rapt with interest I leaned in closer to Mom, Dennis, and Dad huddled in front of the double-arched doorway.

In a contemplative mood, Dad looked up from the guidebook and said, "Listen up, guys; this church is the entrance to the Holy Sepulchre, the coffin in which Jesus was entombed and the name of the church constructed on the established place of his crucifixion and interment.[63] As stated in the Bible, the coffin was adjacent to the spot of the crucifixion (John 19:41-42); hence the church was designed to surround the location of both cross and coffin. The Crusaders reconstructed the Church of the Holy Sepulchre around the twelfth century. Since that period, constant improvement and renovation has been crucial. The current church dates primarily back to 1810. This location has been continuously acknowledged since the fourth century as the spot where many believed Jesus died, was entombed, and ascended from the dead. It is the holiest site in Christianity."

Jerusalem enchanted me with one sacred place after another. I didn't anticipate the sudden rush of "traveling" back to the medieval period. At one site, Dennis pointed out a man behind me. He wore a lengthy black robe with a white belt. He exposed his head, and he leaned forward hurrying toward the arched entrance. *He must be a monk,* I thought to myself. Both an ancient and modern feeling overwhelmed me.

I wonder if from that day forward I began to really believe in Jesus. I visited the holiest site in the world—the center of the world. Until then I found it difficult to believe in anything that I couldn't witness with my own eyes. The gleaming interior of the Church of the Holy Sepulchre glistened with gold altars, candles glowing around flowers, holy pictures, and golden mosaic murals. A reverential ambience embraced and soothed me. The dank air smelled of myrrh incense. I heard monks chanting in the background. My eyes rejoiced at the exquisite stained-glass windows—it was like looking at an eternal rainbow. I strolled across stone and marble floors toward a set of circular steps under a surreal stoned archway.

"*Du, ach du lieber Gott! Wunderschön! Sehr Schön!*" Mom kept saying, remarking at the beauty of the place.

Dad grinned. "Indeed, Schatzi."

"Follow me, guys. I'm sure you don't want to miss this next site," Dad said.

"I know, I know, Dad. Jesus' grave, right?" Dennis deadpanned.

"Dad, how do we know that all of this really happened?" I asked, puckering my lips.

"Well, Carina, great question," Dad said. "All of these facts have been passed down to us through history. It's up to you to believe it or not."

I followed them to the supposed burial site with enchanted thoughts. An air of surrealism permeated while I gazed in awe at the remains of a lonely stone bench. I wondered how much truth lay in this exact spot that was known as Jesus' burial site. I believed that we were so close to the truth. Soothed with the presence of Jesus and what He'd done for humanity, I felt reassured that I'd find the strength to forgive my parents.

We climbed to the top of the Mount of Olives. I turned my head to admire an iconic view of Old Jerusalem.

"Oh my gosh! Dad, what's that area down there in the clusters of zigzagging trees?" I asked.

Dad informed us that olive trees used to grow during ancient times on the Mount of Olives.

I observed a spectacular view and found myself both surprised and blessed. Magnificent churches adorned the side of the Mount of Olives—an intense divineness descended upon me, and I felt a calm wash over me. It seemed as though the prophets—past and present—were smiling down on me. I couldn't help feeling the sacred air as I gazed at the holy view. An amazing church with orthodox-style gold domes stood majestically among tall green trees. Further down the hill a beautiful sand-colored church featured three arches under a colorful biblical façade.

Reflecting back upon this momentous sight, I'm sure that in my own way I felt someone's presence guiding me along my personal journey to forgiveness and gratitude. Much the same way Jesus asked for God's help. This was His favorite spot to pray.[64]

We walked all over the place that day, including the Via Dolorosa.

"Guys, this is the Via Dolorosa," Dad said, clutching his guidebook.

Heaving a deep sigh, I attempted to assimilate my day's pilgrimage.

"Via what?" Dennis asked with a puzzled appearance.

"It's called Via Dolorosa,[65] the course Jesus walked, carrying the crucifixion cross. I guess you could say that we might possibly be walking the same path Jesus walked." Dad raised his voice an octave. We could tell by the tone of his voice that we had better listen. Dad took a picture of us standing next to a shrine-like stone wall enclosed by a wrought-iron gate with a tablet of Jesus falling on the floor under the cross. Thin clouds streaked across an azure sky.

Mom turned to me. "How are you doing, Carina?"

I kept my sunglasses on to shield my eyes from the glaring sun. "I'm OK." I gently bit my bottom lip.

••••••••••••••••••••••••••••

Once we descended the Mount of Olives, I walked toward an ornate brass-gilded fence and parked myself between Dennis and Mom, who were chatting.

Dad called to us, "Guys, let me take your picture in the Garden of Gethsemane. The name Gethsemane (Hebrew *gat shemanim*, 'oil press') hints that the garden was a cluster of olive trees in which was situated an oil press.[66] I bet these are some of the oldest olive trees in the world." He grinned from ear to ear.

Mom and Dennis turned their heads to be photographed. The ancient olive grove with its red roses and fresh-smelling peacefulness enchanted me. I grabbed my instant camera and clicked away. I tried to picture Jesus praying. I too prayed for strength to find forgiveness someday. For a brief moment, I escaped my suffering and felt connected. My imperfect world diminished.

Summer's vibrantly colored flowers covered the garden beds, and ancient olive trunks writhed up to the heavens. I listened to the soft sounds of branches and leaves rustling in a summer breeze and breathed in the smells typical of Jewish life here centuries ago.

••••••••••••••••••••••••••••

Damascus, Syria

Years later, Dad reminded me that we spent the night in Damascus, Syria, while visiting the grand *souq* and Great Mosque of Damascus. I grew up under the spell and lure of Jeddah's *souqs*. My only memory of this *souq* is that it continued on forever. Mom and Dad confessed that the Souq al-Hamidiyya[67] was phenomenal.

I looked back at photographs and reminisced over that glorious visit. The Umayyad Mosque was magnificent, and the massive marble courtyard held a plethora of arcades supported by ornate Roman pillars and arched windows.[68] Mom and I each slipped on a long black robe to cover our clothes and placed our shoes in a remote spot alongside Dad's and Dennis's.

What I only subconsciously felt then, I now keenly feel that the prayer hall's grandeur and glamour enchanted me. We entered the prayer hall with the afternoon sunlight peeking through vibrant-colored arched stained-glass windows. Ornate Middle Eastern red rugs throughout softened my saunter. Men kneeled on a rug performing their adulation. I passed women and a handful of tourists. Nearby stood a dazzling gold shrine surrounded by emerald green arched glass windows. I distinctly recall Dad mentioning that this chapel was dedicated to Saint John the Baptist and purported to contain his head. Low-lying crystal chandeliers adorned the mosque's palatial architecture.

Confirming my curiosity over what Dad said, I now know that this divine masterpiece contains a chapel allegedly encircling an artifact, St. John the Baptist's head, which both the Muslims and Christians treat with respect.[69] The Great Mosque of Damascus is also named Umayyad Mosque. This stone masterpiece is the first extant stone mosque constructed from 705-715 AD by the Umayyad Caliph al-Walid I. The mosque covers a rectangle measuring 515 by 330 feet.

Homs, Syria

"Guys, our next stop will be Homs, where there is a huge castle on top of a hill built by the Crusaders—I promise you will love it," Dad said, beaming.

Dad's prediction held true. Krak des Chevaliers sat majestically on a hilltop protecting its environs below. We learned from Dad's guidebook that the Knights of St. John (Hospitallers) constructed this magnificent castle and occupied it from 1142 through 1271, when the Mamluk sultan Baybars I seized it.

My mind conjured up images of what the term Crusader meant to me—massacres, honor, courage, Holy Wars at the time of the Middle Ages. I was a crusader seeking the courageous path to forgiveness.

Dennis giggled. "Holy cow, Dad. Can we check out this cool fort?"

"Of course. I knew you'd love this. Du and Carina, ready to explore?" Dad tilted his head at Mom and me.

"Hey, Dennis, I'll meet you at the top. Bet you can't catch me!" I teased.

The air embraced us, dry as dust under a navy blue sky. Dennis and I buzzed around the hillside, climbing the steep hill to the Crusader castle of Krak des

Chevaliers. No tourists invaded our space, so I routed around the ramparts and stampeded across the drawbridge while Dennis tried to find me. At last I stood on top of the tallest tower of this incredible stone castle, high above the fertile fields below, with the sun beating down. I was both Crusader knight overlooking her lands and damsel in distress in her prison: *Where is my Knight Hospitaller to stop my bleeding heart, to guide me along the road to courage and strength in order to forgive and heal? Will my heart ever heal so that I am able to accept my truth? I yearn for love and acceptance.*

In 2006, UNESCO designated the castle (together with Qal'at Salah al-Din ["Fortress of Saladin"]) a World Heritage location.[70]

Palmyra, Syria

A straight and narrow but well-paved road led on and on for two long afternoon hours. I stared at the endless Syrian Desert. Although I knew we were on our family adventure, I felt like a nomad in the middle of nowhere. I considered that I might be a nomad my entire life. Perhaps I would never know my true heritage. I considered life as a Bedouin. They were doing this all around me. Two wonderful Bedouins rescued us. Was I getting any closer to my truth?

My parents remained reticent, despite their "How are you?" No one offered me any facts about my heritage: who my real father was and why he abandoned me. Where did I really come from? Why did it happen that way? Didn't my parents realize how distraught I was and how I longed for answers? Aimless desert and scorched saltbushes echoed my questions with silence.

On occasion a car passed us. The Bedouins' black goat-hair tents specked the otherwise empty and desolate plain. Small villages with dilapidated cement-box houses and mud-brick beehive dwellings broke up the monotonous sun-baked desert landscape. I saw no evidence of human activity. Then we passed a boundless nest of pillars. We made a turn and four more columns rose in a sea of often crumbled colonnade ruins supported under a beam. *Had I been dreaming?* Dad's announcement jolted me out of a fog.

"We are in Palmyra," Dad proudly announced.

"Can we stretch our legs?" I begged.

"Absolutely! Let's check this place out!" Dad said.

"This must have been quite a wealthy city in its time," Mom said.

"You're absolutely correct, Du," Dad said. He grabbed his guidebook from his bag and slammed the car door shut.

"Come on, Dennis, let's go," I said.

"I'll be out in a minute." Dennis yawned.

"I'm going to give you the history of this ancient place," Dad said cheerfully.

Despite my defiant decision not to listen to any more of his lectures, I couldn't help half-listening to his description of this compelling place and people.

"Palmyra conveys 'city of palm trees,'" Dad began.[71] "She achieved fame in the third century BCE, when a central route through here developed into an east-west commercial crossroad. Palmyra developed over an oasis spread out between the Mediterranean Sea (west) and the Euphrates River (east); she also helped bridge the Romans with Mesopotamia and the East. Its magnificent remains tell of a heroic history amid the reign of Queen Zenobia."

I set out to explore Palmyra's chalky maze of ruins under a scorching sun, abandoned in the stillness of this desert oasis. Not a soul came into sight. The Greek temple called the Parthenon on the Acropolis came to mind from when we visited Greece in 1972. The stillness can sometimes be your innermost turmoil. I wandered the sea of stone ruins, a jumble of pillars, some with their chopped round tops collapsed nearby in a lake of remains. Ornate arched entrances from temples and buildings rose up, sprawling among this devastation in the sands.

Today, the "Silk Road" conjures memories of high school classroom discussions over its significance. I relived my intrigue over this elongated road: what could the importance of a lonely road be in the middle of nowhere? Then I learned about the explorers bearing precious and exotic gifts when they returned from the Orient.

What I now know after my research on Google about Palmyra's importance on the Silk Road is that it is a city of grandiose wealth and beauty. I know now that in 1980, UNESCO designated the ruins of Palmyra a World Heritage site.[72]

The undulating landscape of scattered ruins stretched as far as I could see. Had my young adult self recognized Roman or Greek influences in the elaborate and ornate colonnades? A path led to the Temple Bel, named after a god, according to Dad. This great temple rose up to the heavens over fifteen times my height. As Dennis and Dad disappeared inside, I admired Palmyra's wild romanticism. Romancing an oasis of ruins, I became Queen Zenobia, standing tall and proud of my inheritance.

As we continued through the remaining assemblage of stone towers nestled against the hills, Dad pointed to a far hill. "Guys, see that Arab fortress on top of the highest hill[73]—what you say we climb to the top?"

I couldn't continue anymore. I hoped the others were fatigued as well. "Dad, I'm tired and I need to wash my hair," I said.

"Du, I am very tired," Mom agreed with a sigh.

"Not me, Dad. Not me!" Dennis thrust his right arm toward the sky.

"Well, we could definitely spend another day or two here, but we better make a move on as we still need to find a hotel," Dad said.

The sun set as we continued to look for a hotel. I was sure that we were headed nowhere again when a small rectangular limestone building appeared.

"Welcome to Palmyra's one and only hotel in town," Dad announced triumphantly.

We entered the hotel via a courtyard. A few steps led up to a long stone slab. I swung open the screen door to an empty lobby. My memory was a blur, and next thing I remember I was standing inside of two airy bedrooms. I threw my suitcase on the bed and rummaged for my shampoo. A hot breeze soothed me. I headed to the bathroom and ran the bathwater. Brown, rusty, musty-smelling water gushed into the porcelain tub. Dad arrived and joked, "At least we have water in the middle of the Syrian Desert!"

That night came and went. The next morning, under a cooking sun, we left our bedrooms and entered the familiar slab of stone in front of the hotel. Our breakfast consisted of tiny cups of coffee with a pleasing aroma, Syrian pita bread pieces on a round white plastic plate, a block of cheese, a jar of jam next to a sharp knife on a weathered wooden board, and bottled water displayed upon a rusty cast aluminum five-piece bistro set. We dared only to drink bottled water. Mom and Dad warned us earlier in the trip that we must only drink bottled water. I didn't care for it; but in the middle of the desert, you couldn't be picky. It smelled of too much chlorine.

A friendly man approached us with a large smile. Staring at him, I realized that I hadn't seen any other humans for such a long time.

"A-OK? Amreecan?"

"Yes," we all said.

"You better eat up your breakfast, guys, there isn't anything else," Mom warned.

Dennis and I exchanged wry glances; we knew this was it for breakfast. I washed my pita bread and stale cheese down with gulps of bottled water.

15

DRIVING FROM
JEDDAH TO PARIS (1975)
(Middle East: Part 2)

Aleppo, Syria

We doubled back on the road to Palmyra heading for Aleppo, where we stopped overnight. A colossal medieval fortress overshadowed the peak of Aleppo's massive hill. Soaring and indomitable, the castle prevailed over the city below. This castle's medieval aura of valor struck me along with the peculiar shape of its supporting mound.

After a three-hour drive, I wanted to stretch my legs again. We parked in a large parking courtyard in the town below to climb the steep steps to the citadel. The weather felt comparable to constantly having my hair under a hooded hair dryer.

"Once we get to the top, I'll brief you on the castle's history," Dad said.

"OK, Dad, can't wait to hear it." I pursed my lips, annoyed at Dad's never-ending history lessons.

I hiked up the steep steps past an impressive stone tower with an arched entrance landing me on a humongous stone bridge with arches. We traversed a moat to an imperial arched entrance.

Once at the top, we did the customary huddle to hear Dad recite from his guidebook.

"Guys, no one knows how old Aleppo is, but it's considered one of the world's earliest continuously occupied cities.[74] During the latter part of the twentieth century, excavators found remnants of this temple appearing by the location of Aleppo's medieval fortress, on top of a hill at the city's hub. Earliest pieces of this temple belong to the third millennium BCE, and throughout the ensuing one thousand years, the architecture was restored on many occasions. The denseness of the destroyed walls suggests the appearance of a towering temple, which would have been seen from remote areas. During the twelfth century, Aleppo became a hub of Muslim resistance to the Crusaders, who failed to besiege Aleppo in 1124-25."

Reaching the top of this spectacular medieval castle, I imagined myself a princess. Would I meet my knight in shining armor? But how would he rescue me through these impenetrable walls. Admiring the stupendous moat and standing near the citadel's fortified walls conjured up images of Arab might. I eyed the grassy maze of ruins, and I envisioned grand sultans admiring their panoramic view of wealthy Aleppo below. For now I frolicked in the rubble of bathhouses, and I fantasized of my servants dousing their Arabian princess with precious oils.

Now older and wiser, I recognize that this sophisticated citadel—complete with palaces, baths, religious mosques, and shrines—prevailed many years and accommodated several civilizations endeavoring to protect Islam.

I recall waking up in the Mercedes close to Göreme, Turkey. I must have become exhausted from charging the ruins for hours. I later learned that UNESCO named the ancient city of Aleppo a World Heritage location in 1986.[75]

Göreme, Cappadocia, Turkey

We entered Turkey from Syria at Cilvegözü and headed toward Göreme, known for its "fairy chimney" bizarre rock formations. According to Dad, we traveled a little under four hundred miles. I dozed off and on through endless boring desert roads until we entered a valley of russet and wild stone formations. At first glance, sprawling mesas topped with vegetation soared and protected freakish cone-shaped rock formations. Had we crash-landed on an obscure planet? I thought of *The Planet of the Apes*. Massive bedrock pillars burst out of a moonscape. I strained my eyes against the glare to see beyond disparate green shrubbery and golden brown vegetation. "What is the name of this place, Dad?" I asked, befuddled at this alien-world.

"Göreme, Cappadocia."

I seized my trusty Agfamatic pocket camera. But where was my lunar module to guide me to explore this interstellar landscape?

Dennis's mouth had dropped wide open, and he released a cry. "Wow, those huge rocks look like penises!"

I turned with him to look to the right of the car. He was right! There were indeed phallic-shaped rock formations.

"Why, Dennis! You don't have to shout it out," Mom expostulated.

"Yeah, Dennis," I said with a wry smile.

"Well, they really do resemble them quite astonishingly." Dad chortled.

"Right, Dad!" Dennis added with a chuckle. "See?" he added to me.

I pushed my head forward, flabbergasted at Mother Nature's power. I gawked at these massive phallic mushroom-shaped rock formations. They stood alone or in clusters of three or more in a rough-hewn valley. Dad slowed down and pulled the car over to the side of the asphalt road. I was already clutching my pocket camera and jumped out of the car. Ignoring the tropical heat, I stepped onto a mixture of sand, gravel, and brassy vegetation and photographed these peculiar obelisks. We climbed back into the car and Dad continued along the asphalt road only to stop again. We all piled out.

"I've got to get some more pictures of this wild place," Dad said.

"Du, I wonder how far back these rock oddities date?" Mom said.

As Dad read from his guidebook, I scanned the expanded mesas over cone-shaped spires. Then it was time to move on and check out some caves up the road.

We proceeded toward an undulating maze of hills, a rocky paradise of conical pillars, mushroom-shaped cones, and chimneys. *This place is out of this world, a world of immeasurable capabilities.*

"Wow! This place is cool," Dennis said.

Dad parked the car and we spilled out to explore this surreal valley. Widespread rocks reminded me of hooded robes of ghosts. I gazed up at their rugged sandy and ash-colored peaks. I sauntered to a square carved-out hole. Openings emerged into doors and windows: a possible peek into a bygone culture.

"Let's go inside," Dennis suggested.

"Sure," Dad said.

"I'm right behind you," Mom said.

Cautious, I let Dennis peek first.

I wondered if anything inside had remained.

"Let's walk some more and then we'll drive to Derinkuyu Underground City[76] where people built elaborate homes and churches," Dad said.

An acrid smell permeated the area. Abundant apricot and grape trees sprouted from irrigated fields surrounded by a thickness of lush green shrubs.[77] Peace and quiet abided amid the chirping birds. One particular cave created a semi-dome cut out of the rock, riddled with pigeon holes, some arched, some square.[78] I discovered that one arched cave contained the wall of a square house and the remnants of an attached foundation.

"Hey, guys, over here!" I shouted to the others.

Dennis ran toward me, followed by Mom and Dad.

"Hey, Mom and Dad! Check it out. Did someone live here?" Dennis asked.

"Du, this definitely appears to have been someone's house," Mom said, eying the stone wall.

"It does for sure," Dad said, nodding.

I could be standing in someone's bedroom. I don't precisely recall how my young adult self reacted to the Zelve Open-Air Museum, but I know it affected me. The entire landscape felt like a moonscape or an eerie ghost town dwelling. At one point I entered a cave and raised my head to admire wall paintings.[79] I stared at an archangel with red wings. I know now that these were from "Church of the Grapes (Uzumlu Kilise)."[80] I felt tremendous sorrow for Christian folk who needed to flee from persecution by the Romans. Caves overflowed with artistic religious icons. These caves appeared to be a Christian's spiritual sanctuary.

"Let's head out to the underground tunnels," Dad suggested.

We returned to the car and drove about thirty minutes to the Derinkuyu Underground City.[81] We parked, and I couldn't wait to explore. We got out and walked behind Dad to purchase our tickets.

"OK, this way, guys," Dad said.

"Dad, are we going to see a city here?" Dennis asked.

"Soon, Dennis, patience," I bossed.

"I just hope I don't have to do any crawling and I don't get claustrophobic," Mom said, betraying some apprehension.

I pursued a dank and brightly lit bumpy stone tunnel and passed amicable male bazaar vendors dressed in Western attire selling fresh fruits and vegetables. I rounded a corner and followed our guide through a metal door that opened into a long narrow corridor.

"Mom, you were right about having to stoop low," I reminded her.

An earthy stone smell permeated the cool hall. Occasionally I had to tuck my head toward my chest to avoid the carved "living" rock.

"It's like Bedrock city from the Flintstones." Dennis grinned from ear to ear.

"Yeah, but without the rock furniture," I said.

I entered a maze of corridors, inclined chambers, arched openings, and steps of past settlers.[82]

Gazing now at the image of narrow corridors transports me back in time. I eyed a huge stone wheel with a peephole, perplexed at its use. It conjured up images of the Fred mobile from the Flintstones cartoon.

"Guys, these massive stone wheels were actually doors the Christians used to keep out any attackers," Dad said.

Today, I'm still dazzled at having witnessed this sophisticated community from ancient times. I imagined myself Alice in Wonderland searching for adventure through the diverse multicultural world and grand historic events. I now understand what Dad meant when I asked him about whether this all discombobulated his mind. He'd proudly related to me: "No, my mind is akin to a sponge, soaking up the world's history."

My mind is now close to a sponge: learning about the crusading Christians, Christ's followers, Muslim shrines. I thrive on having experienced these intriguing sights firsthand. My incredible journey to these cities of historical importance opened for me a new perspective, one that would eventually lead to my own healing.

Alanya, Turkey

During one of our reminiscent talks, Dad reminded me that we visited Alanya along Turkey's coastline or Riviera to have lunch on Cleopatra Beach. He told me that after the death of Julius Caesar, the Egyptian queen toured the Mediterranean and met Antonius at Tarsus. According to Dad, the legend survived that Cleopatra journeyed on canal boat to Tarsus;[83] she was clothed in royalty and entered through the gate in 41 BCE with the full intention to seduce Mark Antony.[84] Cleopatra enchanted Antony, and they embarked on a romance. Dad also mentioned that Antony offered territorial presents to Cleopatra.[85] In hindsight, I'm not sure if Dad teased me during our discussion about Alanya. According to him, Antony gave Cleopatra the city Alanya as part of his numerous and benevolent land presents.[86] I wondered: were Cleopatra and Antonius seduced by Alanya Castle and the cliffs that plunged into the passionate untamed waters of the Turkish Riviera. Had they yearned for love, for identity, for happiness, for belonging…like me?

Alanya Castle dates back to the thirteenth century.[87] Seljuq Sultanate of Rûm constructed the bulk of this castle. I later learned that the castle was built on a rocky point 820 feet high. I remember being spellbound by its massive stone wall that zigzagged down the slope into the Mediterranean. I slipped into Cleopatra's Egyptian sandals under a puffy blue sky with a sea-salt wind teasing my long blonde hair. Nearby, the majestic Seljuq Alanya Castle dominated breathtaking views of the billowy Mediterranean. I intended to speak several languages like that exotic queen and aspired to receive many lands as gifts.

Selçuk, İzmir Province, and Ephesus, Turkey

We were on our way to Ephesus just after Dad detoured off the main road toward a hilltop along a sinuous sandy road. Clusters of red poppies dotted a carpet of lush green—a tonic for my sore eyes, tired from the sandy brown desert. Rubble covered the slopes.

We spilled out of the car and I stumbled through archaeological debris. *Oh no, not more piles of rubble*, I thought. I'd had my share of touring ancient sites with rocks. I wasn't sure how many more cities I could handle. And then I'd have to grit my teeth listening to one more of Dad's history lessons. I gazed past a lonely erect stone column to a castle dominating inaccessible mountains. A mid-morning sun and ninety-degree heat beat down. I listened to the bird's whisper sweet nothings into my ear. No tourists loitered here.

"Du, how are you?" Dad asked Mom.

"It's hot, but these are fantastic ruins," Mom said, sighing.

"I knew you would enjoy seeing Selçuk, which is a nearby town from the ancient ruins of Ephesus.[88] We are heading there afterward." Dad pursed his lips, opening his guidebook, and I prepared myself for another lecture. Dad turned to us with a slight frown. "Dennis and Carina, how are you guys doing?"

"It's hot but great to get out of the car," I said, fatigued.

"Dad, can we visit that castle?" Dennis begged.

"If we have time, Dennis, because we'll be spending several hours here. There are a ton of ruins to discover. This is only the beginning. Let me tell you the importance of this lone pillar first." Dad smiled, pointing to a totem-type pole. "This is the remnant of the great Temple of Artemis, known as one of the Seven Wonders of the World.[89] You all recall the Parthenon of Athens, right?"

"Absolutely!" I had purchased my gladiator sandals in Athens and always felt like a Greek goddess when I wore them. Sadly, they broke.

"Well, this Temple of Artemis measured larger at over 350 feet by 180 feet.[90] Today only one lonely marble pillar remains—imagine that?" Dad said.

"Impressive," Mom said.

I sauntered along dirt paths from the top of the hill and gazed at a stone square mosque surrounded by gray turquoise arched windows and twin gray turquoise domes. Today I admire Dad's stunning photo. I felt a peaceful serenity, gazing at this ornate monastery.

The others caught up with me.

"This mosque is a wonderful model of Seljuq Turkish design constructed under the control of the Emir of Aydin.[91] It's called the Isabey Mosque and was built in 1375. Come on, let's carry on to check out the next site," Dad said.

In my opinion, this splendid mosque, dating back to the fourteenth century, depicts simple yet elegant architecture. After researching the word *bey*, I learned that in Turkish *bey* was a heading for Turkish folk routinely offered to rulers of limited ancestral classes, representatives of governing kin and eminent administrators.[92] Under the Ottoman Empire, a *bey* meant administrator of a district acclaimed by his inherent banner.

The mosque's stone and clay bricks looked like marble in the surrounding fertile farmland. A stunning gray turquoise tiled roof and twin domes evoked tranquility and wisdom. Had this wise and eminent *bey* taken this into consideration? It amazed me that this civilization accomplished such a marvel. People all around the world fled hardship and succeeded; then so would I—somehow.

Ephesus

We drove a short distance to the ruins of Ephesus, or what Dad called the most magnificent ruins of all.

I straggled behind Dad along the main roadway. The blazing sun's rays peaked through patches of clouds, highlighting the roadway's peach-colored marble slabs lined with Corinthian columns—many intact. Some places were obvious excavation sites for archaeologists.

A glorious Roman amphitheater fanned out from a massive hill slope. Three sections of seats divided this spectacular theater. I climbed the summit and gazed far below, inspecting a semicircle stage in front of erect Roman-style pillars and an associated excavation site.

I sat down on the stone seat to imagine history.

Dad's guidebook said the theater dates back to the Hellenistic Period.[93] It had seated twenty-five thousand people in its heyday and hosted concerts and plays, as well as gladiator and animal fights.

"Wow! Too bad we can't see one now!" Dennis said.

Hoping to help, I said, "You could imagine, though, Dennis. Picture powerful, athletic swordsmen sticking out their chests protected by gleaming armor—their glistening costumes, mighty helmets, and daggers in full glory ready to strike down their opponents."

"Yeah, right, Carina." Dennis smirked, mimicking a silly child.

I didn't anticipate the sudden rush of happiness I felt there. I became absorbed in my own reverie about love; I couldn't fathom its potency, let alone control it. I sat engrossed in the eye of my own storm. I thought I would travel the world to resolve my cyclonic sorrow of identity loss.

I pretended to watch a Romeo and Juliet performance. My thoughts centered on my biology teacher and the luscious Hershey's candy bar he'd left for me. I cherished the concealed milk chocolate wrapper which lay tucked away in my wallet, the tiny white paper with his scribble "For Carina Rourke, 3rd period." I lamented over the thought of never seeing him again. And in the still of the night with not a soul in sight, I'd gingerly unwrapped my gift—his love—pure and simple matching that first bite. You never forget your first crush...

Mom's announcement shook me back to reality. "Du, I think it's time we eat soon," she said.

"OK, Du. We'll wrap it up with the Temple of Hadrian.[94] This temple goes all the way back to the Roman Era. It's devoted to the Emperor Hadrian and is situated on Curetes Street. Many of these ancient roads and baths, in addition to a lot of Ephesus's superb remnants, go back to the Roman times," Dad said.

Today I admire and reminisce over Dad's photo. An arched portico adorned the entrance supported by four Corinthian columns. Their capitals of intricate leaf designs embellished this royal room.

"Say cheese, Carina," Dad called, pointing his camera at me.

I pretended to be Hadrian's empress, entering her imperial bedroom on her honeymoon. I delighted Emperor Hadrian, one of the Five Good Emperors.[95] I stood inside the temple under a square door, fixated on the elaborately decorated moldings. I imagined being a Christian guarding her faith. Saint Paul planted Christianity in Ephesus and in the region." [96]

While I know that I cherished visiting various cities and discovering new cultures, I also lived in a "bubble" centered on anger and denial. I continued to harbor great anger toward my biological father and toward my mother and non-biological father for their deception. I replayed Mom's words: "Your father is your real father—that is the truth—the truth is right in front of you." The tremendous shock of not being blood-related to Dad remained too daunting to grasp. I simply had to find a way to heal my broken heart.

As I look on it now, once I finally forgave my biological father and my mother, my true healing began. The key was to forgive even though I was still angry. Forgiveness created the mind shift, returning me to my "authentic self." Authenticity is the driving force to happiness. Dad loved me as his own daughter. He sacrificed his life for me, and he performed to the best of his ability. I could never imagine life without Dad—he *was* my real father.

The way I saw it then, I'd become a citizen of the world: a girl of a German mother, adopted by an American father, with a birth father of unknown origin. Like my ancestors, I clashed and struggled to form my future identity. And so it was that I genuinely journeyed the wonders of the world, finding my own wonders inside me.

Troy, Turkey

Three hours later, we parked at Troy's ruins under a warm wind and dusky sky. I climbed out of the car and made my way along a deep stonewalled path planted on a disheveled archaeological site. Half-crumbled walls and rubble sprawled chaotically throughout the ancient hillside, Hisarlik. [97] Gnarly green trees and shrubs spotted the fields and farmland beyond.

We listened as Dad told us about the Trojan War, a legendary disagreement among the early Greeks and the citizens of Troy, around the twelfth or thirteenth century. [98] According to the legend, Paris of Troy traveled to Sparta to snatch Helen, one of the world's most alluring women. Her husband, Menelaus, was the king of Sparta. He and his brother, Agamemnon, then went on a reprisal crusade to Troy. The Trojan War lasted for ten years. It ended with the Greeks' bluff departure when they abandoned a majestic wooden horse full of ransacking soldiers. The Trojans delivered the horse just as the concealed Greeks exposed themselves. The Greeks plundered Troy by killing their men and kidnapping their women.

I plunked myself down in the shade next to an olive tree. The antique stones warmed my tanned legs. I peeked over at Mom standing inside a deep trench fortified by a stone wall. Tall grass and shrubs thrust themselves between ancient stone cracks. A muggy breeze swept through her hair. She removed her sunglasses and faced Dad, who stood opposite her.

"Du and Carina, look up here. I want to take your picture," Dad shouted.

I studied my mother's expression. Was she replaying our conversation and wishing that it had never happened? Could she simply be proudly watching her daughter bloom into womanhood? Or was she thinking about how Dad came along and swept her off her feet?

Admiring Dad's photograph today makes me wonder: was Dad thinking about how he rescued two women?

I later learned that in 1998, UNESCO named the archaeological site of Troy a World Heritage location.[99]

Istanbul, Turkey

We'd traveled just over three hundred miles since Troy when I awoke from a long nap. My fantasy thoughts idled on a tapestry of archaeological sites. We'd finished with the Greeks and Romans—so I hoped. I glanced at the map mindful that Europe existed around the corner. I lit up. Stretching my arms, I sat up in my car seat. But first we'd visit Istanbul; I overhead Dad's announcement.

"Guys, we've arrived in Istanbul. We're crossing the Bosporus water channel linking the Sea of Marmara and the Black Sea, and dividing portions of Asian Turkey (Anatolia) from European Turkey,"[100] Dad said. "Also, did you know that Istanbul was once known as Constantinople? Istanbul is located in both Europe and Asia."

"So one minute we're in Asia, and now that we are crossing the Bosporus, we're actually entering Europe. I'm looking forward to seeing the difference," I said.

"Once you've had a chance to scout about, Carina, let me know what side you prefer," Dad joshed.

"It will be fascinating to see how both cultures mix together," Mom said.

"That's right, Du. Istanbul is Turkey's cultural hub," Dad said.

"Are we going to stay in a fancy hotel?" Dennis asked.

"Actually, I booked us two rooms in Istanbul's new five-star Sheraton Hotel, which has a pool." Dad chuckled.

"We'll finally be able to eat hamburgers and French fries!" Dennis beamed.

I shot up in my seat. "Cool, and a pool too."

I stared ahead over the wavy Bosporus and noticed an alluring white mosque with two minarets as we left Asia toward Europe.

"Hey, Mom and Dad, did you notice that beautiful white mosque ahead of us?" I asked.

"I barely got a glimpse. So now you're getting an introduction to Ottoman- or Turkish-style mosques. They're all over the place."

"Isn't it gorgeous, Carina?" Mom said, admiring the view.

Puffy clouds hovered in a pale blue sky as we crossed the elegant Bosporus suspension bridge to the European side of Turkey. The Bosporus's seaport bustled with cruise ships, tankers, and boats.

"Wow! Check out those neat cruise ships and tankers!" Dennis said.

"Du, let's find our hotel so we can freshen up," Mom said with a yawn.

"Yeah, I want to go swimming." Dennis threw his hands into the air.

"I could go with that idea," I added.

"We just crossed the longest suspension bridge on the planet,"[101] Dad said.

"Wow, how cool is that!" Dennis said.

"Du, I love this," Mom said with a slanted smile, scanning the scenery of churches, mosques, and modern houses with red-tiled roofs.

"Me too, Schatzi, I can hardly wait to see it all," Dad said.

"I can't believe that we just left Asia, soon to be in Europe in a matter of minutes," I said.

"It's pretty wild, Carina, right?" Dad said.

::::::::::::::::::::::::::::::

"Holy mackerel, our hotel is a palace!" Dennis shot up in his seat as the tall tower of the Sheraton came into view.

"Nothing but the best for us, Du." Dad winked at Mom.

Mom gently pursed her lips, smiling. "*Wunderschön, Du.*"

"Wow, luxurious, Dad, you certainly splurged this time." I threw him a crooked grin.

Our rooms looked out onto the choppy Bosporus, its shoreline speckled by traditional red-tiled roofs. I felt like a princess, swimming in the hotel's outdoor pool and charging my sodas to our hotel room. I gobbled up a whopper hamburger and French fries that first night.

::::::::::::::::::::::::::::::

According to Dad, we stayed several days in Istanbul. Memories of Istanbul awaken images of domes and minarets sprouting out of undulating hills. These awe-inspiring mosques built by sultans over four hundred years ago endure beside modern buildings, palaces, and posh mansions. Istanbul's multiculturalism enamored me through her vibrant and unique architecture.

After a luxurious overnight rest and breakfast, we walked a short distance to the Grand Bazaar. A tropical sun beamed through fluffy clouds. I hiked down one of the seven hills located around Istanbul,[102] listening to the sigh of a dusty breeze. A plethora of doner kebabs' seasoned meat found around every corner. The mosques of modern Istanbul helped create a blend of antiquity and modern.

"I'd love to purchase a couple of Turkish rugs," Dad said like a boy in a candy store. Then he added, "But first, listen up and I'll tell you about this huge *souq*."

I stood next to an ornate stone arched gate and listened to Dad's history lesson.

"Guys, this is one of the biggest and oldest covered *souqs* in the world. It's called the Grand Bazaar (*Kapali Çarsi*), which was established in the beginning of the Turkish reign; despite blazes and earthquakes, over four thousand shops flourished in the *souq*,"[103] Dad said.

"OK, Du, I can hardly wait to head inside," Mom said.

Memories from my father's photos remind me that this extravagant covered market included a maze of dazzling shops that displayed rugs, jewelry, handmade pottery wares, clothing, spices, and so much more. Ornate church-style vaulted ceilings shielded me from the heat but not from the crowds. Hordes of people dressed in modern attire hustled and bustled. Stale air wafted by me. In recalling that scene about Dad's mission to buy a rug or two, I found a picture of a marble drinking fountain near a rug vendor. I passed by bedecked marble square fountains with brass knobs as I tried to keep up with Dad.

"Dennis and Carina, you guys OK?" Mom said.

"I'm ready to head out," I said.

"Yeah, I've had enough," Dennis said.

Across the way, a tapestry of rugs with hues of deep red, gold, and beige hung against a stone wall. I thought about Jeddah's *souq*. Fiery aromas from the spice stalls teased my nostrils. I dreamed about vendors from the East who delivered silk, precious stones, and spices to the vendors in the West. I'm sure that a plethora of influential recipes, stories, and new knowledge arrived and thrived from the Silk Road's ancestry. The heart and soul of Istanbul's trade clearly resides in her awe-inspiring Grand Bazaar. Amidst the strong scent of Turkish coffee, I heard the familiar and beautiful muezzin's resonant voice calling all Muslims to prayer.

<hr>

"Du, I'm now ready to head to the Hagia Sophia mosque," Mom said impatiently.

"OK, I'll come back later to buy a Turkish rug," Dad said. We learned that the Hagia Sophia cathedral is also known as the Church of the Holy Wisdom or Church of the Divine Wisdom, and she's considered the most valuable of Byzantine architecture and one of the globe's most celebrated memorials.[104]

I studied Dad's photos and compared them to my research on Google. Four minarets, a blue-gray central dome, and several mini-domes adorned the imperial mosque. Once inside, I sauntered over a marble floor. Low-lying chandeliers and daylight shone through stained-glass windows effusing the mosque with a gleaming brilliance. I tilted my head back to stare up at dazzling stained-glass windows and the apse mosaic of Mary holding baby Jesus. Two massive plates with black and gold Arabic script surrounded this holy relic. One of the plate's script reminded me of my gold Allah pendant. I gazed up to the alluring yellow dome bordered with arched windows and glittering gold Arabic script. I wondered if this depicted the sun. The huge plates with Arabic script blended in beautifully with breathtaking details of a typical Christian church. Both Christian and Islamic aspects stood side by side.

The others joined me.

"Guys, this area is called a *mihrab*," Dad said. "The *mihrab* is a little nook or apse in the wall of a mosque which points toward Mecca."[105]

"That looks like Arabic handwriting," Dennis said.

"You're absolutely right, Dennis," Dad said.

"Du, the yellow Byzantine domes are truly magnificent," Mom said.

"Yes, Du, this interior is exquisite."

"Guys, I want to go outside and get a bite," I said.

"OK, everyone, let's head out," Dad said.

Once outside in the fresh but muggy air, I bought myself a succulent beef doner kebab and soda from one of the street vendors. I used the pocket money that Dad gave me. Dennis followed suit and Dad bought himself and Mom a chicken kebab. I wove my way among crowds of tourists and sat on a bench beneath lush green trees, blooming flowers, and spewing fountains.

The Hagia Sophia is part of a UNESCO World Heritage location named the Historic Areas of Istanbul (assigned in 1985) that contains Istanbul's other important historic architecture and areas.[106]

"Guys, are you ready to visit the Blue Mosque?" said Dad. "I'd be curious to know which one you prefer."

How could I forget that I'd been absolutely blown away by Turkey's beautiful Blue Mosque?

The Blue Mosque reminded me of Aladdin with its six minarets and layers of domes puncturing the sky close to a mighty alcazar. It finally dawned on me because the book called *The Golden Treasury of Children's Literature* contained the story "Aladdin and the Wonderful Lamp" that Mom and Dad used to read to me at bedtime. I loved staring at those onion-shaped domes.

I walked to the hexagonal fountain in the center of the mosque and eyed the far-reaching courtyard of vaulted arcades topped with smaller domes. Luckily, not too many tourists populated the courtyard.

"Carina, we're going inside," Mom called from the entrance.

I took off my shoes and covered my head with a black scarf provided by an attendant. I entered the mosque with gleaming chandeliers, amplified by stained-glass windows. Sweeping red rugs cushioned my achy feet. Men bowed or kneeled on the rugs, performing their adulation. I passed women and a handful of tourists and caught a faint dirty sock odor.

I lifted my head to study the effusive rainbow colors. Cascading domes of bluish tiles with starry patterns enraptured me. Had the floodtide of the heavens opened up? Were the Olympian gods and goddesses gazing down upon me? I tried to forgive my parents for their deception right there under an arc of prismatic colors where azure and gold dominated. I was still a wanderer, traveling without residence. Had my parents told me the truth early on, I wouldn't be having these thoughts now, I considered. I loved my family, but I didn't know myself anymore. To forgive people of deception is the hardest task in life.

Then I remembered what Dad had often said to me in conversation while growing up: *"If there is anything we have, it's unconditional love within our family."* Dad's heartfelt words encouraged me to pursue my journey and to seek clarity.

Yet how soon would clarity and wisdom come?

Years later Dad reiterated that he went back to the Grand Bazaar where he bargained for two Turkish carpets, which reside in my parents' house to this day.

Massive posh mansions and imperial palaces flanked the Bosporus's embankments. Doner kebab street vendors flocked outside of the grand mosques fit only for sultans. Shopaholics sprinted through the Grand Bazaar's dazzling four thousand shops which dotted the zigzagging potholed streets. Vendors proudly displayed commodities from high-end to basic essentials under a prism of glittering lights. Imperial mosques beautified with Islamic features stood beside Christian icons. Istanbul's cultural hub offered me a touch of Europe under the charm of Islam. I saw truly the most resplendent structure on earth. And today I would have to agree with Mom and Dad's comment about Istanbul being a "wild" city.

DRIVING FROM JEDDAH TO PARIS (1975)
(Europe: Part 1)

Sofia, Bulgaria

I was giddy with joy that we'd reached the halfway mark of our five-thousand-mile trek to Paris. According to Dad's map, we'd driven three hundred fifty miles since Istanbul when we arrived in Sofia, Bulgaria. In looking for a hotel, we encountered a series of "no vacancy" signs. The first night, we slept in the car parked in a closed gas station. Dad booked us in a first-class hotel the next day.

I bolted awake flushed in spite of the coolness of the car. In the pre-dawn morning while it remained still dark outside, I heard a tapping on my window. I watched Dad roll down the window and come face-to-face with a police officer. The policeman mumbled something in Bulgarian and gestured his hand, motioning us to move on.

Dad tilted his head to the side to gaze at the officer. Annoyed, he said, "Hotel full! No room!"

The officer replied gruffly, "No sleep, you leave now!"

Dad raised his voice. "What to do? Hotel no room!"

"You go now!" The officer flared his nostrils and raised his arm forcefully.

Dad pulled into another closed station.

"Welcome to Sofia, Schatzi. And, guys, I promise to book us in a first-classer tomorrow morning. Now let's get some sleep," Dad said.

"That was a close call, Dad," I said, yawning.

"Du, I'm glad we didn't have an incident," Mom said.

Dad chortled. "He wasn't going to do anything."

"You showed him, Dad!" Dennis said.

I stared at the moon. I couldn't go back to sleep; my head swam in a distraction of thoughts. On this night, I felt safe and secure with my family. Yet I felt uprooted. I was still part of this family, yet apart somehow. Like I belonged but didn't all at the same time. It was all a haze. And I hoped that I would someday break through. I longed not to feel different. I watched the dawn break. Streaks of sunlight flared through a jumble of clouds. I tucked a loose strand of hair behind my ear and stared at the morning of another world.

"*Guten Morgen*, how did you all sleep?" Mom stretched her arms and laughed.

I sat up and yawned. "OK. I can't wait to freshen up."

"Yeah, I'm hungry," Dennis said.

"Schatzi, what you say we find a five-star hotel and get some piping hot coffee and freshen up." Dad smiled.

"*Wunderschön*," Mom agreed.

Dad started the engine and the car pulled out of the gas station. We searched for our five-star hotel—known today as the Radisson Blu Grand Hotel, Sofia.[107] Dad pulled over to the side of the road and, after perusing the map, finally found it. He pulled up the driveway of the hotel and came to a stop while I followed Mom and Dennis to the reception area. Dad parked the car. Bedazzled with excitement and hoping that the receptionist could accommodate us, I gaped at the luxurious lobby. Dennis ran over and shouted, "They have rooms for us!"

I shifted my gaze to greet Dad.

"We're in luck, Dad. They actually have two rooms for us," I said.

"I had a good feeling about this place," Dad said, smiling. "OK, go freshen up and be ready in an hour to take on Sofia."

"Can you believe it, Dennis? We're in a five-star hotel!" I giggled as we entered our room.

I pulled open the curtain to an impressive view of the city. The surrounding area brimmed with trees, greenery, parliament buildings, and a grand church with gold-plated domes. A majestic black statue of a general riding on his horse dominated the square below, filled with tour buses and parked cars. People bustled through the square. I quickly freshened up, realizing that I was very hungry. Once Dennis was ready, we tore off to breakfast, and after breakfast we met Mom and Dad in the deluxe lobby.

We strolled along cheerful yellow cobblestones in this immaculate city center. Billowy clouds drifted against a pale blue sky. The day turned out pleasantly warm. I welcomed the cacophony of cars stumbling over yellow bricks.

"This is called the Yellow Brick Road," Dad said with a slanted grin. "Apparently in the late 1800s pedestrians lost their shoes in these muddy streets. The streets were inlaid with yellow bricks so that women wouldn't get their feet dirty."

Surely Dad joshed us, I thought. I recently discovered that while Prince Ferdinand of Bulgaria espoused Princess Marie Louise of Bourbon-Parma in 1893, he envisioned changing Sofia into a trendy main city like Vienna and Budapest.[108] However, asphalted streets were nonexistent in the nineteenth-century uncomplicated and cramped Sofia. To assist, Hapsburg relatives delivered yellow cobblestones evidently as a bridal gift; however, the cinder blocks were guarded in a depository until 1907 and only then rendered Sofia its yellow brick road. We followed the yellow brick road to an opulent church that reminded me of Mom and Dad's photos from Moscow. The church resembled a Russian Orthodox cathedral.

Memories of visiting this gold-domed cathedral brought to mind a four-tiered wedding cake surrounded by gold and green-turquoise domes. In addition, mosaics of saints adorned the exterior arched doorways. I found my way through the open wooden door into a dark and dank interior. Chandeliers hung from a cathedral ceiling and flickered. They illuminated religious icons like a shimmering forest in a Rembrandt painting—*The Night Watch*. I arrived at the magical Emerald City journeying along my yellow brick road to discover my rainbow.

••••••••••••••••••••••••••••••

Giurgiu, Romania

We left Sofia behind, on the hunt for Dracula. Dad informed us that the bridge over the Danube River in Ruse, Bulgaria, would connect us with Giurgiu, Romania.[109] Construction of this steel bridge occurred in 1954. It's called the Friendship Bridge.

As I look back on it, I remember that we all needed to get out of the car so the police could inspect it.

We exited and Dad handed our passports over to the officials as we stood by.

"Where are you traveling from, Mr. Rourke?" one officer inquired in broken English.

"We lived in Saudi Arabia. We're visiting Europe on our way to our new home in Paris," Dad responded.

"Who is traveling with you, and do you have anything to declare?"

"My wife and two children. We have our luggage, gifts, and the two rugs from Istanbul, Turkey."

"We will let you know when we are done inspecting your car. Would you please open your suitcases?"

I watched the officers rummage through my suitcase. I didn't appreciate them rummaging through my personal possessions—what right did they have? This reminded me of Checkpoint Charlie, the Berlin Wall crossing point between East Berlin and West Berlin. I swung my head toward the Danube River; I waited impatiently under a hazy sky. The wind slapped against my hair. A marshy odor wafted by me. Seagulls bobbed up and down over an inclement blue Danube where lush green trees lined the dirt banks. I heaved a sigh and distracted myself with thoughts centered on soon being able to visit Dracula's castle. It would be fun sharing the experience with my friends. I would just have to convince them—maybe buying postcards would do the trick.

I turned to watch the officers open our car doors and thoroughly inspect our car—even under the chassis. They removed the Turkish rugs and placed them against the border hut. One of the border patrolmen pointed at the suitcase. He held his hands together, then opened them—gesturing for Mom to open up the suitcase. He scrutinized and rummaged through. Once we received the go-ahead signal, we reloaded our belongings and crossed the bridge over the Danube to enter Romania.

Bucharest, Romania

On a hot afternoon, we made our way into Bucharest and parked near a major square. Gazing at one of Bucharest's photos made me feel that these following sights impacted me the most.

"Guys, you know that Vladimir Ilich Lenin was Russia's leader and founder of the Russian Communist Party (Bolsheviks).[110] He believed in the ideas of Karl Marx—the German philosopher—who believed in socialism. Let me know if you see the Communist symbolism of a golden hammer and sickle." Dad tilted his head forward.

"OK, Du, enough," Mom blurted.

"Du, I was just getting started," he responded, trying to humor her.

"So what is your impression of this monument, Mom?" I asked.

Shaking her head, she replied, "I hate it."

"I kind of like it." Dennis laughed.

"I do too." Dad chortled.

I stumbled over cobblestones to view a colossal and imposing grey stone monument of Lenin. He appeared to be leaning on a wall or grasping something for support. His left hand rested over his trench coat, flapping in the wind. Behind him stood an imposing wall painted in red and white, dotted with several of the Communist golden hammer and sickles.

"And you, Carina?" Dad asked.

Tilting my head to one side, I said, "I sense a compelling and cold starkness from the bleak stone monument."

"And although I somewhat like it, I couldn't have said it better." Dad threw me a wink.

Gray and sand-colored high-rises surrounded us. They reminded me of the bleak and gray apartments I'd seen in East Germany.

After seeing Lenin's statue and the hammer and sickle, I felt as if this was my introduction to the Communist era of the time.

"These buildings bear a resemblance to Berlin's Gartenstrasse, where I grew up," Mom said.

We strolled among a profusion of white painted houses with thatched roofs and ornately painted blue windows and doors. Their interior furniture reminded me of a simple Amish home. But the hand-woven quilts and home decor were a bounty of colorful floral patterns and geometric designs. I caught a sweet and earthy fragrance as we headed toward a luscious park of dirt paths, trees, and delicate flowers and farmhouses. Some mimicked real-life country hobbit houses. Miniscule mushroom-shaped houses with roofs covered in hay emerged out of the ground. I witnessed a rare glimpse at Romania's local cultures and rich ancestry. I peacefully gazed for the first time at wooden churches with remarkably tall spires hovering above this small village—a delight compared to bustling Bucharest. I longed for the natural beauty and simplicity of this life. Nature doesn't expect anything in return. This seemed a pleasant diversion and contrast to the Communist era during that time.

"Guys, you know who Dracula is, right?" Dad joshed.

"Duh, Dad, yeah, I know," I said.

"He's the vampire who sucks blood from people." Dennis smirked.

"Well, I have a surprise for us. Let's continue our hunt for Dracula's hometown," Dad said.

"This is going to be awesome," I said.

"Cool, man. Is there a museum?" Dennis asked.

"Better yet, there's a castle where he used to live," Dad said.

Transylvania, Romania

We piled into the Mercedes and wound our way through the Carpathian Mountains.[111] I fell asleep dreaming about Dracula's castle.

I heard Dennis shout excitedly, "Wow, I see Dracula's castle!"

I raised my head and turned to view the commanding Bran Castle, located in the medieval city of Brasov. The castle loomed from behind a lush green forest like an ominous painting, her majestic red towers perched atop a hill under swollen clouds.

"Hey everyone, I thought you'd be interested in knowing the following. It has been hinted that Bram Stoker, who wrote *Dracula*, derived Dracula's personality from the Romanian prince Vlad Țepeș.[112] He was known as Vlad the Impaler, who ruled the region of Walachia, not far from here, throughout the mid to late 1400s. He was reputed to use barbarous techniques for discipline," Dad said.

Dennis gawked at Dad with widened eyes. "We're going to check it out, right?"

"Absolutely," Dad said.

We parked at the bottom of a hill and piled out of the car to buy our entrance tickets. The embellished white courtyard and red-tiled roofs reminded me of the setting for Rapunzel and her charming prince.

I listened to Dad brief us on the surrounding history.

"Listen up, guys, the Bran Castle sits on a rock two hundred feet up. Teutonic knights constructed a fortress on this spot in 1212. The citadel was originally chronicled in a decree dated 1377; Louis I of Hungary allowed the Saxons of Kronstadt (Brasov) to construct the castle. Between 1920 and 1957, the palace existed as a royal residence. Citizens of Brasov gave the palace to Queen Marie of Romania as a present."[113]

We ate in a nearby café. Smitten by its old-world charm akin to Heidelberg, Germany, Mom and Dad drank beer over a typical Romanian dish. I can't remember but I'm sure that Dennis and I gobbled down the usual hamburger and fries accompanied by soda refills.

After my meal, I listened to Dad reiterate the story behind the Black Church.

"The Teutonic knights established Brasov in 1211, and originally it was recorded as Brasov in 1251. It developed into a Saxon hub for the exchanging of fabric, ammunition, metalwork, and wax all over much of Walachia and Moldavia. The Black Church, formerly the Gothic Protestant Church, was constructed during 1385-1477 and improved in 1711-1715. It derived its name from a blaze which occurred in 1689, smearing its entire surface with soot."[114] Dad heaved a sigh.

The Black Church's long and narrow façade and gothic architecture reminded me of Notre-Dame Cathedral in Paris. Although the church wasn't black, it appeared darker than normal.

Memories of a windy drive to Dracula's castle make me feel that it was most certainly the name of this humorous road Dad mentioned: "Guys, the only way up to Dracula's castle is via the Transfagarasan Highway,[115] which will be sure to knot up your stomach."

"I just hope this castle isn't as tacky as the other one," Mom said.

"Aw, come on, Mom, it really wasn't that bad," Dennis said.

The never-ending twisting and curving made me constantly hold on. Then we were there. Dad parked the car and I dashed outside to inhale the dense pine forest smell. The only way up to Poenari castle was by way of fourteen hundred steps that led to the top. Vlad the Impaler built Poenari castle in the fifteenth century overlooking the Argeş River valley.[116]

"Isn't there another way?" Dennis whined.

Dad chuckled. "Nope, this is the only way up."

A forest of sweet pine offered a panacea for my upset stomach. I grasped the metal handrail and prepared for a marathon climb. My thoughts drifted to Vlad the Impaler galloping through a thick and eerie forest in pursuit of Ottoman invaders. Shafts of sunlight blazed through the pine-dense forest. A soothing symphony of birds chirped, leaves rustled, and twigs crackled to reassure me. When would I ever reach the top?

I surfaced from a boundless forest and gazed upward. The ruined castle intimidated me with its daunting foundation. Handrails sheltered narrow passageways of crumbling ruins. The Carpathians' steep slopes, splashed with lush green pine trees, protected the valleys below and made my trek worth it. Had anything altered in the past five-hundred-plus years in the impenetrable and legendary forest—apart from the Transfagarasan Highway?

Dad often talked about visiting wooden churches while driving through rural Romania. I recall that this village, Maramureş, consisted of oak churches and shingled roofs dating back to the eighteenth century.[117] Today, I researched on Google and uncovered yet another déjà vu. I shall always recall that the rural road we passed had a profound effect on me.[118] I wouldn't be offering Romania the justice that she so deserves if I didn't offer you a peek.

We cruised through the heart of Transylvania and uncovered a rural jewel during the Communist era of that time. This section of Romania tugged at my heart like a long forgotten Brothers Grimm fairytale. Yellow and white houses with red roofs and flower-filled wooden balconies mimicked Hansel and Gretel's. Undulating lush green hills and grazing sheep lay tucked against the Carpathians. Grass-growing valleys dotted with bundled hay shaped like Nestlé Kisses and sprouting church spires made me smile. Hills alive with ringing church bells and horse-drawn buggies lulled me into a fairytale sleep.

There is no doubt in my mind that the heart and soul of Romania prevailed in the landscape. I witnessed that pulse of life—the ebb and flow of rural Transylvania—where provincial culture survived and embraced medieval manners.

Budapest, Hungary

The picture of us huddled together on the embankment of the Danube reminds me that I felt rapt with splendor gazing across at the flamboyant building swathed in Gothic architecture. While my young adult self had no idea of the history surrounding Budapest and the Danube, today I appreciate how Dad informed us.

I plunked myself onto a bench under a sky filled with clouds and admired this Gothic masterpiece straddling the Danube. Unaffected by the warmness, I half-listened to Dad recite from his guide. "Did you know that the Danube, or the Donau in German, runs through this magnificent city of Budapest? This European river flows through nine countries and numerous cities. The Danube is the second longest river after the Russian Volga River."[119]

I nurture beautiful memories of my parents listening to "The Blue Danube" by Johann Strauss.[120]

"Dad, what's the name of that beautiful building across the Danube?" I asked. "All the Gothic spires remind me of Notre-Dame Cathedral of Paris."

"Very good, Carina," Dad said.

"I studied about Notre-Dame in French class," I said.

"That's called the Parliament Building.[121] This is Gothic Revival architecture, and the Houses of Parliament in London motivated her splendid design."

Dad insisted on reading some more. "In times past, Budapest was referred to as 'Queen of the Danube.'[122] This glorious city sits on both flanks of the Danube. One is called Buda; the other side is Pest. A set of bridges joins Buda and Pest. We're standing on the Buda side overlooking Pest. We'll be sure to drive across the Széchenyi Chain Bridge—a suspension bridge connecting the Danube from Buda to Pest."

Admiring the photo, I recall a star which sat on the main dome's steeple. After my comparative research on Google today, I learned that the red star fell with the Berlin Wall. We must have raced madly around Castle Hill[123] in two days, viewing the decorative ancient spire from Matthias Church and running hungrily behind Dad. He continued on a mission to find a restaurant dating back several hundred years. I know today that this restaurant is called Arany Hordo Vendeglo.[124] I remember eating Hungarian goulash inside a dungeon-type restaurant. Apparently the restaurant existed as an ancient home, which contained the king's head sommelier.

The Széchenyi Chain Bridge impressed me with her two massive arches resembling Paris's L'Arc de Triomphe protected by stone lions on either side.[125] Dad added in his later years, "Budapest has the reputation of being called the Pearl of the Danube or Paris of Central Europe."

By the waning twilight, charming and lush green Budapest had taken me in her arms with memories of hustling and bustling over cobblestones, sheathed with Gothic architectural delights, and dining on goulash—a mildly spicy and delectable stew. I yearn to someday return to the "Pearl of the Danube."

DRIVING FROM
JEDDAH TO PARIS (1975)
(Europe: Part 2)

Sopron, Hungary

G uys, we've driven just under three hours; what you say we take a lunch break near Hungary's border town, Sopron.[126] I read that Sopron's buildings have been around longer than many other Hungarian cities. So how about we check her out?" Dad said.

"*Sehr gut,*" Mom said.

"Do you remember when we discussed how the Danube flows through nine countries? Du, don't answer, but who knows what country Vienna is in?" Dad said.

Mom waited patiently with her poker face.

"Everyone knows that answer, Dad. Austria, of course," I blurted.

"Great, Carina," Dad said.

Mom looked at me. "Carina, who's one of Austria's famous composers?"

"Mozart is, of course!" I joshed.

"I'm impressed, Carina."

"So, we're headed for Vienna?" I said.

"That's right; she's only an hour from here," Dad said.

A surge of delight overwhelmed me; I knew that beautiful Paris awaited me before long.

Dad parked the car near a small town square. I got out and sauntered along a small cobblestoned street with striking architecture.

We learned from Dad's guidebook that Sopron sits on the outskirts of Hungary at the base of the Alps.[127] Twelve churches existed during the time of medieval Sopron.[128] The fortification is situated at the boundary of Hungary and Austria. King Ottokar II invaded the fortification on numerous occasions. And during 1253-1278, it was inhabited and destroyed several times. To get assurance of Sopron's loyalty, Ottokar's soldiers kidnapped children and held them hostage. In 1277, the citizens of Sopron allowed King Ladislaus IV (Kun) access to their city. The king united with the remaining royal city superiors to safeguard the city.

"What a captivating story, Dad. And I'm so glad that King Ladislaus rescued all the abandoned children."

Grinning from ear to ear, Dad put his arm around my shoulder protectively and said, "A true saint indeed, Carina."

I wondered if Dad thought about how he rescued me way back when I was a toddler. I smacked my lips. "I could go for some goulash again."

I'm so glad that I experienced our charming but brief sojourn, even though being a young adult I wasn't overtly aware of its effect on me. I realize now that medieval Sopron provided me with a delightful rest before arriving in Vienna.

We found a café and I sat down at one of the tables under an umbrella and stared at the alluring building. White-laced filigree surrounded it with patterns reminding me of wedding cake frosting. For the time being I welcomed the fresh air over the tropical weather. Pastel-painted houses dominated this hidden gem-like city; red geraniums adorned the windowsills.

After we all enjoyed our goulash, Mom threw Dad a smile. "Well, Du, *dankeschön* for this appealing tour."

"Yeah, Dad, this is a cool city," Dennis added.

"I'm ready to head to Vienna, the beautiful city," I said.

"Sounds good; let me pay our bill and we'll be on our way to the city of music," Dad said.

<hr>

Vienna, Austria

"Du, we must be sure to eat *Schnitzel* in our favorite restaurant," Mom said.

Dad winked at Mom. "Schatzi, I haven't forgotten."

"Mom, so what's this about a restaurant we're going to check out?" I asked.

"If you recall a few years back when on vacation here, we ate dinner at our favorite *Wiener Schnitzel* place. But we also visited a stunning palace. The Habsburg Dynasty owned a royal summer home with over a thousand rooms in baroque style." Mom arched her brows to punctuate what she'd said. "The resemblance to Chateau de Versailles impressed me."

"Wasn't it though, Du," Dad said.

Shifting his eyes and head away, Dennis said, "Sounds boring to me."

I nodded, "Yeah, yeah, of course I remember because we sauntered along luxurious and sculptured gardens. Why, are we visiting it again?"

"Carina, I'm not so sure that we'll have time, because I have to be in Paris for work by mid-August. At the same time, we're planning on visiting your cousin Ina in Grafenau. It'll be on the way to Nürnberg." Dad winked.

"Ah, all right. Cool, then Ina and I can go discoing in the *Tenne*."

"In addition, we want to visit Nürnberg and Omi's grave," Dad said. "And I recall that you kids delighted in eating Vienna's specialty—the *Wiener Schnitzel*."

"We certainly couldn't leave Vienna without eating one," Mom said.

"Yeah, I remember those huge slabs of veal were yummy," Dennis said.

I salivated over Vienna's specialty of a slab of thinly hammered veal coated with flour, eggs, and breadcrumbs, fried to perfection. "Remember the time we visited the Prater amusement park. Vienna sparkled under her giant Ferris wheel. In the meantime I marveled from a whirling red box car one shimmering night. It sure would be fun to do that again; but heck, I'm psyched to see Ina soon. One thing for sure, I could definitely eat an entire huge *Schnitzel* for dinner," I boasted.

"Me too, and can I order French fries, please, Mom?" Dennis begged.

"Don't you worry, they come with them anyways, Dennis," Mom said. "So if you promise to be patient with some sightseeing, then you can pig out on *Schnitzel*." Mom giggled, joking.

"Me too, Schatzi—add a nice cold Pilsner."

"*Wunderbar*." Mom glanced at Dad.

"First let's find Vienna's famous roundabout called the Ringstrasse," Dad said.

<hr />

Memories of our hunt for *Schnitzel* reminded me of playing ring around the Ringstrasse, the intersection encircling historic Vienna.[129] Glancing over the photo of an ornate column surrounded by angels makes me feel that an important story resided there. Although my young adult self had no idea about the Plague Column,[130] I now appreciate its hidden story. I pictured us standing relaxed nearby and absorbed by Dad's history lesson.

"Listen up to this one, guys. This ritzy avenue is called the Graben.[131] It is full of elegant homes and high-end boutiques. Straight ahead, check out the prodigious stone column crowned with the Holy Trinity in gold. Way back in 1679 and 1713, Vienna endured the bubonic plague. This amazing statue was constructed to memorialize the end of the plague. Isn't this a feast for your eyes?" Dad said.

Most of all, I contentedly gazed upon horse-drawn black carriages all around Vienna. I know now that the term *Fiaker* comes from the French.[132] Hackney carriage stations existed on Rue de Saint Fiacre in Paris. Accordingly, *Fiaker* became the word of choice over the Viennese word *Janschky* by 1720.

<hr />

"You guys hungry?" Dad winked. "OK, follow me. Let's go find that place that serves the world's best *Schnitzel*."

I salivated hearing the mention of *Schnitzel* and hiked to our parked car.

On our quest for *Schnitzel* we traipsed toward the restaurant's terrace under a serenade of classical music. Thickly settled trees hovered over quaint red- and blue-checkered tablecloths. I sank into a wooden chair, content to cradle my *Schnitzel* appetite. The aroma of something frying made me hungry. Mom and Dad ordered in German.

"*Guten Tag*," the waitress replied.

I knew that Mom ordered four *Schnitzels*, two beers, and two cokes.

The waitress quickly came back with our drinks.

Mom and Dad nursed their tall Pilsners. Meanwhile I savored my coke.

A *Schnitzel* aroma intensified. I faced our waitress to watch her carrying our order. My *Schnitzel* hung over the plate's edge topped with a lemon slice. She hastily returned with our French fries accompanied by a bottle of ketchup.

We stuffed ourselves with *Schnitzel*—although I really couldn't eat the whole thing because it was too big, so I left the rest on my plate.

Today, I could still anticipate the gently fried *Schnitzel's* lingering aftertaste.

"The bill please," Dad said.

A smiling waitress reappeared and uttered a number to Dad in German. Dad took his wallet and offered her some colorful bills.

We said our goodbyes.

———

Grand boulevards shimmered with baroque architecture. Traditional cafes around every corner displayed endless shelves of exquisite desserts. I wonder if I indulged in *Apfelstrudel* (apple strudel). I bet Mom and Dad luxuriated over the *Sacher torte* (chocolate torte) with whipped cream.

I later learned that the chateau of Schönbrunn and its lavish surroundings were designated a UNESCO World Heritage site in 1996.[133]

I developed a love affair with Austria's most renowned *Mozartkugel* chocolate rounds. I still savor memories of these round chocolate balls filled with pistachio marzipan melting in my mouth. These delectable delicacies were named after Wolfgang Amadeus Mozart. Elegant horse-drawn carriages and their picturesque drivers added a final aristocratic touch. I felt like a queen in Vienna—the city of dreams.

###################################

Grafenau, Bavaria, Germany

We drove past small scenic villages. The thick of the countryside boasted a variety of tall pine-like trees and rural farms. Historic houses dotted with brown roofs often featured red geraniums hanging outside the windows. Now in Grafenau, Hotel Sonnenhof emerged out of a lush green hill nestled in the Bavarian Forest. I reflected back upon my recent childhood visits with my favorite cousin, Ina. I sat giddy with enthusiasm when Dad rounded the corner. To my right stood the familiar coat of arms sign—Grafenau's mascot is a bear climbing a wall.

In the summertime, I often rode the train solo from Paris to vacation with Ina. *Onkel* Herbert, *Tante* Helga, and Ina picked me up at Passau's train station less than an hour from Grafenau. Passau borders with Austria and the Czech Republic. I delighted in gazing at Passau's charming pastel-colored houses. They reminded me of sherbet ice cream flavors. I listened to Onkel Herbert mention pleasingly how Passau resides where three rivers meet: the Danube, Inn, and Ilz.[134] Once back in Grafenau, *Tante* Helga recited how Grafenau is a climatic spa town with the freshest air in the world. I often heard her mention "Stifter." Adalbert Stifter said, "Never declare anything beautiful before you have seen the Bavarian Forest."[135]

Euphoria overpowered me. I thought about spending time with my cousin Ina, who's a year younger than me. After all, we were attached like sisters—how I cherished waking up to fresh *Brötchen, German* hard roll, and sucking on tart, chewy Haribo Gummi-Bears. *Tante* Helga and *Onkel* Herbert, Mom's oldest brother, and their two daughters, Ina and Sissy, greeted us.

"*Grüß Gott*," we all said in German, hugging one another. I loved to hear this unique Bavarian greeting for "hello."

Their airy two-story quaint Bavarian-style home sat opposite the hill of the Sonnenhof with exquisite views of the Bavarian Forest. *Tante* Helga mentioned to me during my previous visit, "Carina, I rise at 5:30 a.m. every day and love smelling the *frische Luft* [fresh air]."

Tante Helga reminded me of a movie star with velvety brown eyes and platinum blonde hair perfectly styled in an elegant French twist. She hugged me

186 | THE SYRIAN JEWELRY BOX

with her tall, slender physique. I hoped that she would treat me to her succulent *Sauerbraten* and *Semmelknödel* (pickled beef with dumplings). *Onkel* Herbert, my favorite uncle, threw me a wink as he approached me with a bear hug—a tall, handsome man with a receding brown hairline and green eyes. *Onkel* Herbert did not use his left arm because of a war wound. He fought in World War II stationed in Stalingrad.

I hugged Ina, a tall, shy, curly blonde-haired girl with gorgeous hazelnut-colored eyes—*the sister I never had.* Sissy, a slightly taller, slender girl with short auburn hair coifed similar to her mother's, had stunning green eyes.

I entered through the large living room with two picture windows and a balcony overlooking the Bavarian Forest. Aromatic German coffee wafted by me; all the while I honed in on the tray of German pastries, *Käsekuchen* (cheesecake) and *Schlagsahne* (whipped cream) on the long wooden table opposite a brown leather couch.

"Carina, let's go to my bedroom and hang out," Ina said.

I followed Ina upstairs, leaving Mom, Dad, and Dennis with the others chatting in German.

"So do you want to go dancing tonight?" Ina beamed.

"Are you kidding? Of course! And we can stay out late. My parents booked a room in the Sonnenhof. We're leaving for Nürnberg tomorrow to visit Omi's grave."

Ina lowered her chin.

"She lived a hard life," I added.

Trying to change the subject...

"Here, Carina, I bought you your favorite sweets—your very own private stash." Ina grinned.

"Wow, you remembered how much I love Haribo Gummi-Bears—remember *'Haribo makes children happy—and adults as well'*? Cool, you also remembered the famous chocolate-covered marzipan *brot*. You're the best, Ina."

"Yeah, you were very much into sweets and had gummy bears and marzipan throughout the night, waking me up by opening the packages." Ina furrowed her brows and laughed.

"All along my drive over, I thought how great it would be to see you again. Eating gummy bears with marzipan and sleeping under the cozy *Federbetten* cover. I love them because they are warmer than many blankets and lighter than only one."

"Let's go meet up with the others for some *Käsekuchen*, and then we'll get dolled up for the *Tenne*."

"Sounds great, and maybe we'll meet some cute guy!" I laughed.

"Possibly!"

I followed Ina back to the tray of German pastries and grabbed a slice of *Käsekuchen* and scooped a generous dollop of *Schlagsahne* on top. I squeezed in between Tanta Helga, *Onkel* Herbert, and Ina on the comfortable leather couch. Sissy, Mom, Dad, and Dennis sat in wooden chairs on the other side of the table. Everyone savored the delectable pastries.

"Mom and Dad, Ina and I want to go dancing in the *Tenne* tonight. We'll be home by midnight." I winked at Ina.

"Is this all right with you and Herbert?" Mom asked *Tante* Helga.

"Renate, of course, yes, of course," *Tante* Helga said.

Although *Tante* Helga, *Onkel* Herbert, Ina, and Sissy all spoke English fluently, Mom and Dad always spoke in German.

"*Muttl, kann Carina heute übernachten? Sie fahren doch morgen weiter.* [Can Carina sleep over tonight before they leave tomorrow?]"

"*Natürlich ja, natürlich.*"

I loved how Ina affectionately called her mom "Muttle."

I threw my hands up into the air then hugged *Tante* Helga. I glanced at Mom and Dad and said, "*Danke, danke.*"

Ina hugged her mom. She smiled at Mom and Dad and thanked them too.

I nudged Ina and whispered, "We should go upstairs and get ready."

We both excused ourselves then shot upstairs, leaving the others to talk about our long journey and exciting Paris.

Ina's bedroom with two windows slightly ajar had a fresh clean lavender scent with two pine beds. The puffed up *Federbetten* covers resembled oversized pillows. The Abbey Road Beatles poster hung with pushpins against her white wall.

"So you still have a crush on Paul McCartney, Ina?" I asked.

"Yes, he's adorable." Ina blushed.

"I think George Harrison is handsome," I said.

"Carina, I need to use the hot curling iron to recreate some curls."

"Sounds good, Ina. I can't wait to go dancing!"

"What are you going to wear?" Ina asked.

"I'm going to wear my blue bell-bottom jeans and red shirt."

"OK, I also have a pair of bell-bottom jeans. Only I'll wear a white shirt. You can borrow some of my Fiji perfume," Ina offered.

"Thanks, you're the best. We're going to have so much fun. This refreshing flowery scent smells great." I chuckled.

While I dabbed some on my wrists, chest, and behind my ears, we admired ourselves in front of the long mirror behind Ina's bedroom door.

"We look great, huh, Ina?"

"Smashing—one American broad, one German broad," Ina added.

"So, we are ready to hit the disco scene?" I twirled around.

"Let's go and knock them dead," Ina announced.

We walked downstairs and waved goodbye to the others, still in conversation.

"*Tschüss,*" we hollered simultaneously.

We walked toward the picturesque, rural Grafenau, passing by several Bavarian-style inns, cafes, and pastry shops.

"This is the *Tenne*, Carina."

We entered a dim, dank little pub off the main cobblestone street. From across the bar, I spotted a free round-top with a pedestal attached.

"Come on, Ina, there's a free spot," I hollered over the loud music.

"Good eye, Carina."

We pushed our bodies through the pulsating crowd, finding our way to the empty spot. Over the clinking of glasses and drone-like German chatter of people, the mingled smells of smoke and sweat and too many people instantly attacked my nostrils. I motioned to the waitress. She arrived shortly thereafter.

"*Zwei Coca Colas, bitte,*" I ordered.

"That was good German," Ina complimented me.

The waitress nodded and melted away into the bellows of all the other thirsty folk.

"This is great, Ina. Are you having fun yet?"

My eyes finally adjusted to the darkness. Bright neon lights boomeranged off the wall, revealing faces and gyrating bodies in staccato glimpses as Gloria Gaynor's "Never Can Say Good-bye" boomed.

"You bet. Oh, don't do anything, but there are two men coming our way," Ina said.

We continued sipping our cold cokes. Two young men around twenty-five years old parked themselves next to us. One had curly blond hair with the most beautiful blue eyes. He wore an olive green shirt over long pants, and the other had straight black hair in a white shirt over black pants.

"*Guten Abend,*" they both said in unison.

My entire conversation with Hans—the cute blond one—took place in German.

"My name is Hans." He looked at me with a steady gaze.

"I'm Carina."

"You're an American?" He gazed at me with his mesmerizing blue eyes. "You speak good German, Carina. Would you like to dance?"

"Sure." I batted my baby blues.

Ina and Peter soon followed under the beat of "Honey Bee" by Gloria Gaynor.

That night was the first time I began to feel quite special again. I wondered if I was on the road to recovery.

DRIVING FROM JEDDAH TO PARIS (1975)
(Europe: Part 3)

Nürnberg, Germany

I loved Nürnberg. Oh, Germany, how I cherished your romanticism. Visions of red-roof tops, colored gable-front houses, cobbled streets, Gothic spires, and castles etched peacefully in my memory.

The sun beamed under a bright cerulean sky on this summer's day. I saw it all in a daze. Nürnberg was my birth city. I rejoiced in the familiar cobbled streets of *Altstadt* (Old City) and her intimate aura.

Dad parked the car near the main market in downtown. I sprang off my seat and bolted into the warm fresh air. The others followed. Meanwhile I soaked up my quaint and serene surroundings. I felt giddy with elation.

"We definitely can't leave here without eating a huge pretzel and *Bratwurst mit Brötchen*," I said to Mom and Dad.

"Topped off with a tall Pilsner beer," Dad said. "I can't complain."

Mom let out a satisfied sigh. "Me too. But don't forget about my favorite dark rye bread."

"I wouldn't dream of it, Schatzi." Dad smiled tenderly at Mom. "Come on, guys. Let's explore the grounds a bit first to build up an appetite."

I sauntered toward the spectacular *Kaiserburg*, or "imperial castle," leaving the *Hauptmarkt* behind. I have always felt a deep affinity for Nürnberg. This picturesque city endured severe damage during World War II.

I hiked the steep cobbled street lined with pastel-colored houses and ornamented black bay windows. This neighborhood brought cheerful thoughts of my parents' numerous visits, with me lagging beside Omi at age two.

Two lofty towers, namely *Simwellturm* and *Heidenturm* (Heiden Tower), dominated a large stonewall.[136] These two towers rekindled a long forgotten intimacy, a passionate belonging that spawned a connection. I had a strong image of Dad walking with me at an early age. He lovingly and safely held my hand at this same place.

And I yearned for my father's heartfelt protection and devoted security.

As I ogled the proud *Simwellturm*, I wondered: had this tower influenced the Brothers Grimm?

The castle hill bustled with people snapping photos or parents with children and lovers holding hands. I entered the castle through a stone archway.

"Wow, this is one mighty castle," Dennis said.

A delightful medieval village emerged from within the castle's walls. Birds darted about the budding trees, and luscious grass beds dotted the castle's cobbled streets. Windowsills of vibrant flowers adorned half-timbered houses with their traditional red- and white-colored shutters. I plopped myself onto a wooden bench over a cobbled patio and looked up to admire this obliterated image. An immense red-brick wall adorned with ivy and flower boxes speckled its second floor. I listened to Dad talk about Albrecht Dürer.

"Before we head back to the *Altstadt*, let's check out where Albrecht Dürer, Nürnberg's painter, lived.[137] He was born here in 1471."

Dad paid the bill. I stood up and loitered on the cobbled street dotted with cafes, shops, and restaurants in more of the same pastel colors near red-timbered houses. No doubt Dennis soaked up the castle's museum filled with the emperor's memorabilia. I simply tagged along throughout the humdrum tour. I preferred marveling over the view of Dürer's sensational house. It reminded me of a stately dollhouse. Plentiful windowsills filled with splashy flowers bedecked its lower stone level. Dormers jutted from the upper level, adorned in typical red-timbered fashion against white paint. Once inside, squeaky floors transported me back five hundred years into a dark and dank medieval kitchen. It contained an original stone block stove and a few dangling pots.

On my descent back to *Altstadt*, my stomach grumbled from the baking aroma. I gawked at huge pretzels hanging behind the plastic window of a pretzel stand. I found several *Deutschmark* coins in my pocket and walked over to order.

"Three please," I said in German.

A friendly man shot up from his plastic bin. He offered me a piping hot pretzel wrapped in wax paper. He laughed and said, "*Bitte Schön.*"

"*Dankeschön.*"

Then I called over, "Hey guys, I bought you a pretzel."

Dennis charged over begging for a bite.

"Whoa, slow down, Dennis. OK, here, you can have your very own." I handed one over.

"Thanks, sis," he said.

I shifted my gaze to Mom. "You'll have to share with Dad, OK?"

Overhearing me, Dad winked at me. "How did you know that I wanted one of those? Thanks, Carina."

I wolfed down the last of my pretzel as Mom said, "Now here comes some of my favorite places in Nürnberg: the *Hauptmarkt* with the *Frauenkirche* (Church of Our Lady) and the *Schöner Brunnen* (Beautiful Fountain)." She grinned.

I wondered what my mother was feeling right then. Were her thoughts centered on my birth and how she would have to tell me the truth someday? I remembered what she told me after my discovery: "*After you were born, I always knew that someday I would have to tell you the truth.*"

The *Hauptmarkt* pulsed with life—people contemplating the surrounding baroque half-timbered houses in pastel colors and the magnificent Gothic church. Vendors sold neatly displayed fruits, vegetables, and flowers under red-striped umbrellas. I watched Mom choose a colorful rose plant for Omi's grave. I stood next to Dad and inhaled the fresh fruit smell, enraptured by the backdrop of little shops and stone houses on the cobbled streets.

Turning his head to the plaza's elaborate fountain, "Guys, I can't forget to tell you about the beautiful fourteenth century golden fountain, *Schöner Brunnen*, across the way.[138] Her Gothic spire soars over sixty-two feet high. Forty ornate and noteworthy stone 14th century figurines symbolize the Holy Roman Empire's worldly perspective. So let me pay up and we'll continue our excursion."

I ran over to the glistening fountain. Tilting my head upward, I eyed her gleaming spire. Red-, blue- and green-colored figurines of emperors in gold robes surrounded this gothic masterpiece. I spun one of the two bronze rings buried in the embroidered wrought-iron fence just how Dad had instructed me. Nürnberg's legend portrayed that my dream to forgive and heal through love and acceptance would come true.

I stood wide-eyed, marveling over the colorful images of Nürnberg. Today I'm still charmed by the fairytale façades and Gothic spires of this tantalizing city.

"We're ready to move on. So how are you enjoying Nürnberg, Carina?" Dad asked me.

"I love it here."

I always felt special and gladly received Dad's endearing glance every time we toured this charming medieval city together. Upon our numerous returns here, I always experienced a deeply rooted connection. A jovial camaraderie abided between us. "I could eat German food all day long," I said.

Dad laughed. "Me too. What do you say we get the car and visit the *Heilig-Geist Spital*. I'm sure Mom will want to buy some pastries there. Then we'll go to Omi's grave." Dad hugged me.

Biting my lip, I nodded. Oh, how I wanted so much to carry on and show Dad my extreme love for him. He was larger than life for me. But then learning that Dad wasn't my biological father made the act of forgiveness the most difficult chore to accomplish. My heart ached. Anger seethed inside me too.

I followed behind thinking that I would be coming back to Nürnberg on my own in a few years. I would purchase the Eurail Pass and travel by train, visiting castles all over Europe.

Dad drove a short distance to Fürth so that we could visit Omi's grave. I stood in front of her tombstone gazing at the engraving there: *Unvergessen* (Unforgotten). I dug a hole with my shoes and offered to plant the roses. Mom, still and silent, dabbed her tears. Dad and Dennis stood close by in silence. It felt good remembering the good times we had together, and I cherished Nürnberg's idyllic setting.

Nothing beat this perfect ending of a precious journey back to my birth home. Now, though, I longed for a home with my heart in it. Had I succumbed to being a nomad? Would I ever get over such a withdrawn feeling in the world? Would I ever be able to love myself, fully knowing that my biological father had rejected me? Would anyone ever love me again? Somehow or another, Nürnberg held a key to my own existence. Nürnberg remained a miracle since being almost entirely reconstructed after such devastation from the war.

Wiesbaden, Germany

Over one hundred miles later, I stood gazing up at the world's largest cuckoo clock located in Wiesbaden. A giant reindeer's head above green antlers protruded from an oversized chocolate brown A-framed cuckoo clock. I hoped to see a huge pendulum instead of this tacky ornament.

Memories of Wiesbaden jogged my memory of the prevailing sulfur odor floating by me. Today I can still hear Dad lecturing, "So guys, in addition to Dennis being born in Wiesbaden, she is popular as a well-known spa town, an early community noted as a spa during the Roman era. Evidence of a Roman barricade exists from around 370."[139]

I recollect that ornate thermal fountains prevailed throughout the city; meantime I detested the relentless sulfur stench.

Years later, Dad mentioned to me that we passed through quaint Mainz, Rüdesheim, and Lorelei along the Rhine River. I must have dozed off and on throughout our drive. However, I distinctly remember awakening to sweeping green hills brimming with vineyards and a medieval castle. I know now, after researching, that ruined Ehrenfels Castle came into view.[140]

During our drive through the Rhine, castles in the air loomed over lush green vineyard-swept hills. Ancient towns and church spires speckled the Rhine's cluttered embankments. Barges cruised along the river's waters. Castles along the Rhine unfolded a medieval romanticism that I thought you could only obtain in books.

I knew that we would soon be arriving in Paris since I overheard Dad say to Mom, "Schatzi, soon we will be living in the most beautiful city in the world."

Paris, France

Driving almost five thousand miles, my seven-week journey was on the verge of ending right here: in Paris. Pressing my nose to the window, I felt on top of the world. "I can see her!" I shrieked. "I can see Notre-Dame!"

"Schatzi, I give you the most beautiful city in the world," Dad sang affectionately to Mom.

"*Wunderschön*. It's absolutely amazing to be back here again, Du," Mom said, smiling broadly.

"That's one big whopper of a church," Dennis cried out.

"She's actually a cathedral, Dennis. And, guys, she sits precisely in the center of Paris on Île de la Cité.[141] Notre-Dame's construction took place over the debris of two previous churches, which were preceded by a Gallo-Roman house of worship committed to Jupiter.[142] The bishop of Paris, Maurice de Sully, in around 1160, thought about altering her into an individual structure on a grander scale using the remains of two previous shrines. Construction of Notre-Dame began in 1163 and continued for over 180 years. And isn't she absolutely perfect?" Dad swung his head toward us with a smile that lit up his face.

In the act of rounding alongside the Seine River near Île de la Cité, there she was! Notre-Dame majestically emerged in front of me—she glowed under the five o'clock afternoon sun. Rapt with glee, I gaped at the immensity of this majestic cathedral along with her surrounding ornate detail and gargoyles. Her royal beauty was stunning. I had left the deserts of Arabia only seven weeks ago. And today that nomadic life etched in my memory—a distant memory—a long forgotten song that enfolded my heart. Notre-Dame welcomed me with all her grandeur. I couldn't help but adore such awe-inspiring beauty. I'd heard about "falling for Paris"...had I fallen under the Parisian spell already?

Notre-Dame beamed through the sun's rays. Driving alongside her northern façade reemphasized her incredible vastness. Her rose window resembled a lace-crocheted doily. An incandescent lighting highlighted her Gothic architecture. Rose beds, myriad-colored flowers, and evenly groomed hedges swiftly captivated me—a time warp of infinite splendor. *What does a fifteen-year-old girl in Paris do?* I embraced my surroundings with all my heart—*my new life is dawning.*

Parisian ambience enveloped me—and something transformed that afternoon. A self-professed young lady, I was eager to embrace and enjoy the Parisian culture, ready to break through and move closer to myself.

19

PARIS (1975–1979)

P aris awakened my spirit. We continued past Notre-Dame. Mom held both the roadmap and Michelin Guide open in her lap. While my young adult self had no idea of the challenges of driving in Paris, I now appreciate how Dad cruised through it.

Pinching his lips, he said, "Darn it, I took the wrong turn. I wanted to land on the Left Bank."

When the traffic cleared, Dad raced into an empty parking spot.

Anxious, Dad leaned in next to Mom. "Schatzi, can you hold the map open so I can find our way? You see," he said, pointing. "The Seine River runs toward the northwest through the middle of Paris and through half of her twenty city sections, or how the French people say *arrondissements*.[143] OK, I got it now. Somehow or another we ended up on the Right Bank. Hey, no problem, guys; we can pick up Pont d'Iéna over to the Eiffel Tower." Dad nodded to himself.

A plethora of cafés cluttered the sidewalks. Customers settled back in wicker bistro chairs absorbing the Parisian flair. We weaved in and out of traffic.

"Du, remember this magnificent building?" Dad said, turning his head slightly to Mom.

"Absolutely. Dennis and Carina, look at the Louvre's exquisite baroque architecture," Mom said, gazing out her window.

"So who knows what museum is the topmost globe-trotted?" Dad grinned.

"It's the Louvre of course. It goes on forever." I stared at her flamboyant design.

A happy expression stole onto Mom's face. "Carina and Dennis, are you glad we're finally in Paris?"

"I'm so glad that we're all done traveling!" Dennis rejoiced.

"Well, don't be surprised if you feel a bit of culture shock. Remember we spent *so* many years in the desert," Mom advised.

"Not me. Look at that huge barge next to the tour boat," Dennis said.

"I remember from French class that they're called *Bateaux Mouches*, and they offer excursions along the Seine. Wow, this is unreal! No culture shock for me. I plan on devouring all Paris has to offer me," I declared.

Bateaux Mouches peacefully cruised under arched bridges that straddled the Seine River.

"Dennis, check out the Eiffel Tower. It's gigantic!" I cried.

"I saw it before you did!"

I asked Mom and Dad, "Can we get out and look at it as soon as we get there?"

Dad glanced at me through the rear-view mirror. "Sure, we should arrive momentarily."

"OK, Carina, you want to be our chaperone? I bet you remember every one of these from French class, right?" Dad winked.

"Yeah, it's amazing how it's all coming back to me. That's OK, Dad, I'll let you have the honors. I wouldn't want to make a mistake," I humored him.

"We're now circling Place de la Concorde where both King Louis XVI and Marie- Antoinette were beheaded,"[144] Dad said. "And who can tell me the name of the most famous street in Paris? I anticipate finding it soon."

"The Champs-Élysées, actually the most famous street in the world," Mom said.

I checked out the sleek obelisk and ornate surrounding buildings and cringed as I thought about executions. I turned to Dennis. "Pretty gruesome, don't you think?"

"I suppose," Dennis said.

"One thing you'll notice is that Paris is a symmetrical city," Dad said. "We're heading down the Champs-Élysées, and the Arc de Triomphe should be straight ahead. Haussmann, a city planner, modernized Paris into a city of symmetry during the mid to late 1800s.[145] Check out the entire common mansard roofs, wrought-iron balconies, and ornamental buildings.

"We're circling Paris's most influential memorial," Dad said. "In 1806, Napoleon I authorized the triumphal arch to honor the French armed force's success. The Tomb of the Unknown Soldier is situated below the arch. A memorial candle first illuminated in 1923 is revived every night."[146]

"The arch is humongous!" Dennis cried out.

I rolled down my window to the rush of Peugeots and Citroens busily swirling around as horns honked constantly. I tilted my head upward and studied her mammoth size bug-eyed. I'd become one of Spindrift's little passengers from the television series *Land of the Giants*.

"That guy just cut me off!" Dad yelled. Then he added wryly, "Well, it will definitely require some getting used to since I'm supposed to yield to the guy on my right side."

"You'll get the hang of it soon enough, Du," Mom reassured Dad.

"What do you say we circle another time? Maybe I won't get cut off? By the way, the French refer to this roundabout as Place Charles de Gaulle, which replaced the former name, Place de l'Étoile.[147] Be sure to check out the surrounding twelve boulevards which spread out from this intersection in the shape of a star," Dad explained.

"That means Square of the Star," I said.

Dad glanced at me. "*Merci*, Carina."

I chortled at the sound of his funny accent.

He pulled over safely and quickly onto Champs-Élysées to study the map. I gazed out onto the wide tree-lined boulevards bedecked in Haussmann architecture and admired the cafés and glamorous shops.

"OK, we need to go down Avenue d'Iéna to Trocadéro, catch Pont d'Iéna over the Seine to the Eiffel Tower. And if we get lost we just ask directions for the Hilton Hotel," Dad said.

The Place du Trocadéro in front of Palais de Chaillot and spewing fountains brought me back to those guidebook pictures Dad showed me.[148] I gaped at the spellbinding Eiffel Tower. We drove over Pont d'Iéna and somehow landed under her base. Dad parked the car.

"Hold on. I'll pull over because the Hilton Hotel should emerge," Dad said.

In recalling this scene, I wonder if we did indeed get lost, because Dad parked the car on a side street nearby. He and Mom lingered to study the map. I jumped out and ran over to the gargantuan Eiffel Tower, where people milled about with cameras. A lingering French fries odor wafted past me over the cacophony of international chatter, and I spotted a fry truck. I peered straight up at the tower, admiring her strength and sleek beauty. Visitors hustled and bustled trying to get a photo opportunity. A large field of grass was filled with flower gardens and trees. I know today that the Champ-de-Mars extends from under the Eiffel Tower to the École Militaire, constructed from 1769-1772.[149] After this, it became the War College (École Supérieure de Guerre).

I returned to the car looking up at Paris's residential architecture. I reveled in the tall French patio windows. Black wrought-iron balconies ran alongside the width of the windows.

I relaxed and reminisced over the fact that seven weeks ago, I had departed on the longest journey of my life.

We drove to the entrance of the Paris Hilton Hotel where the valet and doorman welcomed us.

"*Bonjour, monsieur*," a lean, dapper gentleman in a black top hat said to Dad.

Dad smiled. "*Bonjour, monsieur.*"

"Du, I will wait here with the kids while you book us into our rooms," Dad said.

Mom got out of the car. "OK, *gut.*"

Two rolled-up Middle Eastern rugs were wedged snugly between Mom and Dad on the armrest with their tail end stuck between Dennis and me in the back. I couldn't help but notice people staring at us as we got out of our car. Did they think we were gypsies? I then considered our dark tans and the rear-displayed Arabic license plate of our filthy-white car.

I ran over to Mom. "I don't want to wait here. Can I help you sign us in?"

"Sure, come and help me. Dennis, you can stay with Dad and help him unload the car. Carina and I will meet you two back in the lobby near the registration desk."

Mom and I stepped through the revolving glass doors.

"*Bonjour*," Mom said in broken French to the receptionist behind the registration desk.

"*Bonjour, madame*," the woman replied politely.

"We have a reservation under the name of Rourke for two rooms."

"The first name of the reservation, please?" she asked in a thick French accent.

"Joseph," Mom said.

"Ah, yes. I see you will be staying with us for a month. Yes?"

"That's correct."

"We have you on our fifth floor with two bedrooms. If you would kindly sign here and we will get you your keys."

Dad showed up from behind us. "Du, how's it going?"

"OK, all done, everyone. Let's check into our rooms and then meet the landlord downstairs," Mom said.

We walked the white marble floors to the silver elevators that took us to the fifth floor where our rooms were.

I claimed my space. "I want the bed next to the window."

"Cool, we get our own TV!" Dennis exclaimed.

"We better hurry up to Mom and Dad's room to meet the landlord," I added. "Don't forget the key, Dennis. You ready?"

"How do you guys like your room?" Mom said.

"It's neato," Dennis replied.

"Great view of the Eiffel Tower," I added.

"OK, guys, Madam and Mr. Shu are waiting for us downstairs."

"There they are, in the revolving glass doorway," Dad said, excited.

Dennis yelled out, "They're speaking German!"

This was a welcoming relief, since Mom and Dad spoke German—but not French like Dennis and me.

Our landlords accompanied us to 22 Avenue de Suffren, a mostly residential street lined with elegant Haussmann-style buildings. A modern green stone apartment building with about ten balconies and green shrubbery decorated the twin-door glass entrance blending in nicely with the neighborhood.

"Your newsstand, *boulangerie*, cheese shop, and bistro are only a few doors down the street. A wine shop and Vietnamese restaurant might come in handy across the street," boasted our petite Asian landlady.

I entered through a secured glass door. The lady concierge knitted behind a glass window. She slid the glass panel open and introduced herself—Madame so and so, I couldn't remember her name, let alone pronounce it. We took the brass-door elevator to the sixth floor. Mr. Shu unlocked a varnished door onto a sunny open floor plan overlooking the back of the Hilton. I rounded the corner to a kitchen hallway. Right in front of me a balcony faced the first floor of the Eiffel Tower. I admired our spectacular view of the Eiffel Tower and Champ-de-Mars. The Shus stepped out onto the balcony and I followed to two adjacent bedrooms.

"Please, I prefer the bedroom next to the kitchen," I pleaded with Mom and Dad.

"Sure."

"Then can I get the other one also overlooking the Eiffel Tower?" Dennis asked.

Mom appeared satisfied with our choices. "Absolutely."

I butted into the conversation, "I hope you'll be able to study and not get distracted."

Two bathrooms stood side by side. Mom and Dad's bedroom had a balcony looking out onto the back of the Hilton.

"*Dankeschön. Auf wiedersehen*," we all said to each other. We headed back to unpack and eat dinner.

I gobbled down French onion soup with morsels of baguette floating about and remnants of thick crusty gruyere cheese stuck on the sides of the bowl's rim.

I pulled the cheese off my spoon like bubble gum and savored the dissolving succulent cheese combined with the onion broth.

***

After dinner, we made our way past our apartment, the *brasserie*, and the newsstand to the *boulangerie*. Pedestrians strolled and families dined in the *brasserie* under a wonderfully warm summer night. A delectable display of pastries made me want one of each. My all-time favorite was the *gâteau moka*, a multilayered cake with delicate tiers of vanilla sponge and coffee-flavored butter cream. Dad loved the *tarte au citron* (lemon tart) as did Mom. Dennis chose the chocolate éclair. We returned to the front of our apartment and sat on the ledge of the flowerbed. I bit into my pastry and savored every bite. This perfect night caressed my five senses; somehow I knew that in Paris I would discover my dormant sixth sense.

***

"Guys, I hate to mention this, but we can't move in for another month. We'll have to live in the Hilton."

Dennis and I exchanged glances of glee. The frenzy of finally being home and in Paris, the most beautiful city in the world, began to inspire me.

"Carina and Dennis, close to 7:45 every morning, the school bus will pick you up by the corner bringing you to the American School, located about forty minutes outside of Paris."

Dennis and I stared at each other and asked, "Can we have hot chocolate every morning in the hotel?"

"Probably, we'll see," Mom said.

"In addition, guys, it will be your job every morning to pick up some *pains aux raisins* [spiral-shaped pastry with raisins and a pastry cream filling], croissants, and a fresh baguette along with a copy of the *International Herald Tribune* before you go to school," Dad said.

I didn't mind. I was in Paris after all.

***

By the end of the month, we'd had enough of hotel living. Dad arrived home to playfully announce, "Movers are arriving tomorrow to unload our belongings. Within a week, you will be sleeping in your beds overlooking the Eiffel Tower and Champ-de-Mars."

I no longer heard the humming of the air conditioner to lull me to sleep—only the constant buzzing of cars six floors below and occasional late-night chatter. I earned a weekly stipend of twenty francs, about five dollars, for cleaning the bathrooms. I had just enough money to buy a movie pass. My happy life in Paris coexisted with the enduring pain of my earlier discovery. I believed that I would overcome the shock of my truth in a short period of time. But I realize now that I underestimated the time it would take to heal. Now, after all of my nomadic traveling, I was in a new "home"—so the contrast of *not* feeling at home grew ever more intense. A part of me told me that I should feel settled now. But I knew that I wasn't, and the pain increased right then and here. People everywhere were happily savoring Paris and everything this lovely city offered.

In English class during a discussion on William Faulkner's *Light in August*, Mr. Packard asked me to explain the significance of a particular sentence. I became tongue-tied and turned fifty shades of red hoping that the teacher would ask another student since I didn't know the answer. I still felt lost. My future scared me.

I threw myself into discovering Paris.

I borrowed Dennis's skateboard, a gift from Dad after one of his occasional business trips to America. I turned into a skateboard thrill seeker on the esplanade of Palais de Chaillot, riding down the steep ramps.

Under the Palais de Chaillot's terrace, I discovered that a small room held nighttime movies that displayed many of the classic black-and-white films, which I think best suited Greta Garbo. I pampered and lost myself in Garbo's portrayal of pure love and bliss. Here I inhabited the world's most beautiful and romantic city. I attended high school at the American School of Paris, and seeing all the girls happy unsettled me. I yearned for love, happiness, and a home. I watched Parisian lovers kissing on the benches by the Seine River. Seeing everyone so alive and happy reminded me of my own depression.

Although Mom controlled my desserts, I often desired more than our daily allotment. I wondered if I would have recovered more quickly if Dad or Mom had shared the truth with me earlier. The thought nagged me more and more.

"Carina, would you mind picking up four *tartes aux citrons* and three *religieuses* for dessert." Mom gave me thirty francs.

The *religieuse* mimicked a nun in practice, well almost. Its concoction consisted of two *choux* pastry buns filled with *crème pâtissière* (confectioner's custard), a large one on the bottom and a smaller one on top, traditionally iced with a chocolate- or coffee-infused icing and joined together by butter cream.[150]

"Sure, Mom," I agreed.

I strolled to the *boulangerie*. In addition to Mom's order, I bought two extra *gâteaux mokas* and two *pains au chocolats*. That day, I had enough leftover allowance. I made sure the attendant gave me separate boxes.

On the way home, I sat down on a stone wall and luxuriated in the painful pleasure of French pastries. I licked the velvety smooth butter coffee cream and cherished how it soothed my tongue followed by a divine melting. A force of gravity lured me to carelessly indulge in this exquisite sponge cake. I blissfully anticipated this decadent bite filled with yet more of a creamy texture. Momentarily entranced, I had no care in the world. I wanted my hypnosis to linger, so I nimbly took out a *pain au chocolat*. I shut my eyes and bit into this golden, crispy, and buttery pastry dough blanketing two chocolate sticks, then groaned and welcomed an explosion of light and flaky layers with chocolate.

I financed my sweet-tooth addiction with a meager allowance. I let the exquisite flavors and luscious textures embrace me, and for a brief moment I was in a world of delicious ecstasy—a world devoid of betrayal, anger, and loneliness.

Before going inside our apartment, I hid my box behind the elevator door outside the kitchen to retrieve when Mom didn't notice.

"I'm home, Mom!" I yelled from the kitchen.

"*Dankeschön*, Carina. Just leave them on the counter," Mom called out from the other side of the apartment.

"I will, along with your change."

I hastily fetched my box and ran across the balcony to my room and hid the pastries under my bed covers. Before falling asleep, I tucked my cache in the back of my clothes closet.

On any occasion that I shopped for groceries, I always bought an extra package of LU Prince Chocolate Sandwich Biscuits for my very own private wardrobe stash. Once I started on one cookie, I simply had to eat the six left over—all of my worries vanished instantly. Mom would never know. I allowed myself special permission to indulge and soothe my pain.

"Hey, guys, I think it would be a great idea to go to a private French school—it's the fastest way to learn the language. You now have the opportunity to communicate it and become fluent," Dad announced.

"Come on, Mom, Dad! Do we really have to?" we both whined.

"Hearing, speaking, and studying it—you'll be fluent in no time," Mom said firmly.

I knew that I was going to have to listen to Dad, even if I didn't like the idea—Dennis knew it too, I figured. After one year attending the American School of Paris, St. Cloud, Dennis and I enrolled in a private French school—without debate. Every morning I boarded the local bus and metro train to a private École Alsacienne, a two-story red-brick building with a huge courtyard. Every professor taught in French. I took philosophy, algebra, and the basics. I discovered how hard trying to learn a subject in another language is. One day the director walked into my philosophy class. Fatigued, I rested my head on my shoulders at the same time that I felt a nudge.

"Get up!" my classmate Natalie insisted.

I noticed that everyone was standing except me. The director of the school stood near the head of the classroom. I shot up immediately, bright red, wishing nobody noticed.

During those two years, I became fluent in writing and communicating in French—although the French classics such as *Candide* and *Madame Bovary* presented a chore. Dennis and I both tried to endure the Baccalauréat (or, in French vernacular, known as the "Bac" or "Le Bac"). In France, this hugely important and extremely complicated examination is given at the completion of high school.[151] I stayed up that entire night studying—not knowing upon which subject I would be interrogated. The following day the examiner asked me a question about the significance of something to do with Emma Bovary. I froze and rambled in French, hoping he would sympathize. I received an unofficial note of eleven points out of twenty. I believed that this arose out of his lone act of kindness. I returned to the American School for my senior year and graduated in 1979.

Being an American family living in Paris, every weekend we went on daytrips. We visited the Louvre—sometimes spending three hours, looking at statues like *The Winged Victory* and *Venus de Milo* and Impressionist paintings. I thought that if I looked at another voluptuous naked woman after viewing so many of the Rubens paintings, I might have to throw up. I loved Leonardo da Vinci's *Mona Lisa*, which remained continuously hard to get a close-up view of because of the constant swarm of people. I also admired the manner in which Vermeer used light in *The Milkmaid*.

I'm so glad that I experienced the following event. Even as a young adult, I'd become overtly aware of its effect on me. That fall, Mom and Dad's wish came true. Dad bought tickets for us to attend a trumpet concerto and listen to world-famous trumpeter Maurice André perform at the phenomenal Sainte-Chapelle.[152] In my mind's eye, I can envision Dad's lecture: "This sublime chapel's construction took place under Louis IX's control from 1243-1248. Sainte-Chapelle means Holy Chapel and it represents the epitome of Gothic Rayonnant design."

We drove to Île de la Cité. Once inside the chapel, I sat basking in the rainbow radiance of the Gothic stained-glass windows. During one of Maurice

André's solos, he hit the high notes—only by pushing down on a trumpet's three buttons. Time stood still and my heart sang with bliss. I surrendered myself to his magic spell. A melodic Garden of Eden sent me to another dimension.

<hr>

For months, weekends seemed consumed with trying to see every exhibit at the Louvre.

"Come on, guys, it's time to get up and continue our exploration of the Louvre. It's one of the most famous landmarks in Paris. You'll thank me later on in life. With almost three thousand pieces on display, we better get started."

"Aw, Dad, I only want to sleep in some more," Dennis whined.

"Come on, Dennis, you might discover a new treasure," I coaxed.

"Dennis, Dad bought your favorite *religieuse*."

"Cool. I'll be there shortly."

After this treat, Dennis would definitely need to go to confession. I passed through the open glass door into the long narrow balcony overlooking the grassy field of Champ-de-Mars and the Eiffel Tower.

"Hi, Mom."

"*Guten Morgen*, Carina."

Mom wore bell-bottom blue jeans and leaned against the balcony, admiring the view. Through the glass window, I saw Dad in jeans sitting on one of our lime-green padded vinyl barstools reading the *International Herald Tribune*, accompanied by his favorite *pain aux raisins*.

Over the coffee aroma, I groaned. "Where's my favorite?"

"Go look in the bag. Dad picked up more *pains aux raisins*," Mom said.

"Thanks, Dad," I added over a grumbling stomach.

"No problem."

Dennis showed up with disheveled dark brown hair wearing jeans. He grabbed his *religieuse* from the box and plopped himself down on the other lime-green vinyl stool.

"Eat up, guys, because there's always a long line in front of the Louvre," Dad said.

<hr>

We cruised Paris under a crisp and sunny autumn day. We crossed the Seine via Pont d'Iéna onto the Right Bank and arrived at Place du Trocadéro. Then we drove down Avenue Kléber to L'Arc de Triomphe. This colossal monument never failed to enthrall me as we continued down the elegant Champs-Élysées with all its designer clothes and shoe stores, opulent perfumeries, high-end chocolate shops, cafés, and cinemas lined with perfectly clipped chestnut trees.

"Did you know that this boulevard is one of the most expensive pieces of real estate?"

"I don't doubt it," Mom agreed, gazing out the window.

"The traffic here is always crazy. For instance, the goal is to get to the center as soon as possible. Remember that right-of-way rule. One guy cut me off and it infuriated me."

I kept my eyes peeled for all the fancy restaurants, cafés, *boulangeries*, and people strolling about.

"There's the place where they beheaded Marie-Antoinette," Dennis said.

Dad nodded and threw him a wink.

"Remember it's called Place de la Concorde, and after passing the Tuileries Palace, we will be near to the Louvre."

Dad found a parking place nearby and added some coins just as we got out. He clutched his guidebooks in one hand. "OK, guys, are we ready for the grand tour of the best château about and former home to the kings of France?"[153]

"Sure, sure, Dad. How long are we going to be here?" Dennis appealed.

"Come on, Dennis, they even have some ancient relics that you might like." Mom smiled wryly.

"What do you guys think of the baroque architecture of the Louvre?" Dad said.

"It's very ornate and fit for the lifestyle of a king and queen," I said.

"This place is too gigantic," Dennis pouted.

Mom laughed. "It's glorious."

As we approached the *Mona Lisa*, the room was so crowded that we couldn't see it right away. International chatter floated by me. Everyone waited their turn to see the *Mona Lisa*. I tried to get an intimate view of her in spite of everyone taking pictures. Finally I found my spot. I adored that faint smile of such a beautiful and serene-looking woman. What did I feel then? I'm not sure; I do know how it affects me today. The *Mona Lisa* is portrayed at almost dusk, which adds to her mysticism. She resembles a saint; might she be mulling worldly travels?

<hr />

We played sightseer inside and outside of Paris, visiting sites such as the cathedral in Chartres, about an hour away, and another in Rouen. All majestic, they imposed their own beauty of Gothic architecture. The entire D-Day landing area including Omaha Beach and Utah Beach of Normandy touched me deeply. I paid homage to those honorable soldiers whose perfectly aligned crosses stretched the length of the vast cemetery.

It would be difficult to describe my favorite French excursion; they all shone in their own beauty. However, a daytrip to Mont-Saint-Michel impressed me. This desolate castle, perched on a rocky island surrounded by the English Channel's tides, appeared to soar up into the sky.

"Guys, around the eighth century, cleric St. Aubert, bishop of Avranches, perceived to have seen the archangel Michael. So he constructed a place to speak publicly. Pilgrims quickly flocked here, and a Benedictine abbey's construction came to pass in 966 [Mont-Saint-Michel].[154] If they didn't return prior to the tide arriving in the afternoon, they would drown underwater," Dad jested and winked through the rear-view mirror. "Let's get out and steal a picture while we still have time."

I jumped out of the car under a billowy sky, letting the wind tease my hair. The tide was out. Dad quickly snapped away. Two cars sped by us. I returned to my seat and we drove along a wetland of the vast English Channel.

"If you look way up you might be able to see archangel Michael crowned on the spire," Dad said.

"Hopefully we'll be able to get closer," I said.

If memory serves me correctly, I climbed almost a thousand steps to the top of the isolated abbey. I wasn't expecting such enchantment on that bleak day. Gazing out onto the turbulent English Channel, I stood there desolate—while a cascade of serene happiness overcame me. It was divine.

I later learned that Mont-Saint-Michel was named a UNESCO World Heritage site in 1979.[155]

———————————

Six months before turning eighteen, I had had enough of Paris's sweets and wanted my figure back. *Had my depression dissipated?* For one entire month, I ate healthy and shed fifteen pounds. After graduating from high school and now eighteen, I began looking for a job to earn some extra money. I responded to an ad in the local paper from an elderly Russian Jewish lady needing care in her home to cook meals and do some light cleaning. Madame had a very strict diet, which included no salts or fats. I had to boil a calf's brain and ensure that she ate it without any condiments.

Cennet, the young lady I would replace, became my best friend. Cennet's long straight black hair fell over her sleek five-foot-eleven body. She had the most beautiful dark eyes. Her mother was American and her father was Turkish. During our one-year friendship, we went to the movies, chatted and ate at various cafés, window-shopped at gleaming boutiques, and danced the night away at sizzling discos.

"Carina, since you've traveled the world, I think that you and Miyaz would get along great," Cennet said one day. "He's extremely kindhearted. I would like you to meet him."

Giddy with excitement, I responded, "Absolutely! I welcome meeting people from all over the world."

"I'm not sure if he's still at his old address; it's been some time since we last spoke. I'll try his number, though," she said.

A couple of days later Cennet called to tell me that she had spoken to Miyaz. He still lived in the same neighborhood. He invited us both to his apartment for a cup of coffee on the weekend.

———————————

On Saturday, we took the metro to visit him. He lived near the Latin Quarter in the Rive Gauche (Left Bank). Cennet rang the doorbell to his quaint apartment. My heart rate sped up. I remembered Cennet mentioning what a kindhearted man he was. The door opened and a six-foot-tall man with brown eyes and black hair and mustache stepped out. He wore a colorfully striped robe.

"How are you, Cennet. It's been a while," he said, glancing at me.

"It has, Miyaz. I'm well. I'd like to introduce you to my good friend, Carina."

"Good evening, Carina. It's a pleasure to meet you," Miyaz said.

"It's a pleasure to meet you likewise, Miyaz."

"Won't you both kindly come in?"

I sat on the white leather couch next to Cennet. Miyaz grabbed a chair and sat across from us.

"I understand that you're returning to Turkey to visit with your family," Miyaz said to Cennet.

"Yes, I've worked now for the past two years for Madame, and I miss my family terribly. My parents are also getting on in their years."

The room we sat in had white walls with colorful paintings and a large hardwood floor. A TV and a tall black floor lamp decorated the corner.

"I've just brewed some fresh coffee. Would either of you like a cup?"

We both agreed.

Miyaz headed to the nearby kitchen to bring the coffees.

"And, Carina, I understand that you will be working for Madame now," Miyaz said. He placed the coffee tray on a glass round table opposite us.

"How do you prefer your coffee?" he asked.

"With some cream only, thank you," I said.

"And you, Cennet?"

"Black, thank you."

He offered us each a mug, a biscuit, and a napkin. Grabbing a mug, he sat down in the chair facing us and prompted me to continue.

"Yes, I'm looking forward to practicing my French and earning some money," I said.

We all talked for at least an hour and a half about my past road trip, Miyaz's lawyer's job, and Cennet's enthusiasm about returning to Turkey. I checked my watch and realized it was late and time to leave. Cennet and I stood up.

We thanked Miyaz and bid him well.

I threw him a sweet grin. "Goodbye, Miyaz. It was a pleasure meeting you."

He shook my hand graciously. "Goodbye, Carina, it was a pleasure to meet you too, and good luck with everything. Here's my business card. If you ever need anything, please don't hesitate to call me. Cennet, it was great seeing you again. I wish you the best of luck on your return journey home."

***

What Paris and traveling to exotic places with my parents has given me is a fondness for exploring the unique value of our inherent and interesting cultures. This all helped me to discover how each culture played a unique role in determining who I am. As we embrace and enjoy these cultures, we break through and move closer to one another.

***

Miyaz and I hit it off from the start. We both felt at ease with each other, and conversing came with utmost ease. I thought about Miyaz every day all day for that entire week. I couldn't wait any longer. At noon I rang his office and he answered.

"Bonjour, Miyaz. I wanted to thank you again for your—"

"Carina, I'm glad you called. Why, there's no need to thank me seeing that I would like to invite you out for dinner. Are you free tomorrow night?"

"I look forward to it."

"Why don't we meet near the Montparnasse Tower and then head into the Latin Quarter to listen to jazz. How's six o'clock?"

I wanted tomorrow night to already be here. I hunted through my closet debating whether to wear a skirt or jeans, heels or no heels. I resorted to my heather gray French pleated skirt with three-inch Charles Jordan pumps, which cost me close to $150 on the Champs-Élysées. In case it got chilly after dinner, I chose a black cashmere cardigan to wear over my crepe cowl-neck silk white blouse.

***

The temperature dipped to a delightful seventy-five degrees so I quickly washed my hair and let it dry naturally. I sprayed my favorite Jolie Madame perfume behind my ears and on my wrists and chest. I slipped into my skirt and blouse eyeing myself in the mirror. Pleased, I stepped into my pumps, heaved a sigh, and grabbed my cardigan. In a dreamy state, I walked past the Hilton and took the metro to Montparnasse Tower and eagerly waited for Miyaz, looking forward to showing off my French.

I felt a tap on my right shoulder and turned to greet Miyaz, dressed in a black dress shirt over faded blue jeans.

He smiled. "Good evening, Carina. It's nice to see you again. You look very pretty."

I tried not to blush. "Good evening, Miyaz. Thank you." At that moment he absolutely stole my heart.

My heart skipped a beat as I admired Miyaz's lean athletic physique. He appeared manly in his black shirt and tight blue jeans.

"How about we walk over to the Latin Quarter to find an outdoor café on Boulevard St. Germain?"

We found a quaint and lively café with a guitarist playing jazz. I listened to the harmony of people chatting in French as they ate and drank merrily. Miyaz pulled out a bistro chair for me to sit down. Then he sat across from me.

"So, Carina, how long have you known Cennet?"

"We've been friends for about a year. We often went to the movies and discos together."

He smiled. "I also appreciate going to movies and dancing. My favorite song is 'Let's Groove Tonight.' Do you know it?"

"Of course, and it's actually my favorite!"

"Well, that settles it. We simply must go dancing sometime soon." His eyes twinkled with a warm light.

"That sounds marvelous!"

Leaning closer to me, he said, "I am so glad that we met. You speak French fluently, and you're a fascinating young lady with all of your travels—plus very attractive may I add."

Blushing shades of pink, I simply pursed my lips and gazed at his beautiful brown eyes. "You're too kind; thank you for those lovely compliments."

"My pleasure, I'm starving. How about you?"

"I could eat some French onion soup, my favorite with the stringy gruyere." I beamed.

"OK, I can go for one along with you. Do you drink?"

"Yes, I would enjoy a Kronenbourg."

I thought to myself: *I'm sitting across from this handsome man with sexy black mustache in a French café in the Latin Quarter.* I was floating on happiness. I had surrendered to a kind of abandoned doldrums. But something had rekindled this evening. Was I falling in love again?

After he placed our orders, I had to ask: "I'm curious, how old you are, Miyaz?"

"How old do you think I am, Carina?"

"Not sure, about late thirties?" I tilted my head sideways.

The waiter arrived, setting frosted frothy beers in front of us.

"Not too far off, actually. I'm thirty, and you?"

I couldn't lie about my age.

The waiter returned, this time with two onion soups and two slices of baguette. We both nodded and thanked him once again.

I twirled a strand of loose hair. "I'm eighteen."

"I would have guessed older since you're very mature."

What I liked about Miyaz was his happy-go-lucky, adventurous, and exciting nature.

I had so much fun hearing and learning about Tunisia's beach resort Sidi Bouzid near Carthage. I loved his descriptions of fluffy Tunisian couscous and fresh white fish made spicy with a fiery harissa sauce. He introduced me to all of his wonderful friends, and for two blissful years Miyaz and I courted. I eventually fell in love, yet again. We danced at the disco on the Champs-Élysées, attended weekly movies, socialized with friends, and simply devoured this vibrant city full of world-class art and culture, alongside architectural delights.

Two years flew by and then Miyaz decided to leave Paris to return to his hometown of Tunis. Tears pooled in his eyes. "I love you, Carina, with all my heart, but I cannot marry you for the reason that your life would be over if we married and you lived with me in Tunis. Although it breaks my heart to tell you this, I'm doing this for your own good, even though you can't understand now: you and I are not meant to marry each other." He hugged me tightly.

I brooded over how Dad and I hadn't spoken for a year other than hello and goodbye. Though he had not outright said anything, I knew he considered what I'd done fearfully promiscuous, and he feared what every father fears: that I'd get hurt and lose myself to a foreigner and his foreign world.

Tears ran down my cheeks. "I love you too and will forever. I am trying; I'm really trying to understand all of this. But it's really hard." I hugged him and cried.

I cried for three days straight.

I simply had to see him one last time before leaving for secretarial school in America.

Tunis, Tunisia (1979)

Still an au pair, I took a week off work and flew to Tunis, where I discovered jasmine, Tunisia's national flower. I had the most memorable mini-vacation with Miyaz. His two beautiful sisters and parents treated me with utmost kindness and embraced me as one of their own. May's hot and sticky temperature in Tunis reminded me of Jeddah. I discovered paradise visiting the seaside village of Sidi Bouzid facing an exquisite emerald sea.[156] I've never experienced such an unbelievable color scheme of purity and sky blue: shockingly white houses accented with azure-blue-painted windows and railings.

I didn't want to say goodbye so I called my employer and notified her that I'd missed that day's last flight back to Paris. The weekend flights were booked solid. I would have to wait over the weekend, and I couldn't get back to work until Monday.

We spent several days swimming alongside the beautiful golden-sand beach, Al-Hammamet, about an hour away from Tunis and well known for its ubiquitous jasmine. On our last night together, we made passionate love. Two bonding souls on fire from that charismatic attraction we'd felt from the onset. Something I had never experienced before.

I boarded the plane with a hole in my heart.

In retrospect, I know that we visited Carthage on the outskirts of Tunis.[157] We drove by intriguing stone structures. Today these stone structures jogged my memory, and I discovered the following: according to Encyclopedia Britannica, Carthage was established during the period of the Phoenicians of Tyre during 814 BCE. The surviving rock formations and pillars resembled ruins from a bygone city, with a sensational beach view of the Mediterranean Sea. This Roman city had a theatre built by Hadrian, an auditorium based on the design of the Roman Colosseum, a plethora of baths and temples, and a circus. The excavation location of Carthage became a UNESCO World Heritage site in 1979.

20

STANDING STILL
Ridgefield, Connecticut (2002)

y husband, Geoffrey, furrowed his brows. "How would you like to live in Holland?"

Leaning my head forward, I asked, "Holland? How about Paris?"

"Paris is way too expensive—sorry. You'll have to settle for windmills and tulips." Geoffrey smiled affectionately.

"When are we leaving?"

"My boss wants us there by Christmas."

My heart skipped a beat. My craving to live overseas returned.

Our three sons, Jacob, eight years old, and his six-year-old twin brothers, Conor and Markus, initially resisted. However, I knew all too well that it would eventually work out.

"Guys, Mom and Dad have some news for you," I said.

"How would you like to live in another country?" Geoffrey said.

"I don't want to leave America, my friends, or my school," Jacob whined.

"Yeah, me neither. I don't want to leave my school or friends," Conor and Markus mimicked.

"Aw, come on, guys, Holland will be great fun!" Geoffrey insisted, eager to win their approval. "And you'll make new friends real soon. Plus, they have the biggest and best candy stores in the world. You'll be able to ride your bikes everywhere, with a helmet, of course—they have a special lane for bikes only."

I nodded. "That's right; Holland is a beautiful country with wonderful desserts. In the international school, everyone speaks English. Maybe you guys have already seen pictures of wooden Dutch shoes?" I tried joking with them.

"I'm not going," Jacob said, staring down.

"I don't want to go," Conor copycatted, scrunching his nose.

"I'm staying here," Markus whined.

"All right, we don't have to discuss it anymore, but I promise you all that once you're there, you'll be glad you went," Geoffrey said, glancing at me.

Waalre, The Netherlands (2002-2003)

In 2002, a week before Christmas, I arrived in Eindhoven with my young family. Eindhoven is situated in the southern part of the Netherlands onward of the Dommel River, just over sixty miles southeast of Rotterdam.[158]

Geoffrey worked for Koninklijke Philips N.V. as research director. Philips provided us with a quaint house temporarily in Waalre, a prosperous town south of Eindhoven. We lived across from a lush forest brimming with trails, fields, and tall, slender trees.

We endured nothing but rain for a two-week period, and not just plain old rain but a raw, cold, windy rain with the kind of chill that seeps into your bones. Everyone rode a *fiets* (pronounced feets), Dutch for bike. Our car would not arrive for another three weeks from America.

It was the night before Christmas, and we'd all biked forty minutes to Toys R Us in freezing cold rain and wind. We had forty-five minutes until closing time. We came home with two huge plastic bags that Geoffrey and I contentedly carried, jostling in the persistent rain and wind. In a peeve over getting drenched, the boys wrestled biking behind us. I slept soundly that Christmas Eve, knowing our boys would have a gift on Christmas morning. Jacob later confessed that he'd stopped believing in Santa!

Frequent visits to the local cafés for piping hot pea soup with sausage and cappuccino took me through the lengthy cold and snowy winters. Jacob, Conor, and Markus attended the Regional International School (RIS) in Eindhoven with classes in English, except mandatory Dutch. Jacob entered Level Five while Conor and Markus entered Level Three. Culture shock in the first year resulted in the boys objecting to participate in homework.

Valkenswaard, The Netherlands (March 2003)

Philips provided us with lasting housing in Valkenswaard, a nearby city only two miles away from Eindhoven. The boys reveled in eating chocolate sprinkles or *hagelslag* for breakfast. And, yes, even adults take pride in eating chocolate sprinkles. Once Jacob, Conor, and Markus uncovered chocolate and fruit sprinkles over soft white bread for breakfast, there was no turning back.

On Jacob's ninth birthday, I sat down on the edge of his bed and wondered, *am I making the same mistake?*

"Jacob, there is something I want to share with you, and I wanted to be sure you heard this first from me. Opa is not your biological grandfather."

Jacob lowered his chin onto his chest. He stared against his bedroom's white wall. His baby blues pooled with tears. He heaved a deep sigh. "Mom, am I adopted?"

"No. You're not," I said and smiled tenderly, taking his hand in mine. "It's just that Opa is not my biological father."

Jacob pinched his lips. "Is Omi your real mother?"

"Yes." I patted his hand reassuringly. "Jacob, Opa loves you and your brothers very much. This doesn't at all change Opa's love for you. This is very important for you to understand."

"I know, Mom."

"Opa confided in me that you boys remind him of everything he ever wanted to be at your age. Let's keep this between us for now. We can tell your brothers real soon." I cracked a smile.

"You bet, Mom." Jacob grinned.

When Mom and Dad visited us in Valkenswaard that spring for vacation, I heard Dad's words of wisdom for the first time. One sunny afternoon in May, Geoffrey and I grabbed our *fiets*. We biked with Jacob, Conor, and Markus trailing behind us. We were off to pick up Mom and Dad, who stayed at the Hotel de Valk in Valkenswaard center. They would rent their own *fiets* from the hotel. We all agreed on a leisure nature bike ride to a neighboring *heide* (Dutch for heath) called "the Malpie." This huge nature preserve of marshland surrounded us. We biked on both flat roads and hills for a good hour. We could have biked for another three hours since the wetlands continued. Hawks hovered above us and birds chirped. Families on bikes, joggers, and pedestrians with their dogs passed us by.

"Opa, try and catch up with me," Jacob cried out to Dad over the seagulls' squawking.

Huffing and puffing, Dad said, "Jacob, I'll be right there."

Conor hollered over to Mom, "Catch me if you can, Omi."

"Omi, I'm passing you," Markus cried out.

Mom pursed her lips. "Wow, yeah, Markus and Conor!"

Geoffrey whizzed by everyone, waving with an ear-to-ear grin. I waited for Dad to slow down behind the boys. Mom trailed behind us now. I peeked behind me to be sure the coast remained clear; I hurriedly biked over and turned to him.

"Hey, Dad." I threw him a sweet grin.

"Hey, Carina, so what can I do for you?"

"You know, Dad, all I ever wish is forever to be happy—like that innocent young girl growing up on the compound with the joy of sun, sand, and the Red Sea at my fingertips."

He nodded. "To be happy is all anyone ever wants. And, if there is any advice I would give you, it would be this. Stand still and appreciate what you have around you." Dad threw me a tender expression and winked. There were many times when I wanted to sit down to tell Mom and Dad how betrayed I felt. However, I never found the strength to have a heart-to-heart conversation with them. Mom reacted in an unsupportive manner right after my discovery, adamantly telling me that she had nothing else to discuss. I realized at that moment that I would have to resolve my issues entirely on my own. Dad only approached me once to try and have a heart-to-heart. That occurred shortly after I learned my truth. I will never forget that day when Dad pulled the jeep over and parked next to the Red Sea, eyeing me with concern.

"How's it going? It's not so bad after all, is it?"

I couldn't find the strength, nor had I the heart to disclose how distraught and frightened I felt. How would I begin to explain my infinite set of emotions that arose during that momentous day? Instead I stared out onto a choppy Red Sea. The familiar desert road reminded me of how boundless and deserted my world was. I struggled like a disoriented nomad with no sense of direction.

My anger seethed inside of me well into adulthood. I transformed from a vivacious extrovert into a brooding introvert as depression crept over me, quietly smothering my energy, joy, and vitality. My self-worth and trust deteriorated; I argued with my mother, although we didn't communicate about what really bothered me. I never wanted someone to leave me again. I would never confess my fears. I believed that showing fear meant that I became easily intimidated and/or that people would think something was wrong with me. I resorted to pretending to always be strong. When, in fact, my heart perpetually ached.

Finally summer arrived. Exercise consumed me. My running prolonged distances kept me from standing still and having to face the anger I felt toward my mother. My anger felt like a parasite inside of me. I performed my daily jog through Valkenswaard's vast forest of orderly asphalted bike paths. Tall stick-type trees shielded me. An elegant horseback rider trotted over dirt paths. Traditional thatched-roof farmhouses emerged from nearby fields of corn. A local farmer steered his Gypsy Vanner[159] to pull a cart. Sunrays played with fluttering aspen leaves, and tall grass swayed to and fro. I yearned for my morning ritual to sit upon a low and lonely tree stump. Purple crocuses in full bloom enveloped me. I sat down on the stump and closed my eyes to let the sun's warmth bathe me.

A woodpecker's tapping startled me out of my reverie. Tears gushed uncontrollably from bliss. For but a moment I'd detached myself from my feelings of betrayal by both Mom and Dad. I'd discovered a glorious grace of existence.

I realized that I'd succumbed to being a nomad, always searching for greener pasture. I never knew my destination. The fact that I will never know my background did not help me to heal. I wrote in my journal aspiring to find equal bliss. Words flowed freely from the deepest part of me onto paper. Such an intimate and intellectual relationship amazed me. Words were my feelings. My thoughts centered on when Dad once expressed to me, "Your writing must be very cathartic, Carina."

Feelings flowed. And I discovered the stillness.

Mom and Dad left Holland en route to Belgium to continue their tour through Europe. Everyone slept peacefully in our eighty-year-old detached farmhouse in Valkenswaard.

Late that night, I awoke startled. My thoughts swam in the trance of my recurring dream from Jerusalem—only this time I shot up in my bed and screamed, "Please don't leave me! Please don't leave me!"

Geoffrey bolted awake. "I'll never leave you, sweetie, you're having a bad dream." He hugged me tightly.

I saw the same two shadow faces staring me down. I experienced the same dream three months later. I awoke in frenzy, reassured to see my soul-mate still next to me. I was in a safe home—A-OK.

Eindhoven, The Netherlands (2004)

We moved yet again. I hoped this post-war home would be our last move around Eindhoven. Holland's tulips, canals, wooden shoes, and windmills here, there, and everywhere rendered me giddy with glee. Weekly, I purchased dozens of fresh flowers which only cost me the equivalent of less than five American dollars. A sea of bikes outside of Eindhoven's train station brought me joy on a rainy day. Whenever I gazed out onto the ubiquitous canals, I thought about how the Dutch people had amazingly constructed cities and cathedrals above water.

One weekend morning, we embarked upon an easy daytrip and ventured into the Middle Ages at Kinderdijk, outside of Rotterdam.[160] The Lek and Noord rivers merge near the towns of Kinderdijk and Albasserdam in the colony of (South) Zuid-Holland. Fifty percent of the Netherlands would exist below water if the North Sea coast didn't contain sand dunes and dikes. Nineteen windmills dating to the 1740s operated through to 1950 in the process of draining water out of the marshlands under sea level.

I recently discovered the following during my research. After the great Saint Elizabeth Flood in 1421, a fable lingered.[161] Alblasserwaard's polders remained unscathed, and someone spotted a floating wooden cradle with a cat aboard. Once this cradle arrived on the dike's dry soil, the folks of the region discovered a baby on board—hence the "The Cat and the Cradle." *Kinderdijk* translates into "children's dike." Today, electrical draining devices are employed for this intention. UNESCO named the Mill Network at Kinderdijk-Elshout a World Heritage location in 1997.[162]

I cheerfully clutched the Lonely Planet guidebook and imagined myself reciting to my family. I stepped out of the car, secured my hat over my head, and buttoned up my winter coat. I walked maladroitly against the blustery wind and slight rain. The wetlands boasted tall grass and colorful seasonal flowers with a backdrop of nineteen large windmills, which aligned a bustling canal. Kinderdijk epitomizes an idyllic Dutch setting. I was transported back to the eighteenth century.

Every day I adorned our Dutch home with glorious flowers, which added a colorful splash. Once a year, Keukenhof gardens hosts the biggest display of flowers in the world.[163] This exposition (March to May; originated in 1950), which takes place on a rural manor from about the seventeenth century, De Keukenhof Castle, has boasted carpets of gardens over sixty-five acres.

One warm spring day, we drove roughly one hundred miles to Lisse where we rented *fiets* for everyone. Lisse is situated in the western Netherlands and resides in the hub of the flower farmlands among Haarlem and Leiden. Outside of the Keukenhof gardens, Lisse's local residents grew fields of vibrant-colored flowers. Fluffy clouds drifted. We biked past windmills, alongside canals, and through unfathomable fields of red, pink, purple, yellow, and orange tulips, hyacinths, and daffodils—my eyes pooled with tears from the surrounding splash of colors, a never-ending rainbow. Although we never made it to Keukenhof, an ostensibly perfect afternoon bike ride flooded me with happiness. I was an individual without any care or worry, taking me back to my innocent childhood before my discovery. I felt nature's stillness. I felt at one with the universe. I allowed the present moment to enchant me. I've finally understood the value of the word "present."

I volunteered to supervise the lunch hour at the Regional International School (RIS) in Eindhoven, which invites children ages four through eleven. Children from around the world attend this school taught in either English or Dutch. My children attended classes taught in English, which included a mandatory Dutch class.

On this particular drizzly day, many four- to five-year-old children sat on the floor in front of the overhead television, watching a Dutch children's show. The rest of the students ate lunch at their tables, drew pictures, or chitchatted with friends.

One beautiful girl, Aisha, who had a full head of long curly black hair and big brown eyes, approached me while I scribbled notes for my story.

She asked, "*Wat schrijf jij?*" [What are you writing?]

"*Niks bijzonders.*" [Nothing important.]

Aisha reminded me of the free-spirited girl I was at her age and of my inquisitive nature. Had I not responded to her or ignored her, I would not have received her gift of making me feel special. She accepted me for who I am—simply existing.

We all have unique and special gifts. Aisha stared at me intently with her inquisitive grin. I examined the room. I admired children simply enjoying life, and time stood still. This moment hypnotized me. Inebriated with blissful peace and harmony, I surrendered to pure peace. Such spellbinding peace surpassed my deep-rooted experiences. Falling in love, giving birth, and experiencing joy paled in comparison to this divine bliss falling from the heavens above.

When we stand still and live in the moment, we experience peace and harmony. Tranquil auras permeate everywhere. Some of us never stop running until we go to bed at night, missing that life-altering event. It is my sincere hope that each person encounter this heavenly serenity at least once in his or her life. Afterward, tuck it away in your heart for future reflection.

Veldhoven, The Netherlands (2005)

Spring had sprung, and this is when everyone in Holland anticipates the fields of vibrant tulips and other flowers; however, the landlord of the house on 16 Treurenburgstraat, Eindhoven, wanted to sell his home.

Philips Housing Department mentioned that they had a wonderful semi-detached home on 22 Pastorielaan, Veldhoven, for us to rent. The owners lived abroad, and we could remain until our departure the summer of 2006. Veldhoven is located near Eindhoven.

On Saturday night, my girlfriends and I went out for dinner in the center of Eindhoven to celebrate my birthday. We ate, drank, and chitchatted over what a delightful expatriate experience we'd had. I received spectacular gifts and cherished this special moment. I particularly enjoy my colorful book *Holland*, reminding me of savoring delectable Dutch tarts and visiting windmills, tulip gardens, and quaint cities alongside canals and dikes, in addition to admiring Gothic cathedrals.

We left the restaurant and noticed a trendy dancing bar with an outdoor terrace where people socialized and drank. We entered the nearby pub and continued to celebrate and danced to a variety of songs which dated back to the 1970s until closing time.

My friend Chrissy and I shared a taxi to our respective homes; she knew my story. Intrigued, she asked, "Carina, do you ever have a desire to search for your biological father?"

"No, not anymore. In my twenties, I thought of hiring a private detective; but I don't know anything about him, not even his name," I said earnestly.

She then reached her house and wished me goodnight. "OK, sweetie. Have a good night's rest." Chrissy hugged me.

"Good night, my dear, and thanks for a swell birthday celebration and my beautiful gifts." I hugged her back.

I awoke at noon the next day. I dreamed that my biological father died of a heart attack.

<hr />

I was running on the treadmill at the gym when I whispered Dad's words of wisdom to me given with that familiar endearing laugh and wink: "If there is any advice I would give you, it would be this. Stand still and appreciate what you have around you."

I cried uncontrollably. I was conscious. I stood still. There was not a soul around me. I was forced to stop running. I felt pulled into a tornado of energetic rush, and I felt either alarm, fear, or both. My body started to shake. My entire bodily sensation overwhelmed me, and I knew right then that this was my turning point. I wholeheartedly accepted Dad—I locked his gift of mindfulness in my heart, where it shall remain eternally for our future generations.

Dad is my *real* father.

The peace that surrounded me was only equal to the peace that was within me.

Shocked by this phenomenon, I paid particular attention to the billowy clouds drifting purposely through the azure sky. When I left the gym, I heard birds sing-song that spring had sprung. I wanted to walk around the world in utmost astonishment, appreciating life's marvels. During that timeframe, I lived life in a state of wonder, and I often shed happy tears. What I only subconsciously felt then I now keenly feel after reflecting upon what motivational speaker Anthony Robbins identified: *our six human needs: love/ connection, safety/security, significance, variety, growth, and contribution.*[164] Most of mine were gratefully fulfilled.

It is my dream that others experience "standing still and appreciating what you have around you." Michael Nitti, author of *The Trophy Effect,*[165] and Eckhart Tolle, author of *The Power of Now,*[166] have shared wise truths with me. I embrace this quote by Eckhart Tolle: "*That stillness is also inner peace, and that stillness and peace is the essence of your Being.*"

Palo Alto, California (2009)

Last year, during one of our usual phone conversations with the speaker turned on, I greeted Dad lovingly. "Hi, Dad. How are you?"

"Doing the best I can, Carina, the best I can," Dad said.

Ever since his first stroke in 2008, Dad always replied with that slogan. Prior to the stroke he always said, "Great, fantastic, and how goes it in sunny Palo Alto?"

Since the late 1980s, he and Mom resided in Massachusetts. They'd lived for two years in The Hague, the Netherlands, twenty-two years prior to my young family's relocation to Eindhoven. Now I sensed a change. I heard a catch in his voice. Something wasn't quite right, though I couldn't put my finger on it. Were we both protecting each other? Dad never complained.

"Hey, Carina, you'll never guess what I found," he said.

"What, pray-tell?"

"Remember years ago when you asked Mom and me about an image in your mind. Then I explained how we crossed the Atlantic Ocean to America when you were four years old. Well, I've found those two black-and-white Polaroid snapshots with all of you sitting at a small square table. Dennis is in a wooden highchair, and you're next to the porthole across from Mom. The other is of you and Dennis atop the huge round table with other preschoolers. I'll send you a copy of each of them."

I was stunned and ecstatic. I finally realized that that particular image in my mind was a real place and real event. "Wow, I can't believe it. I love it. I always knew that image meant something. Thanks, Dad. Always, you have the answer to everything that I ask."

"No problem. I'll send it in the mail tomorrow." I could hear that old beam in his voice.

"You're extraordinary, Dad."

"As are you."

"I love you."

"I love you too, Carina. Bye."

"Bye, Dad."

After I returned the cordless phone to its console, I cried.

Palo Alto, California (March 4, 2009)

A few days later, I received the phone call we all dread. Dennis called at 8:15 a.m. PST with news that our father had had a massive stroke. We did not believe that he suffered. He was seventy-five years, seven months, and eight days. He rests in our hearts forever.

On April 11, 2009, I turned on National Public Radio. The program did not intrigue me. I was about to switch channels when something told me to listen...I felt Dad's spirit right there. Somehow I knew there would be a lesson learned and read in the ethers: "Knowledge is power."

I turned up the volume and listened to *Weekend Edition Saturday* with host Scott Simon's interview of Rowan LeCompte, a stained-glass window artisan.[167] He contributed extensively to the Washington National Cathedral's stained-glass windows. Rowan's passion for stained-glass windows began at age fourteen when he first visited the Washington National Cathedral. He spoke about wishing that churches would give more priority to "kindness, kindness to everybody."

Rowan recited a story about the cathedral's volunteer guides who spotted a five-year-old girl dancing in the huge reflected circles as the sunlight shone through the stained-glass window.

When the cathedral's attendant asked the young girl what she was doing, she responded, "I'm dancing because I found the end of the rainbow."

Scott Simon asked Rowan, "Do you believe in God?"

"I believe in kindness and love, and there are those who say that those are God. I don't know, but I respect and love kindness and love and worship them. And if I'm worshipping God, I'm delighted."

It was the most powerful show I've ever heard.

Rowan LeCompte brought me a bountiful, tearful joy—reminding me of my father, who had died only five and a half weeks earlier. I thank Rowan LeCompte from the bottom of my heart for reminding me of my father, a rare gem, a friend to many, a philosopher, but most of all one who embodied love and kindness.

———————————————

Throughout life, I reassure my heart that I will stay with it, pay attention to it, and experience it. When I listen, feel, and acknowledge—therein lies my truth. There is pain and it hurts. Listening and feeling guide me out of pain. Today I am the woman I have always wanted to be.

I found the end of the rainbow.

EPILOGUE

I have now arrived full circle. The day my father died, thoughts of life with him swirled around me like a tornado. I cried uncontrollably, hoping for a miracle. Finally I realized that I would never speak with Dad again—in this life!

Early on in my story, I questioned a reoccurring image in my mind—not at all surprisingly—a carbon copy of one from Dad's library of timeless black-and-white Polaroid snapshots. I shared with you an earlier conversation Dad and I had regarding those two photos. Even today, I can still recall that vivid scene: a lonely glass of orange juice sitting across from us, Dennis and I captivated with a puzzle.

When Dad called me and said the photos mirrored our trip across the Atlantic Ocean to America and that he would send me a copy of each of them, I could hear that old joy: a smile, and then his wink.

Not only did this Polaroid confirm my earliest childhood memory, but it represented the beginning of life for me with Dad. Dad's cradling love touched my heart from the onset. Today I know that a *real* father's love conquers all.

For me, these two Polaroid snapshots are even more powerful today: they represent the ending of life with *my* father—made real with love. Dad knew that he was dying but withheld it from us. He never wished to cause us anguish. He only desired to shield us from harm, yet another one of his endless gifts to us. And Dad made darn sure that I would have a copy in my possession. One day he shared: "You can never do enough for your kids."

As for these two snapshots of my early life, I shall tuck them away in the other corner of my heart across from his gift of mindfulness.

For four months after Dad's passing, I often felt warmth upon my right cheek and across my shoulders. Upon greeting me, he always kissed me first on my right cheek and then on my left cheek; or he gently placed his hand on my shoulder, reminding me of his presence.

Four months after Dad died, I returned to their home, where Mom and Dad lived for thirty years. One sunny morning I prepared for my daily run. My shoulders radiated warmth. I felt Dad's presence—reminding me that he never left me or Mom or Dennis. Only a few minutes into my run, my right cheek suddenly felt warm. Soon I ran by a corner field near a red barn—stealing but a glimpse of pink cosmos. I gravitated back toward it. *Voila*, a huge field spanned the entire length of the red barn. Brilliant lavender and red cosmos swayed to and fro in the hot breeze. I stood still and appreciated what I had around me.

Life never ceases to amaze me, seeing that nature provides such magnificence and vibrancy. I have shared with you my story. And I encourage you to inspire others through your story. I stand still. I listen. Nature awaits my embrace. You see I believe in something larger than life... larger than myself. In honoring my father's soul, I honor my soul. Through the power of a real father's love I heal, and through that same love, I accept.

Dad—you remain forever in my heart. I love you and miss you dearly...

In honor of and completing my father's legacy, duplicates of his photos have subsequently returned home. Dad's timeless images now reside in Jeddah Our Days of Bliss Magad Museum. The museum's founder, Mansour Al Zamil, revealed how a few stolen pictures on the Internet led him to search for me. Mansour graciously and respectfully honored my late father's photos in dedication: "A man whose love for our city is now in full exhibit ... Through his work ... Through his silent yet loudly spoken images ..."

I shall forever value Jeddah, both old and new. In my mind's eye, I envision Dad lecturing about Jeddah's rich heritage, Jeddah's exotic lure. Dad rests in peace, and so should his timeless pictures recently bestowed ... in Jeddah.

ABOUT THE AUTHOR

For over two decades, Carina Burns traveled the globe throughout Europe, Asia, and the Middle East, including Germany, France, the Netherlands, Hong Kong, and Saudi Arabia. She enjoys all aspects of foreign cultures, including exotic cuisines, cultural history, and language. She studied writing at DeAnza College and Stanford and is a member of the California Writers Club South Bay Branch. A speaker and blogger on adoption-related issues, Carina is currently pursuing a bachelor's degree in psychology. She is the author of *What Do You Mean I Was Adopted? 7 Steps to Acceptance, Gratitude & Peace*. When not attending school, she enjoys spending time with her family, reading and nature hiking. She lives in Palo Alto, California. To learn more about Carina, visit her website at www.carinasueburns.com.

ACKNOWLEDGMENTS

Renate E. Rourke, my wonderful mother, your courage and strength *truly* inspire me, and most importantly, thank you for loving me. I love you, Mom. Dennis, my amazing brother, for *always* being there. I love you. And Joseph C. Rourke, my father—Dad, losing you in 2009 was the most painful experience I've ever known. Before you died, I promised you that I would write my book. Dad—I love you. You remain forever in my heart.

To my extraordinary and loving family, who allowed me to write my story:

My husband, Geoffrey, I am privileged and honored to have called you my soul mate for the past twenty-three years. I love you with all my heart.

To my three extraordinary sons, Jacob, Conor, and Markus, for their forgiveness and patience when I needed to write instead of cooking a meal; you all have blossomed into fine young men. I love you all more than you can know.

I would like to extend loving gratitude to my mother's family: Emilie Feder, Georg Feder, Herbert Feder, Hans-Georg Feder, Karl-Heinz Feder; to Helga Feder and Sylvia Feder; and with heartfelt gratitude to my loving soul sister, Ina Feder Krümmel, for graciously assisting me with my German translation. I love you dearly!

To my brother's extended family for their unwavering love and encouragement: Deborah Rourke, Joshua Rourke, Isabel Rourke, Oliver Rourke, Linda Zeltzer, Bob Zeltzer, Steve Zeltzer, Karen Zeltzer, Stephanie Levinson, and Jocelyn Levinson-Fernandez; and to Joanne C. Locke, with loving gratitude, Steven Locke, Alexandra Locke, and Graham Bengen.

To Geoffrey Burns's extended family for their unwavering love and support: James Burns, Cindy McLean-Greeley, Hollis McElwain, Helen McElwain, Jonathan Jay Dubois, Shane Cynthia Dubois, Catherine Burns, Ernie Buford, Seamus Buford, Evie Mae Buford, Sean Burns, Lori Burns, Zachary Burns, Acadia Burns, Jim Burns, Chris Burns, Gwyneth Burns, Harry Burns, Barbara Grace Sullivan, and Howard Taylor.

Kathy Kliskey, my longest and dearest friend, we've endured both marvelous and demanding times, and I love you dearly for that! Robin Levenherz, my mentor, I'm indebted to you; Zvezdana Rashkovich, Joanie Jones-Lefevre, Susan Lee Mun, Susan M. Davis, Karo Caran, Bonnie Chi, Kimberly Dodge, Harini Shekhar, Sandra Aussentine, and Melinda Athey, you are the most incredible friends!

I would like to extend my heartfelt gratitude to Nina Munteanu, who was originally referred to me as an editor and has since become a special friend. Nina, your grace with words transformed promise into story. You contributed both outstanding insight and editing support—and you performed above and beyond the call of duty for setting my story in motion.

I would like to extend gratitude to David Hancock, Scott Frishman, Terry Whalin, Margo Toulouse, Nickcole Watkins, Bethany Marshall, Jim Howard, and the family at Imbue Press and Morgan James Publishing for helping manifest my dream into reality. I extend an extra special thank-you to Rick Frishman for creating Author 101 University. You offered me the means and connections, and most importantly, your belief in me that I am an author and that my words are significant.

Huge heartfelt gratitude goes to Amanda Rooker, Ben Rooker, and Angie Kiesling of SplitSeed—Amanda for your warm and professional editorial assistance; and to Angie Kiesling for her stellar editorial assistance and warm-hearted advice.

To Ashley Goldman, Chrissy Andriola, Lynne Kyffin, Jill Sander, Patricia Gray, Joan Roach, Wendy Klemme—I shall always remember our fun times in Eindhoven! Nora and Ziad Shebaro, for your loving support and Arabic translation assistance. Theda Davids-Muller, with sincere gratitude for your help with my Arabic words. To all of my PCS and Raytheon Compound friends including: Paul Pullen, Fran Pullen, Amy Pullen, Christina Goodwin, Patsy Goodwin, Heidi Lenzen, Charles Webster, Frank Webster, Michael Graham, Philip Graham, and the entire Zamarchi family! Additionally, I offer my special gratitude to the following individuals for their generous contribution and kind support to the realization of my work: Louis Sciortino, Teresa Beer, Glen Grubbs, Patrick Christy, and Delia Rogers.

To Aisha, you're a beautiful soul and my angel. My heartfelt gratitude goes out to the following individuals for their unwavering support and encouragement: Mini Rawat, Sri. Rakesh Kumar Rawat, Thao Tran, Michael Marcil, Gary Nedd, Theresa Nedd, Jean Cook, Ted Aberg, Randy Cook, Judy Cook, and April Topfer.

With heartfelt gratitude to Mansour Al Zamil, founder of Jeddah Our Days of Bliss Magad Museum, for his graciousness, unflappable support, and due diligence in Arabic translation. No doubt, my father is humbled beyond words and smiling down upon you in blissful peace!

I extend my heartfelt gratitude to the following individuals for their gracious and steadfast support and encouragement: Richard Maack, John Mulholland, Gabriella Mulholland, Lucia Fatone, Norman Brooks, Barbara Brooks. And I offer a very special heartfelt thank-you to my incredible and dear friend Lucy Pullen. I would like to extend my heartfelt gratitude to both Renate and Nick Graham for their generous assistance and support. Ute Getz Yaman, for graciously and expeditiously offering me assistance with my German translation. Lorelei Kay for lovingly assisting me with her extensive array of theological knowledge. Caroline and Suha Islam, I shall always remember your kindness. Hussein, you graciously and promptly assisted me in Arabic translation—*Shukran*, my dear friend. Anthony J. Zamarchi Sr., I'm indebted to you, my friend, for your steadfast support and kindness.

I would also like to thank the following individuals for their unwavering support and contribution to the realization of my work: *Oliver Hille*, Joe Soll,

Aminata Toure, Ousmane N. Diallo, Pattie Meyers, Cheryl T. Campbell, Rev. Paula Richards, Kindra Clineff, Michael A. Nitti, Dr. Alexandra Snow, Geraldine Solon, Brendon Burchard, Richard M. Krawczyk, Abby Ross, Mahdokht Khavari, Sevan Balbanian, Candess M. Campbell, Laura Steward, Amid Yousef, Karyn Lutes, Sandra Champlain, Victor Tsaran, Maricel Lennon, and Jozef Kruger; Barbie Lightbody, for your loving friendship and support—may you always shine your light. I love you dearly! Tammy Tiller-Faeth, for your loving friendship, you inspire me so!

I offer my sincere and heartfelt gratitude to Kenneth W. Christian, PhD, as both a friend and colleague. And for his loving support and belief that my story has value—*mon cher ami*. Namaste.

In gratitude to the United States Embassy's Boat and Commissary; Raytheon Middle East Systems; Raytheon Housing Compound and guards; Saudi Airlines and Lufthansa Airlines for their outstanding service during my long flights; our faithful school bus drivers; and to Moosa, whose smile brightened my day. Parents' Cooperative School (PCS), I extend a very special and heartfelt gratitude to each and every amazing teacher, and to the staff at École Alsacienne and my French classmates.

Last but not least, to the reader, I am grateful to you for spending some of your valuable time with the words within this book. I encourage you to inspire others through *your* story. Bless your heart.

ENDNOTES

Chapter 2. The Arrival, Jeddah, Saudi Arabia (1968)

1   "bazaar." *Britannica School.* Encyclopædia Britannica Inc., 2014. Web. 5 Mar. 2014. <http://library.eb.com/levels/referencecenter/article/13892>.

Chapter 3. The Souq, Jeddah, Saudi Arabia (1968)

2   "Saudi Arabia." *Britannica School.* Encyclopædia Britannica Inc., 2014. Web. 5 Mar. 2014. <http://library.eb.com/levels/referencecenter/article/110507#259149.toc>.

3   "Saudi Arabia." *Britannica School.* Encyclopædia Britannica Inc., 2014. Web. 19 Jul. 2014. <http://library.eb.com/levels/high/article/110507#45221.toc>.

4   "Saudi Arabia." *Britannica School.* Encyclopædia Britannica Inc., 2014. Web. 19 Jul. 2014. <http://library.eb.com/levels/high/article/110507#45221.toc>.

5   Angelo Pesce, *Jiddah Portrait of an Arabian City* (Castelfranco Veneto, Italy: Falcon Press, 1974), 114.

6   Ibid.

7   "Saudi Arabia." Encyclopædia Britannica Inc., 2014. Web. 6 Jan. 2014.
     <http://library.eb.com/eb/article-259149>.

8   Angelo Pesce, *Jiddah Portrait of an Arabian* City (Castelfranco Veneto,
     Italy: Falcon Press, 1974), 178.

9   "muezzin." Encyclopædia Britannica Inc., 2013. Web. 17 Dec. 2013.
     <http://library.eb.com/eb/article-9054144>.

10   Ibid.

11   Angelo Pesce, *Jiddah Portrait of an Arabian City* (Castelfranco Veneto,
     Italy: Falcon Press, 1974), 130.

12   "Jiddah." Encyclopædia Britannica Inc., 2013. Web. 21 Dec. 2013.
     <http://library.eb.com/eb/article-9043628>.

13   Angelo Pesce, *Jiddah Portrait of an Arabian City*, (Castelfranco Veneto,
     Italy: Falcon Press, 1974), 126.

14   "adhān." Encyclopædia Britannica Inc., 2014. Web. 15 Apr. 2014.
     <http://library.eb.com/levels/referencecenter/article/3726>.

Chapter 4. Raytheon Compound, Jeddah, Saudi Arabia (1968)

15   "Ramadan." Encyclopædia Britannica Inc., 2013. Web. 17 Dec. 2013.
     <http://library.eb.com/eb/article-9062564>.

16   http://www.sauress.com/en/saudigazette/78489

17   "Ramadan." Encyclopædia Britannica Inc., 2013. Web. 17 Dec. 2013.
     <http://library.eb.com/eb/article-9062564>.

18   http://www.sauress.com/en/saudigaze/78489

19   http://www.sauress.com/en/saudigazette/78489

Chapter 5. The Hajj, Jeddah, Saudi Arabia (February 1969)

20   "Hajj." Encyclopædia Britannica Inc., 2013. Web. 10 Dec. 2013.
     <http://library.eb.com/eb/article-9038834>.

21   Angelo Pesce, *Jidda Portrait of an Arabian City*, (Castelfranco Veneto,
     Italy: Falcon Press, 1974), 132.

22   "Saudi Arabia." Encyclopædia Britannica Inc., 2013. Web. 16 Dec. 2013.
     <http://library.eb.com/eb/article-45218>.

23   "Mecca." Encyclopædia Britannica Inc., 2013. Web. 10 Dec. 2013.
      <http://library.eb.com/eb/article-9109828>.

24   "Hajj." Encyclopædia Britannica, Inc., 2013. Web. 10 Dec. 2013.
      <http://library.eb.com/eb/article-9038834>.

Chapter 6. Mada'in Saleh, Saudi Arabia (1969)

25   "Hejaz Railway." Encyclopædia Britannica Inc., 2013. Web. 6 Dec. 2013.
      <http://library.eb.com/eb/article-9039859>.

26   http://nabataea.net/hejaz.html

27   "Hejaz Railway." Encyclopædia Britannica Inc., 2013. Web. 6 Dec. 2013.
      <http://library.eb.com/eb/article-9039859>.

28   "Lawrence, T.E." Encyclopædia Britannica Inc., 2013.
      Web. 6 Dec. 2013. <http://library.eb.com/eb/article-4099>

29   http://sauditourism.sa/en/Explore/Regions/Medina/Medina/Pages/m-11.
      aspx

30   "Arabian religion." Encyclopædia Britannica Inc., 2014.
      Web. 1 Jan. 2014. <http://library.eb.com/eb/article-68307>.

31   http://sauditourism.sa/en/Explore/Regions/Medina/Medina/Pages/m-11.
      aspx

32   "Bedouin." Encyclopædia Britannica Inc., 2013. Web. 10 Dec. 2013.
      <http://library.eb.com/eb/article-9014079>.

33   "Rub' al-Khali." Encyclopædia Britannica Inc., 2013.
      Web. 10 Dec. 2013. <http://library.eb.com/eb/article-9064311>.

34   http://sauditourism.sa/en/Explore/Regions/Medina/Medina/Pages/m-11.
      aspx

35   http://sauditourism.sa/en/Explore/Regions/Medina/Medina/Pages/m-11.
      aspx

36   Text by Sandra L. Olsen, Photography by Richard T. Bryant, *Stories in
      the Rocks Exploring Saudi Arabian Rock Art* (Pittsburgh, PA: Carnegie
      Museum of Natural History Press, 2013), 22.

37   Angelo Pesce, *Colours of the Arab Fatherland Riyadh, 1972* (Castelfranco
      Veneto, Italy: Oleander Press, 1972), 11-12.

38   http://whc.unesco.org/en/list/1293

39   "Saudi Arabia." Encyclopædia Britannica Inc., 2013. Web. 10 Dec. 2013.
     <http://library.eb.com/eb/article-45218>.

40   "Tabuk." Encyclopædia Britannica Inc., 2013. Web. 20 Dec. 2013.
     <http://library.eb.com/eb/article-9070855>.

41   "Muhammad." Encyclopædia Britannica Inc., 2013. Web. 20 Dec. 2013.
     <http://library.eb.com/eb/article-251798>.

Chapter 7. Petra, Jordan (1969)

42   "Petra." Encyclopædia Britannica Inc., 2013. Web. 10 Dec. 2013.
     <http://library.eb.com/eb/article-9059488>.

43   Ibid.

44   Ibid.

45   Ibid.

46   Ibid.; http://whc.unesco.org/en/list/326.

47   "Petra." Encyclopædia Britannica Inc., 2013. Web. 10 Dec. 2013.
     <http://library.eb.com/eb/article-9059488>.

48   Angelo Pesce, *Colours of the Arab Fatherland Riyadh, 1972* (Castelfranco
     Veneto, Italy: Oleander Press, 1972), 10-11.

49   "Amman." Encyclopædia Britannica Inc., 2013. Web. 12 Dec. 2013.
     <http://library.eb.com/eb/article-9007193>.

50   Ibid.

51   http://www.kinghussein.gov.jo/tourism1.html#Sights of Interest

**Chapter 11. The Parents' Cooperative School (PCS), Jeddah, Saudi Arabia
(1972)**

52   "shamal." Encyclopædia Britannica Inc., 2013. Web. 19 Dec. 2013.
     <http://library.eb.com/eb/article-9067102>.

Chapter 12. The Discovery, Jeddah, Saudi Arabia (1975)

53   Rhonda Byrne, *The Secret Daily Teachings* (New York, NY: Atria Books,
     2006)

Chapter 14. Driving from Jeddah to Paris (1975)—Middle East: Part 1

54   http://www.panoramio.com/photo
     explorer#view=photo&position=347&with_photo_
     id=11053109&order=date_desc&user=1046561

55   "Badr, Battle of." Encyclopædia Britannica Inc., 2013.
     Web. 19 Dec. 2013. <http://library.eb.com/eb/article-9011713>.

56   "Saudi Arabia." Encyclopædia Britannica Inc., 2014. Web. 4 Mar. 2014.
     <http://library.eb.com/levels/referencecenter/article/110507#259149.
     toc>.

57   "Amman." Encyclopædia Britannica Inc., 2013. Web. 22 Dec. 2013.
     <http://library.eb.com/eb/article-9007193>.

58   http://www.art-and-archaeology.com/jordan/amman/cit01.html

59   Ibid.

60   Ibid.

61   "Dome of the Rock." Encyclopædia Britannica Inc., 2013.
     Web. 29 Dec. 2013. <http://library.eb.com/eb/article-9030854>.

62   Ibid .

63   "Holy Sepulchre." Encyclopædia Britannica Inc., 2014.
     Web. 2 Jan. 2014.
     <http://library.eb.com/eb/article-9040858>.

64   "Gethsemane." Encyclopædia Britannica Inc., 2014. Web. 2 Jan. 2014.
     <http://library.eb.com/eb/article-9036633>.

65   "Jerusalem." Encyclopædia Britannica Inc., 2014. Web. 2 Jan. 2014.
     <http://library.eb.com/eb/article-61899>.

66   "Gethsemane." Encyclopædia Britannica Inc., 2014. Web. 2 Jan. 2014.
     <http://library.eb.com/eb/article-9036633>.

67   http://www.lonelyplanet.com/syria/damascus/sights/markets-bazaars/
     souq-al-hamidiyya

68   "Damascus, Great Mosque of." Encyclopædia Britannica Inc., 2014.
     Web. 3 Jan. 2014. <http://library.eb.com/eb/article-9028633>.

69   Ibid.

70   "Krak des Chevaliers." Encyclopædia Britannica Inc., 2014.
     Web. 4 Jan. 2014. <http://library.eb.com/eb/article-9046187>.

71   "Palmyra." Encyclopædia Britannica Inc., 2014. Web. 5 Jan. 2014.
      <http://library.eb.com/eb/article-9058157>.

72   http://whc.unesco.org/en/list/23

73   http://www.pbase.com/bmcmorrow/palmyracastle&page=all

Chapter 15. Driving from Jeddah to Paris (1975)—Middle East: Part 2

74   "Aleppo." Encyclopædia Britannica Inc., 2014. Web. 25 Feb. 2014.
      <http://library.eb.com/levels/referencecenter/article/5570>.

75   "Aleppo." Encyclopædia Britannica Inc., 2014. Web. 25 Feb. 2014.
      <http://library.eb.com/levels/referencecenter/article/5570>.

76   http://www.goreme.com/derinkuyu-underground-city.php

77   http://www.fairychimney.com/english/cappadocia/geology.htm

78   http://www.goreme.com/zelve-open-air-museum.php

79   Ibid.

80   http://www.ephesustoursguide.com/must-see-places-in-turkey/church-of-
      the-grapes- uzumlu-kilise.html

81   http://www.goreme.com/derinkuyu-underground-city.php

82   Ibid.

83   "Cleopatra." Encyclopædia Britannica Inc., 2014. Web. 24 Feb. 2014.
      <http://library.eb.com/levels/referencecenter/article/24335>.

84   "Tarsus." Encyclopædia Britannica Inc., 2014. Web. 24 Feb. 2014.
      <http://library.eb.com/levels/referencecenter/article/71333>.

85   http://www.itsgila.com/headlinerscleo.htm

86   "Mark Antony." Encyclopædia Britannica Inc., 2014. Web. 17 Mar.
      2014. <http://library.eb.com/levels/referencecenter/article/7914>.

87   http://www.azurapark.com/life-in-alanya/alanya-historic-places.html

88   http://www.sacred-destinations.com/turkey/ephesus-isabey-mosque

89   "Temple of Artemis." Encyclopædia Britannica Inc., 2014. Web. 24 Feb.
      2014. <http://library.eb.com/levels/referencecenter/article/9680>.

90   Ibid.

91   http://www.sacred-destinations.com/turkey/ephesus-isabey-mosque

92   "bey." Encyclopædia Britannica Inc., 2014. Web. 24 Feb. 2014. <http://
      library.eb.com/levels/referencecenter/article/79010>.

93   "Ephesus." Encyclopædia Britannica Inc., 2014. Web. 24 Feb. 2014. <http://library.eb.com/levels/referencecenter/article/32766>.

94   http://www.kusadasi.biz/ephesus/hadrian.html

95   "Five Good Emperors." Encyclopædia Britannica Inc., 2014. Web. 25 Feb. 2014. <http://library.eb.com/levels/referencecenter/article/34448>.

96   "Saint Timothy." Encyclopædia Britannica Inc., 2014. Web. 25 Feb. 2014. <http://library.eb.com/levels/referencecenter/article/72539>.

97   Troy." *Britannica School.* Encyclopædia Britannica, Inc., 2014. Web. 28 Oct. 2014. <http://library.eb.com/levels/referencecenter/article/73525>

98   "Trojan War." Encyclopædia Britannica Inc., 2014. Web. 25 Feb. 2014. <http://library.eb.com/levels/referencecenter/article/73476>.

99   http://whc.unesco.org/en/list/849

100 "Bosporus." Encyclopædia Britannica Inc., 2014. Web. 25 Feb. 2014. <http://library.eb.com/levels/referencecenter/article/80817>.

101 "Istanbul." Encyclopædia Britannica Inc., 2014. Web. 25 Feb. 2014. <http://library.eb.com/levels/referencecenter/article/106446>.

102 "Istanbul." Encyclopædia Britannica Inc., 2014. Web. 3 Mar. 2014. <http://library.eb.com/levels/referencecenter/article/106446>.

103 Ibid.

104 "Hagia Sophia." Encyclopædia Britannica Inc., 2014. Web. 4 Mar. 2014. <http://library.eb.com/levels/referencecenter/article/38782>.

105 Ibid.

106 Ibid.

Chapter 16. Driving from Jeddah to Paris (1975)—Europe: Part 1

107 http://www.sofia-guide.com/attraction/tsar-liberator-monument/

108 http://bulstack.com/2011/12/07/sofias-yellow-brick-road/

109 "Ruse." Encyclopædia Britannica Inc., 2014. Web. 15 Jan. 2014. <http://library.eb.com/eb/article-9064449>.

110 "Lenin, Vladimir Ilich." Encyclopædia Britannica Inc., 2014. Web. 15 Jan. 2014. <http://library.eb.com/eb/article-9108666>.

111 "Carpathian Mountains." Encyclopædia Britannica Inc., 2014. Web. 15 Jan. 2014. <http://library.eb.com/eb/article-9106058>

112 "Vlad III." Encyclopædia Britannica Inc., 2014. Web. 16 Jan. 2014. <http://library.eb.com/eb/article-9471442>.

113 http://www.romaniatourism.com/castles-fortresses.html

114 "Brasov." Encyclopædia Britannica Inc., 2014. Web. 16 Jan. 2014. <http://library.eb.com/eb/article-9016245>.

115 http://www.tripadvisor.com/Attraction_Review-g317135-d586315-Reviews-Transfagarasan_Highway-Transylvania.html

116 " Argeș." *Britannica School.* Encyclopædia Britannica, Inc., 2014. Web. 28 Oct. 2014. <http://library.eb.com/levels/referencecenter/article/9376

117 "Maramures." Encyclopædia Britannica Inc., 2014. Web. 15 Jan. 2014. <http://library.eb.com/eb/article-9050735>.

118 http://www.dangerous-business.com/2012/07/village-scenes-life-in-rural-romania/

119 "Danube River." Encyclopædia Britannica Inc., 2014. Web. 18 Jan. 2014. <http://library.eb.com/eb/article-9106065>.

120 Ibid.

121 "Budapest." Encyclopædia Britannica Inc., 2014. Web. 18 Jan. 2014. <http://library.eb.com/eb/article-9106098>.

122 "Budapest." Encyclopædia Britannica Inc., 2014. Web. 18 Jan. 2014. <http://library.eb.com/eb/article-9106098>.

123 Ibid.

124 http://www.stay.com/budapest/restaurant/12336/arany-hordo-vendeglo/

125 "Budapest." Encyclopædia Britannica Inc., 2014. Web. 7 May 2014. <http://library.eb.com/levels/referencecenter/article/106098>

Chapter 17. Driving from Jeddah to Paris (1975)—Europe: Part 2

126 http://www.sopron.hu/Sopron/portal/english

127 Ibid.

128 http://www.sopron.co.hu/tartalom/sopron_tortenete_en.htm

129 "Vienna." Encyclopædia Britannica Inc., 2014. Web. 11 Mar. 2014. <http://library.eb.com/levels/referencecenter/article/108775>.

130 Ibid.

131   Ibid.

132   http://www.wien.info/en/sightseeing/fiaker-horse-drawn-carriage

133   "Schloss Schönbrunn." Encyclopædia Britannica Inc., 2014. Web. 23
       Aug. 2014. http://library.eb.com/levels/referencecenter/article/66198#>.

134   "Passau." Encyclopædia Britannica Inc., 2014. Web. 22 Jan. 2014.
       <http://library.eb.com/eb/article-9058655>.

135   http://www.neureichenau.de/tourism/English.pdf

Chapter 18. Driving from Jeddah to Paris (1975)—Europe: Part 3

136   http://www.tripadvisor.com/LocationPhotoDirectLink-g187310-
       d659773-i41964651-Kaiserburg_Nurnberg_Nuremberg_Castle-
       Nuremberg_Middle_Franconia_Bavaria.html

137   "Nürnberg." Encyclopædia Britannica Inc., 2014. Web. 23 Jan. 2014.
       <http://library.eb.com/eb/article-9056528>.

138   http://tourismus.nuernberg.de/en/sightseeing/places-of-interest/
       monuments-and-fountains/d/nuernberger-denkmaeler-und-brunnen-
       schoener-brunnen.html

139   "Wiesbaden." Encyclopædia Britannica Inc., 2014. Web. 24 Jan. 2014.
       <http://library.eb.com/eb/article-9076938>.

140   http://www.kulturland-rheingau.de/en/travel-experience/well-worth-
       seeing/ensights/enruinsofehrenfelscastle/

141   http://www.frenchfriends.info/travel-paris/visit-cathedral-notre-dame

142   "Notre-Dame de Paris." Encyclopædia Britannica Inc., 2014.
       Web. 26 Jan. 2014. <http://library.eb.com/eb/article-9056343>.

Chapter 19. Paris (1975–1979)

143   "Paris." Encyclopædia Britannica Inc., 2014. Web. 12 Mar. 2014.
       <http://library.eb.com/levels/referencecenter/article/108530>.

144   "Louis XVI." Encyclopædia Britannica Inc., 2014. Web. 13 Mar. 2014.
       <http://library.eb.com/levels/referencecenter/article/49069>.

145   Georges-Eugène, Baron Haussmann." Encyclopædia Britannica Inc.,
       2014. Web. 14 Mar. 2014. <http://library.eb.com/levels/referencecenter/
       article/39555>.

146 "Arc de Triomphe." Encyclopædia Britannica Inc., 2014. Web. 14 Mar. 2014. <http://library.eb.com/levels/referencecenter/article/1547>.

147 Ibid.

148 "Paris." Encyclopædia Britannica Inc., 2014. Web. 15 Mar. 2014. <http://library.eb.com/levels/referencecenter/article/108530#>.

149 Ibid.

150 http://jeparleamericain.com/la-religieuse-%E2%80%94-the-nun/

151 "higher education." Encyclopædia Britannica Inc., 2014. Web. 24 Aug. 2014. <http://library.eb.com/levels/referencecenter/article/40412#284183.toc>.

152 "Paris." Encyclopædia Britannica Inc., 2014. Web. 15 Mar. 2014. <http://library.eb.com/levels/referencecenter/article/108530#>.

153 "Louvre Museum." Encyclopædia Britannica Inc., 2014. Web. 15 Mar. 2014. <http://library.eb.com/levels/referencecenter/article/49115>.

154 "Mont-Saint-Michel." Encyclopædia Britannica Inc., 2014. Web. 27 Jan. 2014. <http://library.eb.com/eb/article-9053456>.

155 Ibid.

156 "Sidi Bouzid." Encyclopædia Britannica Inc., 2014. Web. 12 May 2014. <http://library.eb.com/levels/high/article/105533>.

157 "Carthage." Encyclopædia Britannica Inc., 2014. Web. 12 May 2014. <http://library.eb.com/levels/referencecenter/article/20548>.

Chapter 20. Standing Still, Ridgefield, Connecticut (2002)

158 "Eindhoven." Encyclopædia Britannica Inc., 2014. Web. 27 Jan. 2014. <http://library.eb.com/eb/article-9032147>.

159 http://vanners.org/

160 Bert Van Loo, *Holland* (Houten, The Netherlands: Bert van Loo Produkties. B.V.), 126-27.

161 http://goamsterdam.about.com/od/daytripsexcursions/p/Kinderdijk.htm

162 http://whc.unesco.org/en/list/818

163 "Lisse." Encyclopædia Britannica Inc., 2014. Web. 13 May 2014. <http://library.eb.com/levels/referencecenter/article/48493>.

164   www.econsultant.com/articles/tony-robbins-six-needs.html

165   Michael A. Nitti, *The Trophy Effect* (Carlsbad, CA: Motivational Press, 2009).

166   Eckhart Tolle, *The Power of Now* (Novato, CA: New World Library, 2004).

167   http://www.npr.org/templates/story/story.php?storyId=102977788

CPSIA information can be obtained at www.ICGtesting.com
Printed in the USA
BVOW08s2315111015

421941BV00003B/77/P